THE MYTH OF PRINT CULTURE: ESSAYS ON EVIDENCE, TEXTUALITY, AND BIBLIOGRAPHICAL METHOD

The Myth
of Print Culture

Essays on Evidence, Textuality, and Bibliographical Method

JOSEPH A. DANE

UNIVERSITY OF TORONTO PRESS
Toronto Buffalo London

© University of Toronto Press Incorporated 2003
Toronto Buffalo London
Printed in Canada

ISBN 0-8020-8775-2

Printed on acid-free paper

National Library of Canada Cataloguing in Publication

Dane, Joseph A.

The myth of print culture : essays on evidence, textuality and
bibliographical method / Joseph A. Dane.

(Studies in book and print culture)
Includes bibliographical references and index.
ISBN 0-8020-8775-2   10 06530 157

1. Books – History.   2. Books and reading – History.   3. Bibliography –
Methodology.   4. Criticism, Textual.   I. Title.   II. Series.

Z116.A2D3 2003   002   C2003-902572-1

University of Toronto Press acknowledges the financial assistance to its
publishing program of the Canada Council for the Arts and the Ontario
Arts Council.

University of Toronto Press acknowledges the financial support for its
publishing activities of the Government of Canada through the Book
Publishing Industry Development Program (BPIDP).

Contents

Acknowledgments   vii

Introduction   3

1 **The Myth of Print Culture**   10

    1.1 Print and Scribal Culture (Eisenstein, Johns, Love)   11
    1.2 *The Coming of the Book* and the Departure of Bibliographical
        Inquiry   21

2 **Twenty Million Incunables Can't Be Wrong**   32

    2.1 The Calculus of Book-Copies   32
    2.2 The Quantification of Evidence   41
    2.3 Note on the Relative Popularity of Juvenal and Persius   52

3 **What Is a Book? Classification and Representation of
   Early Books**   57

    3.1 The Cataloguing of Early Book Fragments   57
    3.2 Type Measurement and Facsimile Representation   75

4 **The Notion of Variant and the Zen of Collation**   88

    4.1 Charlton Hinman and the Optical Collator   88
    4.2 The Logic and Description of Press Variation   97

5 Two Studies in Chaucer Editing   114

   5.1 The Presumed Influence of Skeat's *Student's Chaucer* on Manly
      and Rickert's *Text of the Canterbury Tales*   114

   5.2 The Electronic Chaucer and the Relation of the Two Caxton
      Editions   124

6 Editorial Variants   143

   6.1 Early Terence Editions and the Material Transmission
      of the Text   144

   6.2 Richard Bentley: Milton and Terence   148

   6.3 Malone Verbatim: The Description of Editorial Procedures   158

   6.4 W.W. Skeat, Chatterton's Rowley, and the Definition of the
      True Poem   163

7 Bibliographical Myths and Methods   170

   7.1 The Curse of the Mummy Paper   170

   7.2 The History of Irony as a Problem in Descriptive
      Bibliography   185

Conclusion   191

Notes   195

Principal Works Cited   229

Index   237

Acknowledgments

Of the chapters below, two have been previously published in part: the first section of chapter 5 appeared as 'The Presumed Influence of Skeat's *Student's Chaucer* on Manly and Rickert's *Text of the Canterbury Tales*,' *Analytical and Enumerative Bibliography* 7 (1993): 18–27; all but the final section of the first essay in chapter 7 appeared as 'The Curse of the Mummy Paper,' *Printing History* 34 (1995): 18–25. I have also taken some paragraphs from my review of Adrian Johns, *The Nature of the Book*, in *TEXT* 12 (2000): 244–9. I thank the journals for permission to reprint these sections here. The second section of the final chapter, 'The History of Irony as a Problem in Descriptive Bibliography,' appeared in French translation as an appendix to an essay on irony by Pierre Schoentjes (*Poétique de l'ironie*, Paris, 2001); the English version appears here for the first time.

Working through this material is familiar, and certain aspects still annoy me; they are like absurdities of sports or movement of a boat through water, where even good strokes become penalties. There is no trick to any of it. It is not simply that others know what I do not know. The mechanics of even the most routine and trivial of successes are far too complex for conscious thought or even for the language of the most brilliant of coaches or critics. Each swing is a unique swing; breezes are never the same breezes and the sea state always changes. Perhaps if one looks at a thousand books, what one says about the next one might be less ridiculous than what one would have said about the first, but there is no certainty of that, and plenty of evidence to disprove it.

I take this occasion, nonetheless, to thank again Lawrence, Sarah, and Susan Green, and I am grateful for help of various kinds from Lorna Clymer, Alexandra Gillespie, Jaenet Guggenheim, Paulina Kewes, Seth

Lerer, Paul Needham, Sandra Prior, the staffs of the Huntington and the Clark Libraries, Ross Scimeca, and my colleagues Percival Everett, Tim Gustafson, Susan McCabe, Margaret Russett, and less obviously James Kincaid. I also received support from John Detweiler, Catherine Kelley, Fran Leyman, Michaeline Mulvey, and Michael Peterson. There are others as well, yet people being, finally, what they are, I will this time leave the dedication blank.

THE MYTH OF PRINT CULTURE: ESSAYS ON EVIDENCE, TEXTUALITY, AND BIBLIOGRAPHICAL METHOD

Introduction

This study deals with the opposition between evidence and discourse in literary and bibliographical studies. The most basic variant of this opposition, one that I will deal with repeatedly in the chapters below, is that between physical materials and those abstractions that we refer to under the name 'text.' The first of these levels, the material, is generally regarded as the proper focus of bibliography (the book, the materials of a book, the particular historical acts of readings of particular books). What we must in desperation call the 'things' on this level are singularities, and at every moment these singularities challenge the notions of identity, sameness, or fixity. The book I hold is not the book you hold, and when I hold that book tomorrow, the historical conditions under which I hold it will have changed. To speak of identity here may be necessary, but on this level, there can be no absolute manifestation of such identity and no strictly proper use of such a term. The second level is textual (the text, the edition, the reading common to many books). And the things on this level are marked by what I will call their reproducibility. The book I read today is the same one I will ask you to read tomorrow. The author is the same. The culture in which we read them is the same. Much as I will dispute statements on this level throughout this study, I should state here that without such statements, no scholarly discussion or communication of any kind is possible.

This opposition is central to all literary discussion that claims to have a basis in the material facts of book production and distribution. Such claims have become increasingly frequent in literary studies, and their frequency is due to a number of factors: the anecdotal style of New Historicism, the ease of travel to Rare Book libraries, the distribution of materials through electronic media, or even the growing ease with which scholarly studies can be illustrated in journals. However, as those claims become frequent, they also become more problematic, and the desire to found literary criticism and historical research on materials has, I believe, also worked to expose and question the assumptions of that criticism. How do we move from the level of the singular book (or even the book fragment) to discussions of that ominously capitalized Book in general? I will be arguing below that the gap between material and textual levels in bibliographical discussion is one that can never be closed, and it is one that scholarship, in its own advance, discovers new and more mystifying ways to obscure.

The chapters that follow the introductory essay below ('The Myth of Print Culture') are organized to discuss that opposition as it operates in book history on increasingly higher levels of abstraction. The first group (chapters 2 and 3) focuses exclusively on incunables – books printed in the fifteenth century; it is in this context that I discuss questions basic to book history. What is a book, and what do the extant books have to do with the numbers of books produced in the fifteenth century? What are the implications of such quantification, or the assumptions underlying the entries in library catalogues that are the basis for that quantification? What does it mean to illustrate or reproduce such a book?

The next section (chapter 4 and the first section of chapter 5) deals with a task basic to bibliography and editing – collation. The word 'collation' has many uses in these fields, referring both to the structure of books as represented in descriptive bibliography and to the bringing together and comparison of texts in the editorial process. This equivocation on a general level is itself a reflection of ambiguities and problems on its more specific levels. Here I will be discussing particular methods of optical collation of book texts and the abstract methodologies that are implied, but rarely defined, in the textual quantification of the results. What is the actual evidence that is both sought and produced by the optical collator and what is the relation of the evidence as tabulated by the editor to what exists in the actual book-copies themselves? Chapter 5 begins with the first of two problems in Chaucer editing – here on the meaning of collation as used in the construction of critical editions.

The third set concerns editing; it deals on a level more thoroughly textual with the same problem addressed in the earlier chapters – the transferral of the material to the textual. I begin with the second of two problems in Chaucer editing, here involving the assumptions of the recent electronic edition. I then consider cases involving the reception of particular editions, and what I call the critical mythology that accrues to certain historical figures (Erasmus, Bentley, Malone) as they become defined as editors in the modern sense (chapter 6). What is the gap between what the materials indicate was done, and the editorial and critical claims made about these tasks?

I close with two essays that deal with methodology used in book history, the first on the persistence of what might be called an urban myth in paper history and its resistance to proof or refutation, the second on the relation of bibliographical to literary methods in general.

At the core of these discussions is a definition and understanding of just what a book is, and I will address this problem specifically in chapter 3 with a case in early printing. When we go to a panel discussion entitled 'The Book in X,' we understand that 'the Book' here is something quite different from the object we might call up in a library. The word is simply an index of certain types of scholarly discussions that evolve for reasons quite apart from the evolving nature of particular physical books. In general, one will see this word capitalized in English, or connected with a definite article (and no physical referent) – the book, the Book, Book History. This new index of scholarly orientation is probably borrowed from the French, whose system of definite articles allows for greater ambiguity and slippage here. Such slippage is in many ways desirable. Whereas bibliographers (or a caricature of such persons) might be imagined to be concerned with singular books, thinking to increase the stock of bibliographical knowledge on a piecemeal basis, in literary studies that would not be enough to justify their activities or even their existence. Here, the pool of knowledge, insofar as it exists at all, is already far too great, and that singular book must always find its justification within larger contexts, whether literature, culture, reading and writing practices, or The Book itself.[1] There is no defining what such a term means or should mean. And no defining or attempting to define what the scholarly field in literary studies is that announces its concerns as 'the history of the (or that) book.' In the discussion below, I will use the word 'book' most often in a bibliographical sense: it will be in many cases a shortened form of the word 'book-copy,' but I will use this latter term whenever a specific distinction needs to be enforced. I will avoid as much as possible using the word 'book' in the abstract sense, that is, using it in any context where there is a danger or temptation to capitalize it.

Together, the essays focus on two major problems: first, the question of singularity. We all know what a book is – it is something we hold in our hands. We also believe, somewhat preposterously, that that book is something someone else can hold in their hands, at the same time and in a different location. That paradox, or bit of readerly bad faith, is manifested bibliographically in catalogues, particularly union catalogues (the ongoing *Incunabula Short Title Catalogue* [*ISTC*] is one example) or such enumerative catalogues as the Pollard and Redgrave *Short-Title Catalogue* (*STC*). How are such things as editions, states, variants, or even the book itself to be discussed? To what extent is a printed book singular? And to what extent does the (inaccurate) scholarly assumption that it is not, enable reasonable and useful discussion of such objects to proceed?[2]

The second problem is one involving the hermeneutic leap from the level of material to the level of text. That singular book we hold is a material thing, and it cannot occupy two spaces in nature at the same time. What is reproducible, discussable, and transferable is something else – a description of that book, perhaps, or rather the text that book contains. That text exists abstractly despite the various ways it is represented typographically,[3] and it is one that historically has often been felt to be in opposition with the book that contains it.[4] This definition of text is one that is fundamental to my discussion below, and many of the essays deal specifically with that leap from the level of material to the level of text. It is also one that I realize is at first glance opposed to the use of that term in much literary discussion, where 'text,' is defined not in its essence, but rather in terms of its function: to many literary scholars, a text is something that can be interpreted, whether a singular event or a reproducible one. Even this use of the word 'text,' however, involves reproducibility. To interpret, except in a vacuum, assumes the possibility of critical engagement, and where there is engagement, there must be grounds for engagement: that singularity that you interpret is the same singularity on which I base the refutation of your interpretation. And with this sameness – the possibility of critical engagement – arises the notion of the reproducible grounds for that engagement – the text of the engagement.

Note that the same questions arise if we consider text (even in books) as nonverbal. We might ask also what we mean by illustrations? or facsimiles? What do they illustrate? What does the facsimile replace? Are we wrong to consider any of these things ersatz objects or images? Are these merely allusions to their referents? things in the real world? other illustrations in the real world? Does the very formulation of such questions impose a structure of reality onto illustrations that they do not necessarily possess? The failure to ask or even to consider such questions has led, I think, to other universalizing statements about such things: that illustrations must illustrate; that facsimiles must facsimilize; or the often-heard but quite misleading tautology that the business of an editor is 'to edit.' As the discussion of specific cases below will show, each of these banalities must be tested against specific cases.

We will see this in the matter of bibliographical catalogues (the difference between descriptions of particular book-copies and the ideal copy); in editorial collating (whereby the results of an optical collation are textualized); and finally in the matter of edition making, whereby readings on the lower levels of text (that is to say, the particular words in a particular manuscript or a particular version) are transferred to the higher levels of text (they are recorded, evaluated, and disseminated as higher-order scholarly texts.)

It will be obvious from the subject matter of these chapters that the operating assumption behind these essays is that book history and the bibliographical foundations of that history are dependent on the study of individuals and specifics. Both book history and bibliographical study involve acts of categorization, but paradoxically if that categorization is reasonable and useful, the individuals, the singularities and bits of evidence, the very raison d'être of such categorization, risk being subordinated to the categories they seem to generate. Book history, and bibliographical study generally, can promote the view (or illusion) that these fields are either self-contained or self-generating; that they proceed without constant reference to specific individual books, which themselves become less foundational to such fields than merely illustrative of their abstractions. Even Robert Darnton, a historian with deep archival concerns and interests, occasionally caricatures as merely dilettantish traditional bibliographical concerns focusing on individual book-copies.[5]

Neither the book in its singularity, however, nor the more abstract narratives of book history (versions of Fernand Braudel's *grand récit*) provides an adequate version of this implied history. Nor does either level provide a coherent directive as to how other levels of discussion should proceed. My own method of providing the link between material evidence and abstract narrative is a polemical one: for the historian, literary scholar, or bibliographer, what links these levels is the resistance of that material to the scholarly narratives that both explain and misrepresent it.

The chapters below are based on a series of related assumptions and arguments, among them, that no material evidence can ever be fully reproduced nor can evidence from the lower levels of what I call text ever be presented objectively to produce or imply their own coherent narratives. None of this evidence, whether material or textual, is ever completely organized in itself, nor can it be recorded with disinterest.[6] No bibliographical device has been created that could generate more questions than or radically different kinds of questions from those conceived when that device was created. To use bibliographical materials to answer particular questions (as I occasionally do here) is simply to follow the questions already perceived by the composer. There is no way out of the black box of bibliography except perhaps by an assumption so radically perverse it ceases to be bibliographical at all: for example, the bibliographical black box is really about colour coding, not about books.

A second assumption concerns the levels of inquiry. Henry Bradshaw, whose methods influenced an entire generation of English bibliographers of the late nineteenth and early twentieth centuries, claimed that to construct a bibliographical study, one must first arrange one's facts, and that so organized, these facts will speak; 'They always do.' But the arrangement of facts is itself an act of speaking. It is not the facts themselves that speak; it is the act of arrangement that speaks, the act of classification.[7] This particular hermeneutic circle is not the one I critique here. The object of the implied polemic here is a bibliographical sleight of hand of a different sort – the hermeneutic leap, whereby what Bradshaw would have considered facts, instead of organized (mischievously) to appear to speak (to allow the investigator to ventriloquize through them), serve at best an illustrative, and at worst no more than a decorative function.

My own definition of the book is one that comes from Anglo-American scholarship. The book is a physical object that one can own, hold, or call out of a library. It is subject to various levels of abstraction that transform that book slowly into a text or a textlike object. Key to all these levels is the notion of reproducibility; this is what makes a book less a singular material object than a member of a series and the referent (accidental) of a more essential bibliographical description. An ancillary thesis here is that the notion of reproducibility, central to discussions of book production and dissemination, has been projected back onto printing history itself, in such a way that it becomes the central problem associated with printing history, print culture, or The Book. On the one hand, this is bibliographical trickery, and leads to considerable confusion and mistaken information. But on the other hand, the questions generated, legitimate or not, are often the very ones that make the field of book history interesting and productive.

This study differs from other English studies that announce their subject as 'print culture' in the prominence I have given to fifteenth-century books (chapters 2 and 3 deal exclusively with incunables) and to problems of classification and cataloguing basic to the organization and study of such books. That these chapters are first may imply that I consider such cataloguing questions in some way preliminary or spade-work to the more important or interesting bibliographical questions. Nothing could be further from the case. These chapters are first because the books they deal with are the earliest printed books we have, and the problems those books pose are fundamental to all book history; there is not a single question in bibliographical or literary history that could not be considered a variant. To me, dealing with these matters is a great source of amusement; others may find them irritating or simply inconvenient. What do the overly anal conventions for counting and calculating catalogue entries have to do with the grander concerns of The Book? Why not talk about Venice instead? In order to do whatever it is we do, we all must gloss over an arbitrarily defined set of preliminaries, and readers who wish to skip chapters 2 and 3 are certainly welcome to proceed.

The organization of these chapters is not designed to provide a seam-less narrative, narratives I have characterized as bordering on scholarly 'conspiracy-theory'[8] but their relations do reflect the thesis I am arguing. The singularity of bibliographical facts and the singularity of the prob-lems these facts pose can never be entirely overcome. Bibliographers are well aware of this, but in bibliographical scholarship such general con-siderations are often left unstated. Perhaps bibliographers assume that other bibliographers, to whom their studies are addressed, already know about such problems and need no reminder; perhaps they assume fur-ther that literary scholars, who constitute their secondary audience, are interested in something else, or too wrapped up in their own methodolo-gies and conclusions to be much interested in the methodological rumi-nations of others. The essays here are based on a different assumption – that detailed bibliographical study reveals methodological problems that recur in all fields and on all levels of literary scholarship, and that it is just the wrestling with such details, whether one 'gets them right' or 'gets them wrong' that will make bibliographical procedures both meaningful and finally accessible.

1 The Myth of Print Culture

The phrase 'print culture' has grown increasingly popular in scholarship of the late twentieth century, with a surge of studies incorporating this term in the last few years. My check of the MLA Bibliography, in what I believe was a keyword search, produced 249 entries for the years beginning in 1963; 191 of these were from the years 1996–2001. Only two of these were prior to 1980 (Eisenstein and Ong); the decade 1981–90 accounts for only eighteen more; 1991–5 add thirty-eight. Many of these focus on seventeenth- and eighteenth-century England, but others include such seemingly diverse topics as copyright law, late nineteenth-century American popular music, Egyptian nationalism, all somehow related by implication to an undefined but universal form of culture.[1] Abstract as it is, print culture apparently transcends particularities of books or printing history; it is, by definition, that which both encompasses and transcends 'print,' however defined, and all associated levels of bibliographical evidence. What we see here is less a refinement of a critical term, than an increase in the range of materials to which such a term applies.

Studies with the announced subject 'print culture' generally begin with the assumption that such a thing as print culture has real existence, and it is the business of scholarship to discover what that thing is or how it is manifested in terms of some specific historical subject matter. The following chapter is based on a different assumption – that what exists is not print culture at all but rather the modern scholar's invocation of print culture. What exists is not an abstraction such as printing, something instanced by select examples; what exists are those examples themselves, particular actions and products of what we call the printing press and the institutions surrounding it.[2] The phrase 'print culture' thus is a modern one, and the history I trace here spans only the past few decades. There is implied here a generational conflict between an older generation of scholars in English (Elizabeth Eisenstein and Marshall McLuhan) and a younger group (Adrian Johns, Harold Love, and others), and I will be concerned here in part with how the assumptions characteristic of this older group of scholars still operate. Recent English scholars, however, seem to find an even greater affinity with an even older style of scholarship – that associated with the French Groupe Annales; for English scholars, the most familiar example in relation to print culture remains Lucien Febvre and Henri-Jean Martin's 1958 *L'Apparition du livre* and its several reissues in English. The way this book handles particular aspects of printing history will be the subject of the final section.

1.1 Print and Scribal Culture (Eisenstein, Johns, Love)

For English and American scholars, the most influential book on printing history in the last fifty years is Elizabeth Eisenstein, *The Printing Press as an Agent of Change* (1979). It was revised and often reprinted in a more popular form as *The Printing Revolution in Early Modern Europe*, an abridged version, supplemented with illustrations, but with its supporting notes stripped. I will be concerned here with the stance and methods implied by Eisenstein, and what Eisenstein's apparently innocent representation of herself as a newcomer to this field entails.

The inspiration for Eisenstein's study came in a presidential address of the early 1960s by Carl Bridenbaugh for the American Historical Association, 'The Great Mutation' (1: ix). 'While mulling over this question and wondering whether it was wise to turn out more monographs or instruct graduate students to do the same ... I ran across a copy of Marshall McLuhan's *The Gutenberg Galaxy*' (1: x).[3] Eisenstein presents herself as a 'neophyte' (1: xi), and claims repeatedly that no literature was available on her subject:

> As I say in my first chapter, there was not even a small literature available for consultation. Indeed I could not find a single book, or even a sizeable article which attempted to survey the consequences of the fifteenth-century communications shift. (1: xi)

From a methodological point of view, such statements are the most important in the book. Obviously, there was considerable material on early book production available at the time, but Eisenstein defines this material, and in part dismisses it, as 'written for specialists':

> There is, to be sure, a large and ever growing literature devoted to the history of printing and related topics. Although much of it seems to be written by and for specialists – custodians of rare books and other librarians; experts on typography or bibliography, literary scholars concerned with press-variants, and the like – this literature does contain material of more wide-ranging interest. (1: 4)

Such a claim redefines the area of argument; it also places the level of evidence on a higher level of abstraction than that discussed by most such 'specialist' literature.[4] Mainstream bibliographical literature can be gleaned for 'material of more wide-ranging interest,' but it is not central to the discussion.

Before proceeding, we should note how vast this literature is. Gutenberg's name is repeatedly invoked by Eisenstein, but there is no discussion of the many studies produced for the Gutenberg Society earlier this century; works by Paul Schwenke and others on the minutiae of typefonts still provide the basis for the dating and history of this earliest manifestation of print culture.[5] Even if we were to confine ourselves to English, there is a long tradition of work on all aspects of book history. Joseph Ames's still-useful *Typographical Antiquities* of 1749 (a work quoted in the epigraph to Eisenstein's Preface) is never discussed critically, nor are the voluminous publications of Thomas Frognall Dibdin, who, despite his stylistic eccentricities, did much to create the entire field of English bibliography and book collecting in the early nineteenth century. Also removed from consideration are the many publications that came out of the Caxton sesquicentenary over a century ago, as well as the monumental catalogues still basic to the study of fifteenth-century books: Robert Proctor's *An Index to the Early Printed Books in the British Museum*, and the multi-volume *Catalogue of Books Printed in the Fifteenth Century Now in the British Museum*. So too are classic English works on specific groups of early books: E.P. Goldschmidt's work on medieval and Renaissance bookbindings, detailed studies by G.D. Hobson and by J. Basil Oldham of early bindings, and Neil Ker's work on pastedowns. Yet it is precisely these latter works that provide the detailed documentation for how particular physical books were produced and ultimately moved from the continent to England.[6] Eisenstein insists that earlier studies of printing have been too abstract: 'It follows that we need to think less metaphorically and abstractly, more historically and concretely' (1: 91). But with such works marginalized, it is not clear what 'historical and concrete' thinking on the history of printing could be. The area of discussion, print culture, is no longer as dependent on material books as were earlier studies on the early history of printing. Print culture is something different from the institution and a procedure of printing, and something different from print or what one finds in books.

Eisenstein never defines what she means by print culture nor does she deal with the assumptions that term entails. Apparent definitions, such as 'post-Gutenberg developments in the West' (a phrase with obvious roots in McLuhan), are little more than tautologies, and the problematic nature of the term itself is displaced onto opposing terms. What is difficult is not whatever is called 'print culture,' but something to which it is opposed, whether that is orality, Eastern culture, or 'scribal culture':

> There is not even an agreed-upon term in common use which designates the system of written communications that prevailed before print. (1: 9)

> I have found the term 'scribal culture' useful as a shorthand way of refer-ring to such activities as producing and duplicating books, transmitting messages, reporting news and storing data after the invention of writing and before that of movable type ... As noted in my preface, the term 'print culture' is used to refer only to post-Gutenberg developments in the West. (1: 9, n. 18; reference to 1: xiii)

Eisenstein's articulation of a thesis also moves discussion away from the problematic assumptions contained in the central terminology. At issue is not whether the notion of a communication shift is valid – 'Granted that some sort of communications revolution did occur during the late fifteenth century ...' (1: 41, in chapter entitled 'Some Features of Print Culture') but rather what that assumed shift entails, for example, the 'implications of standardization' involved in such a shift (1: 51).

The question Eisenstein asks is 'was the change evolutionary or revolu-tionary,' and there are a limited number of responses to this question. There are those who argue for revolutionary change, such as McLuhan: 'History bears witness to the cataclysmic effect on society of inventions of new media for the transmission of information among persons. The development of writing and later the development of printing are ex-amples ...' (1: 3, with reference to St John). Francis Bacon also argues that print changed 'the appearance and state of the whole world.' There are those who seem to argue for evolutionary change: Jacob Burkhardt makes printing a secondary phenomenon by defining the Renaissance as beginning with Petrarch; Braudel, arguing for 'la longue durée' of most cultural phenomena generally, subordinates printing to artillery and navigation (1: 27); and so do recent scholars on the late medieval book, who stress the continuity between fifteenth-century scribal production and fifteenth-century book production.[7] The basic assumption, one that finds its way into much subsequent scholarship, is not questioned: there are opposing things called 'scribal culture' and 'print culture,' and the scholars and historians of interest are those who argue about the difference.

This conflation of a thesis with a subject explains why Eisenstein can claim: 'I did not find even a small literature available for consultation' (1: x). What restricts this scholarly literature is the definition of the problem. The enormous bibliography of studies of early printing is not ignored; it is simply defined as dealing with a different subject. Earlier bibliographical studies discussed something different: the institution of early printing. They did not discuss the 'shift from scribal to print culture.' That is to say, they did not subscribe to Eisenstein's McLuhanesque view of history and thus cannot be part 'the literature on the subject.'

Cambridge University Press produced two versions of Eisenstein's study. The first, two-volume work, begins with a long sceptical view of the history of scholarship on the question, perhaps the best part of the book. In addition, the extensive footnotes promote a case that seems precisely the opposite of the one finally argued by the text. They are contradictory, detailed, and burdened with unsystematic and problematic information. In the smaller, one-volume abridgement, this oppositional voice is effectively silenced, and notes are replaced by illustrations, which only occasionally are part of the argument, for example, the identical woodcuts used to represent the cities of Verona and Mantua in the Nuremburg Chronicles (*Printing Revolution*, 58). There is in this abridgement an even more radical detachment of evidence from discussion than in the original two-volume work. Whereas in the first version, the notes provided both evidence and an unstated critique of the position argued in the text, in the abridgment, discussion is free-floating, moving through illustrations that in most cases serve no more than a decorative function. The goal of the abridged edition seems not to refine or improve the argument, but rather to rearticulate it in terms of visual examples. The concession that such an argument might be and has been opposed has disappeared.

The most important conclusions are contained within Eisenstein's initial assumption of the coherence of the term 'print culture.' Once that coherence is assumed, there is a level of abstraction to which all material evidence must be subordinated, a level that reduces oppositional voices to the quibbling of 'specialists' and 'typographers' (1: 4). Evidence against her position can be defined as exceptions to presumed rules, the inevitable recalcitrance of detail, proof that the problem defined is both worth addressing and difficult of solution. Negative arguments and evidence do not undermine the concept 'print culture'; they seem rather to reinforce it.

The Nature of the Book

Adrian Johns in *The Nature of the Book* (1998) takes Eisenstein's work as his starting point and characterizes this work as 'probably the most influential anglophonic interpretation of the cultural effects of printing.'[8] Where Eisenstein places all her arguments within the ill-defined context of print culture, Johns declares quite distinguishable events and arguments to be the same:

> Conflicts over the historiography of printing were indistinguishable from these struggles [for ownership of copy]: they took place on the same grounds, with the same evidence, at the same time, and with largely the same combatants. (355)

His book will be the 'first extensive taxonomy of practices labeled piratical – from piracy itself, through abridgment, epitomizing, and translation, to plagiarism and libel' (33). 'This book concentrates on the implications of printing for knowledge, and for knowledge of nature in particular' (41).

Johns brings masses of specific detail to bear on the argument and displays that detail much more prominently than Eisenstein had. He provides a direct critique of the term 'print culture,' but reinstates a version of that term within his own argument:

> The unifying concept of Eisenstein's argument is that of 'print culture.' This 'culture' is characterized primarily in terms of certain traits that print is taken to endow on texts. Specifically, those produced in such an environment are subject to conditions of *standardization*, *dissemination*, and *fixity*. The last of these is perhaps the most important. According to Eisenstein,

printing meant the mass reproduction of precisely the same text, repeatable on subsequent occasions and in different locations. No longer need any work suffer the increasing corruption that Eisenstein assumes to be endemic to any 'script culture.' She focuses on this attribute of fixity as the most important corollary of the press, seeing it as central to most of the effects of print culture.

Johns fairly represents Eisenstein's argument. His critique is focused, however, not on the problematic notion of culture generally, but rather on what is associated with that presumed culture:

> In her work, printing itself stands outside history. The press is something 'sui generis,' we are told lying beyond the reach of conventional historical analysis. Its 'culture' is correspondingly placeless and timeless. It is deemed to exist inasmuch as printed texts *possess* some key characteristic, fixity being the best candidate. (19)

Johns accepts the legitimacy of this notion of fixity, just as he seems to accept the legitimacy of the term 'print culture' generally. But he redefines the term, removing it from the printed object and placing it in history: print culture is the result of certain historical practices, not a cause of them; fixity is not a quality of particular historical institutions and their products (that is, printing); rather, it depends on the psychology of participants in this process:

> There is an alternative. We may consider fixity not as an *inherent* quality, but as a *transitive* one. That is, it may be more useful to reverse our commonsense assumption. We may adopt the principle that fixity exists only inasmuch as it is recognized and acted upon by people – and not otherwise. (19)

To Johns, these people are contemporaries of the press, and he defines his concern as not printing in and of itself, but rather 'how the people of the sixteenth, seventeenth, and eighteenth centuries constructed and construed the craft [or printing]' (5).

All this removes the most naive understandings of Eisenstein's 'fixity' (understandings that Eisenstein herself may not have held). This fixity, however, is more elusive than Johns suggests: it is not something that can inhere in physical books moving through history, nor is it something actually found in the transmission of abstract texts. It is always a psychological entity, and Johns's statement could be taken a step further, beginning with the very questions Johns asks in his conclusion:

> So why do modern readers assert the existence of fixity? If it does not inhere in printed objects simply by virtue of their being printed, where has it come from, and how is it maintained? (629)

Johns's potentially illusory fixity could be associated less with the contemporaries of the press than with the scholars who are looking back on the printing press and its surrounding institutions. Where Johns claims that fixity is related to the historical institution itself – it is imagined by the contemporaries of the press and manifested both in their praise of the press and their distrust of it – that fixity is perhaps better seen as a by-product of the very terms of analysis, a function of the uncritiqued notion of print culture generally. The critical question should not be 'Is there a fixity to the printing press or in print culture?' but rather 'Why should we assume that print culture itself is anything more than a pair of words?'

Johns's book is constructed on two levels, much like that of Eisenstein: the level of narrative (stylized, anecdotal, often generalized, sententious), and the level of documentation consisting of illustrations and often aggressively archival notes. Relationships between these two levels are often unclear. Many of the illustrations are curiously detached from the argument. Fig. 2.6, p. 82, shows the title page from Moxon's *Mechanick Exercises*, yet Johns's text discusses not the book itself, but rather a textual feature of the book: Moxon's analogy of the typographer as the soul and the workmen as the 'Members of the Body.' The illustration thus means only: 'Here is the book in which the following statement is made.' Similar is the portrait of Laurens Coster (fig. 5.1, p. 333), contemporary maps of Gresham College, 'where the Royal Society met from 1660' (figs 7.2 and 7.3, pp. 466–7), and the 'view from the Observatory toward London' (fig. 8.8, p. 580) ('for the aging Flamsteed, a visit to London was increasingly an ordeal'). These are related to specific arguments, but they are not part of those arguments.

The gap between the narrative and the documentary notes is even more extreme:

> When he was eventually freed, in June 1644, Streater almost immediately hastened to establish his own enterprise as a Stationer. It was an exciting moment to become a printer or bookseller. The war, along with the collapse of Caroline licensing and privileges, had witnessed a dramatic

increase in printing and pamphleteering. The result was an explosion
of uncertainty. Printers, booksellers, and readers alike reeled from an
environment of 'counterfeiting,' and the citizenry dissolved into a 'rabble
of all opinions.' Knowledge appeared and disappeared daily, with alarming
transience ... (272–3)

The note to this deeply researched paragraph (I have quoted half)
contains the reference: 'SCB C, fols. 239v, 242v, 248v,' followed by secondary works on the New Model Army. These are pages from the Stationers' Company archives, but readers might well wonder just what they
contain. Where do they speak of 'excitement'? What primary document
could support an 'explosion of uncertainty'? Who is or was alarmed by
the 'transience' of knowledge? Elsewhere, the ordinarily extensive notes
are silent:

> Yet readers did come to trust and use print. Books were, in fact, produced,
> sold, read, and put to use. The epistemological problems of reading them
> were, in practice, superable. And this is the key: such problems were
> soluble *in practice*. While the typographical certainty that modern historians
> all too readily attribute to early printing is a chimera, seventeenth-century
> readers settled for looser, practical criteria of trust – criteria that may have
> been much less absolute than that technological standard, but were far
> more realizable. (188)

Note how Johns's argument works here. The notion of 'typographical
certainty' is first dismissed as chimerical – something modern historians erroneously believe in; it is then reintroduced as something that
seventeenth-century readers overcame. But these historians are not
named, nor is the 'typographical certainty' they presumably believe in
defined, and I am not certain whether this is meant to imply the relation
of particular typefonts to textual content or to particular printers.

Johns has produced what de Man called a 'crisis,' defining his own
area of concern as a particularly problematic one, in an otherwise safe,
fixed context. Good researchers will not find that the evidence in their
fields yields easily to traditional clichés. Johns finds here that certain
vagaries of ordinary printing history, say, fixity, standardization, and
perfect trust in the written word, do not apply. Therefore, fixity must go
elsewhere – to the fifteenth century, to manuscript culture, to a romanticized medieval period, or, as here, to hypothetical scholars less well
informed.[9]

Harold Love and the Notion of Scribal Culture

In *Printing Press as an Agent of Change*, 1: 9, n. 18, Eisenstein defines the problematic term 'print culture' by opposing it to an even more problematic term 'scribal culture.' The term 'scribal culture' is here a methodological convenience, a means of defining a primary area of concern; for other scholars, the emphasis in these opposing terms is reversed, and the most important of these studies is Harold Love's *Scribal Publication in Seventeenth-Century England*.[10] In Love, as in both Eisenstein and Johns, there is a stated (and familiar) distrust in the essential opposition printing vs script. But the polemical force here is redirected; Love attacks not the opposition print/scribal (an opposition basic to the definition of the subject matter) but rather the particular deployment of this opposition as a chronology of cultures. The evidence Love brings implies, of course, that print culture does not historically and chronologically displace scribal culture; yet Love ends by reluctantly conceding the argument he sets out to refute: 'late occurrences of scribal publication' constitute a 'survival,' something that 'remains'; the scribal 'continues to be asserted' (287), and the 'triumph of print' is 'ambiguous' (see chapter 7, pp. 284ff.).

The easiest way to refute the argument of cataclysmic historical displacement is through the examination of specific detail. Any late instance of 'the scribal' challenges the notion of a paradigm shift of culture. Print culture (however defined) does not displace scribal culture (or at least scribal culture understood as scribal production, that is, as something evidenced by products of scribes). Scribal and print culture, if these things exist at all, coexist. They did in the late Middle Ages, they did in the early modern period, and they still do today.[11]

Love uses the same assumption as does Johns: what is of import is not the historical mechanism of the press but the attitude of contemporaries toward it.[12] Writers themselves become participants in the same scholarly argument that Love defines for himself: Spenser, the 'print-fixated poet,' opposes Donne, whose 'knotty and gnarled' stanzas prove he is 'committed to manuscript' (145). But what Love means by 'culture' is no clearer than what Eisenstein means by the same term: he claims he has already 'investigated the position of the handwritten text within the cultural symbologies of the time' (177), but neither the word 'cultural' nor 'symbologies' is at all clear to me, and both are surely abstractions removed from the concrete or material evidence (the products of scribes) that is Love's stated subject.

Love founds his discussion in part on arguments from Ong and Derrida, and Ong's 'oral,' with all its romantic/primitive associations, reappears in a different guise in Love's own discussion as 'scribal,' which assumes an oppositional status to the power exercised by print.[13] What we have is a successive rewriting of Plato's myth of Thoth, with the villain either the technological advance, or, in a Derridean sense, the very nostalgia that rejects technological advance. But for the 'scribal' to assume that laudable oppositional status requires that what it opposes ('print') assume a negative role of some kind. 'Print' becomes monolithic (or, worse, the scholarship on print becomes that), while 'the scribal' maintains its revolutionary status – a revolutionary status that is a product of its singularity, itself manifested by pieces of evidence (individual scribal products), such as those listed in Love's appendix.

Love's rejection of Kernan, for example, while denying the nostalgic view of script, seizes for it the 'critical' aspect, something Kernan had applied to print:[14]

> A further difficulty is posed by Kernan's espousal of the idea that it was print and more specifically 'print logic' that was responsible for the emergence of a 'critical, judging spirit' in the writing of the early eighteenth century. (292)

Love rejects this, but in so doing, returns to the opposition the very banalities he seemed to be removing from it – the construction of this opposition as a Brechtian morality play:

> It is equally the case, and has been demonstrated many times in this book, that in a seventeenth-century context it was script and not print that was the critical, subversive, medium. (292–3)

What makes Love's argument persuasive is the concentration on particulars – particulars that are subversive not only historically, but critically, of the kind of arguments promoted by Kernan. However, through his commitment to the notion that 'the scribal' as an actual thing, a quasi-substance requiring only the scholarly definition of attributes, he is forced back into the same kind of 'culture wars' rhetoric that his entire project seems on one level to oppose.

The arguments of Eisenstein, Johns, and Love are variants of the opposition defined in my introduction: that between levels of evidence and levels of what I will call 'text.' In each case, we have a stylistic variant: the scholarly narrative proceeds on one level with a set of abstractions such as print culture, fixity, printing, scribal; beneath it are arrayed a system of notes. These notes can be variously oppositional or supportive. As singular pieces of evidence, they provide an implied critique of the very generalizations they are intended to instance. Yet the promulgation of that evidence denies this singularity. It becomes part of a larger and abstract system of evidence. It is translated into text, either in the scholar's allusion to it, or, in the case of singular illustrations, in the press's own reproduction of copies. We do not worry about whether we are holding a paperback copy of Johns, a hardback copy, or someone else's copy. In any of the senses in which we use a scholar's argument here, these various books are 'the same.' We do not worry when we cite Love whether our copy has a press variant in it, even a missing page, or happens to be the retitled University of Massachusetts reprint. The very engagement with such arguments reproduces the structure of those arguments. We are thus to some extent forced to become participants in arguments concerning fixity or reproducibility: either these are real things, or they are historical illusions, themselves 'real' in some psychological sense. All these arguments convince because the very process of confronting them regenerates the structure of their assumptions.

1.2 *The Coming of the Book* and the Departure of Bibliographical Inquiry

> Let there be no mistake; do not take this book for something it is not. It was never our intention to write or rewrite a history of printing: there would be no point in doing again what has already been done by such basic works on the subject as Mortet's *Les Origines et débuts de l'imprimerie*. It can safely be assumed that the authors know the history of the book ... and that they are fully aware of all the work done on printing history since Mortet ... There will be no lengthy account of the discovery of printing. Nor will there be any repetition of the hoary old arguments about the primacy of this or that country or about such-and-such a master-printer's significance compared to another's ... or over the provenance of the oldest incunabula.[15]

L'Apparition du livre, by Lucien Febvre and Henri-Jean Martin (1958; Eng. trans. 1976), attempted to define a new style of book history:

> At least we will try to produce something not too unpleasant to read, and once the book is read the reader may at least have the confidence that he has found in it results born of trustworthy statistics and of enquiry which no-one has yet generalised or assessed. (13)

Jules Michelet is cited on page 10, and it was perhaps Michelet's own style of history (that highly stylized narrative built on detailed archival research, only barely alluded to in his notes) that served as a model for Febvre and Martin; their 'le livre' adopted the personality of Michelet's 'le peuple':

> [Le livre] rendered vital service to research by immediately transmitting results from one researcher to another; and speedily and conveniently, without laborious effort or unsupportable cost, it assembled permanently the works of the most sublime creative spirits in all fields – a service which Michelet has described in unforgettable terms. (10)

L'Apparition du livre is divided into categories that attempt to put the material book, rather than the presumed 'hoary old arguments' [*vieux débats sempiternels*] at the focus: 'Technical Problems and Their Solutions' (on type), 'Its Visual Appearance,' 'The Book as Commodity,' 'The Little World of the Book,' 'The Geography of the Book,' 'The Book Trade,' and finally, 'The Book as a Force of Change.' The progression appears to be all-inclusive, but it elides a great deal of mainstream bibliographical scholarship, scholarship often derided by Febvre and Martin. By 'Technical Problems and Solutions' is meant problems faced by historical printers and compositors, not problems sorted out by twentieth-century book collectors or bibliographers, in whom Febvre and Martin pretend to have no interest.

Yet the people and the concrete times in which they lived soon disappear in a larger level of abstraction. Febvre and Martin reject one version of historical periodization: 'We will not use those quite puerile subdivisions based on the artificial distinctions of dates.' But they provide in its place a much looser notion of dates; rather than historical times during which real people lived, we have 'epochs' and 'ages of confusion.'[16] As in Johns, and as in Eisenstein, that the material evidence does not by itself coalesce in a coherent pattern seems to justify the invention of coherence on the much grander, abstract level of scholarly narrative. The fragmentation of individual studies or individual pieces of evidence is overcome by relegating all of it uncritically to the notes.[17]

Gothic/Roman

Let us take as one example of the conflict between evidence and abstraction the section on typography, and the opposition 'gothic/roman' that is at its base.[18] The grand narrative of *L'Apparition du livre* is built, not on a strong evidentiary base, but rather on the 'hoary old arguments' the authors renounce so impatiently in their introduction.

> Thus when printing first appeared certain small groups, lovers of belles lettres (let us not say humanists), appreciated and knew how to read the new script [roman script], but of course the vast majority at that time were faithful to the traditional gothic. (8)

No support is offered for these statements. Presumably we all know that roman type (or script) replaced gothic or black-letter type (or script) at some point in history. Or do we? Just what is it we could be said to 'know'?

> The distinctive story of roman was a triumph of the humanist spirit, the story of a victory which deserves telling. (30)

From a critical standpoint, the important question to be asked here is not whether the narrative is true, since there is no way of determining whether such a narrative would be true. Rather, how does one advance from claims about 'gothic' and 'roman' to claims about the 'humanist spirit'?

The opposition gothic/roman is traditional and has had serious cultural implications since at least the sixteenth century. The adoption of these terms by typographers is in many ways unfortunate, since the opposition does not classify type so much as project onto a field of evidence the ideological assumptions of the terminology itself. The triumph of the 'humanist spirit' (however defined) as a function of the renunciation of the 'gothic' (however defined) is a story more from the sixteenth century than about it.

Febvre and Martin define groups of typefaces as do other historians of type; categories of typefaces are a development of categories used in palaeographical histories. The following statements presumably concern palaeographical matters as they were 'about 1450'; at this time, each style, Febvre and Martin claim, has its own 'proper destination.' The discussion itself, however, blurs into discussion of actual typefonts of the late fifteenth century. The English translators have understandable difficulty here:

> Vers 1450 ... On pouvait distinguer quatre types principaux d'écriture, dont chacune avait sa destination propre [citation to Guignard, Bischoff, Batelli, and Morison]. D'abord la gothique des écrits scolastiques, la traditionelle

'lettre de somme' [trans. 'black letter'!], chère aux théologiens et aux universitaires. Ensuite, la gothique plus grande, moins ronde, avec des traits droits et des brisures dans les caractères: la 'lettre de missel' employée pour les livres d'eglise. Puis un dérivé calligraphié de l'écriture cursive employée dans les chancelleries ... la gothique 'bâtarde' ... Enfin, une dernière venue, promise à un grand avenir puisqu'elle deviendra l'écriture normale des textes imprimés dans une grande partie de l'Europe occidentale: l'écriture humanistique, la 'littera antiqua,' la future 'romaine.' (109)

[Firstly the gothic of scholastic texts, the traditional 'black letter' beloved of theologians and university professors. Then the larger size gothic, less rounded, with straight uprights and fractured letters: the missal letter used for ecclesiastical books. Next a script derived from that used in the Chancelleries ... the 'bastard' gothic, a hand current in luxury manuscripts ... Finally, the last to emerge ... the 'littera antiqua,' the humanist, or roman script ... With this roman script there can be associated a cursive script, the Cancelleresca ... [There are] intermediate styles of all kinds ... the gothic used by the scribes of Bologna ... the Parisian bastarda type.] (111)[19]

That the passage is only marginally intelligible in English points out one of the problems of the discussion here: typefaces and palaeographical styles are not universals that can be pointed to by equivalent terms in different languages. A particular typefont or class of typefont (i.e., a typeface) when used in France or discussed in French is not the same typefont when used in England or discussed in English. Febvre and Martin are attempting to distinguish roman/gothic, subdividing gothic into three subclasses, a system found in several works on early typography.[20] It is somewhat exasperating to critique such statements, since to supply the illustrations necessary to make the above passage at all intelligible lends it a coherence that is to a large extent illusory. There are several standard illustrations readily available (see, for example, the illustration in Updike's *Printing Types*, 1: 61); I provide instead the more mischievous illustration from Isaac's *English Printing Types*. Here, all three types are shown on a single page of the 1528 *Regimen sanitatis Salerni* by Berthelet (*STC* 21596) (see fig. 1). The English text is in textura; the smaller of the two fonts for Latin is a rotunda; the larger is a bastard.

Let us consider the three categories in turn. The first given by Febvre and Martin, 'lettre de somme,' is what English typographers call round, rounded, or rotunda, but even the illustration provided here should not

meth in bloud and suche lyke. The. xiij. is/the
swetenes of spittyll/through swetenes of blud.
Here is to be noted/that lyke as there be tokens
of abundance of bloud/ so there be signes of the
abundance of other humours /as in these verses folowynge.

Accusat coleram dextre dolor aspera lingua.
Tinnitus/ vomitusq frequens/vigilantia multa.
Multa sitis/ pinguis/egestio/ torsio ventris.
Nausea sit motus cordis/languescit orexis.
Pulsus adest gracilis/durus/veloxq calescens.
Aret/amarescit/incendia somnis fingit.

The tokens of abundace of fleme are cõteined in
these verses folowyng.

Flegma supergrediens proprias in corpore leges
Os facit incipidum/fastidia crebra/salinas.
Cõstarum stomachi/simul occipitisq dolores.
Pulsus adest rarus/et tardus/mollis/inanis.
Precedit fallax/fantasmata/somnus aquosus.

The signes of abundance of melancoly are con-
teyned in these verses folowyng.

Humorum pleno dum sex in corpore regnat.
Nigra cutis/durus/pulsus/tenuis et vrina.
Sollicitudo timor/et tristicia/somnia tempus.
Accrescet rugitus sapor/et sputaminis idem.
Leuaq precipue tinnit et sibilat auris.

Denus septenus Bip sseuBotpomiam petit annus.

Spiritus Bertior erit per sseuBotpomiam.

Spiritus ex potu Bini mox multiplicatur.

Humorumq cibo damnum sente reparatur.

Lumina clarificat, sincerat sseuBotpomia.

Mentes, et cerebrum, calidas facit esse medullas.

Viscera purgabit, stomachum, ventremq coercet.

Puros dat sensus, dat somnum/tedia tollit.

Auditus/ Vocem/ Vires producit et auget.

Here the auctour speakynge of bluдde lettynge/
sayth/that at, xbij, yere of age one may be lette
bloудde.

Fig. 63. T. BERTHELET. 95 a TEXTURA (Greg 1) with s^3, w^2 small, v^3, y^2.
54 ROTUNDA (Greg 2) with a^2, both d's, s^1, v^1.
95 BASTARD with a curiously cut h.

Regimen sanitatis Salerni. 1528. S.T.C. 21596.

1. Frank Isaac, *English and Scottish Printing Types, 1501–35, 1508–41* (Oxford, 1930), fig. 63.

be taken to imply that the various scholars using these terms are referring to the same thing.[21] The defining word 'somme' itself points to a
'destination propre,' coming from 'Summa' and presumably to the style
used to copy bulky theological works in small type; 'beloved' though it
may have been by theologians, its existence as a definable category of
type in printing history has been doubted. Theologians and university
professors read what was provided them; there is little evidence as to
what they loved typographically, nor is there evidence that their printers
much cared. The term used in the above passage to translate this is
'black letter,' but this term, in all uses I have seen, refers to the squarish
typeface modelled on the Dutch fonts of de Worde that maintains a life
in English printing through the nineteenth century. (The image that
most English readers will conjure up when they see the term 'black
letter' is as good as any illustration I could provide.) It has no equivalent
linguistically or historically in French, German, or Italian, nor does it
accurately translate the French term 'lettre de somme' (note that what
you imagined for black letter a few sentences ago is closer to Isaac's
example of textura or 'letter de forme' in fig. 1 than to what he describes
as 'rotunda.')

The second class of typeface ('lettre de forme' or textura) is associated
in its larger varieties with missals, although most varieties of English
black letter would also be classified by typographers as texturas. The
term 'livres d'eglise' is unfortunate, even in French, and generates the
English 'ecclesiastical books.' What seems to be meant is 'service books.'
This is inaccurate, as anyone who has studied actual service books of the
period would know: type used in missals is large, since it must be seen at
a distance; type used in breviaries is small. And this difference supersedes differences in form. Obviously, it cannot be accurate to speak of a
'destination propre' for such types, since readers of French missals are
different from readers of English vernacular books even though what
they read might appear similar.

The third type, bastard, is, when applied to early printing, various.
Examples from early French printing would include some of the types of
Colard Mansion and William Caxton – types cut in imitation of the script
in luxurious vernacular manuscripts.[22] In the sixteenth century this term
would include type used in routine vernacular printing; in the example
in fig. 1, it is used to distinguish Latin in a vernacular English text.

The final group, 'littera antiqua,' is presumably a forerunner of roman type. As the 'future roman' type, this classification seems secure
enough: gothic (or is it Gothic?) is in some way opposed to roman (or

Roman), but by the time that roman type is clearly distinguished from the various gothic varieties, there are other types (italic) that complicate the scheme further. The text in bastard type in the example in fig. 1 (from a book printed in 1528) is replaced in Berthelet's line-for-line reprint of 1541 by italic type.[23]

There may be contexts in which the scheme outlined by Febvre and Martin would be useful for discussing early typefaces, but few catalogues that have to deal with real examples of type follow it. The *British Museum Catalogue* (*BMC*) classifies fifteenth-century types differently depending on the region: German types are identified simply by their 20-line measurement; Italian types are classified G (gothic), R (roman), SG (semi-gothic) because of the 'equal rivalry between gothic and roman' in these types (*BMC* 4: xvi). For Dutch and French types, the classification B (bastard) is added, and one of Mansion's types is listed as GR (i.e., gothic-round). Typeforms are not universals, but regional: Mansion's presumed 'rotunda' (*letter de somme*) has nothing to do with what Febvre and Martin mean by this term (see *BMC* 9:132 and their facsimile 1B). The typeface called bastard, when used in sixteenth-century English books, had a different meaning and function from what it had when used to print books in France.[24] What Germans know as Schwabacher would not be used to print a French text, nor would it be available to print one.

The appeal to the level of typography to support a grand cultural narrative is specious. There is no agreement among specialists on how the classifications of such evidence should be made (classifications that are the basis of Febvre and Martin's cultural narrative). Any serious examination of typography reveals that all the terms here must be used in the context of particular books printed with such type, and even further, within the context of particular readers whose shelves and experience may or may not reflect the actual production of such things.

Febvre and Martin do not confront such arguments and appeal instead to such levels of abstraction as the 'people's faith' and 'the triumph of the humanist spirit':

> L'immense majorité des hommes et même des hommes de lettres de leur temps, reste fidèle aux types traditionnels d'écriture gothique. (113)

What precisely is the distinction between the majority of people and the majority of men of letters? And how would these majorities be calculated? What is 'fidelity' to gothic script? And how would such faith be documented? No buyer or reader in the fifteenth or sixteenth century had the opportunity to exercise such a choice, nor did a bookseller ever provide a text in two forms, classified gothic/roman, from which a particular customer could choose.

The discussion then faces several problems. The first is classificatory. Febvre and Martin are interested in the grand narrative built on a few universals, themselves based on particularities of evidence. But the classificatory schemes adopted here do not function simultaneously on these levels, since an opposition that might function intelligibly in one printer's type cases might not function intelligibly or even exist in another printer's type cases. What is represented as a difference between, say, bastard and black letter in one book, might be represented as a difference between roman and black letter in another, even when the book is produced by the same printer (see n. 23).

The second is historical – the attempt to find the micronarratives, the anecdotes, often melodramatic, that fit the grand narrative that is in the process of construction. The anecdote supporting or illustrating this opposition or 'triumph of the spirit' concerns the printing of Rabelais:

> Rabelais' *Gargantua*, to be bought by a huge public at the Lyons fair and elsewhere, was printed in black letter [French *bâtard*]. For a long time, therefore, gothic bastarda was used to print popular books, almanacs and 'gothic booklets.' The poorer printers ran off thousands of these, wearing out their founts in the process and buying cast-offs from their richer colleagues who no longer wanted them. Only later, in the second half of the sixteenth century, when obliged to restock with new types, did they acquire the roman which the public had grown to expect. (83)

The narrative itself is appealing, with its characters of rich printers, poor printers, the poor struggling against the rich. It is a narrative very familiar in Annales histories, but little or no documentation is given for it here. It is not clear what is meant by a typefont here, and the English translators have no clear way of dealing with the technical language of typefaces used in French. The history itself goes against much of what is known in typographical history. Fifteenth-century typefonts were very short-lived, and it was this characteristic that enabled bibliographers to date books without printed dates and to associate them with particular printers – to provide the history of their production, location, and distribution along trade routes.[25]

If I read Febvre and Martin correctly here, the subject is not the obsolescence of typefaces; it is not about, say, the evolution of a typefaces and typographical style. The narrative concerns rather the particular histories of material typefonts in material type cases. These typefonts (the contents of physical type cases) are bought by poor printers in the early sixteenth century; these then survive (the contents of type cases?) until the late sixteenth century when readers were accustomed to roman type. I do not know what Febvre and Martin have in support of such a history, nor do I know of any study that has claimed new fonts, much less worn-out ones, lasted so long. Typefonts did change hands. But this changing of hands is not necessarily a function of economic status. In a fairly well-documented case involving Ulm printers, it seems that the more famous and prolific printer (Johann Zainer) borrowed back a typefont used by one of the more obscure printers (Johann Schaur).[26]

The history of the printing of Rabelais also does not support such a thesis. Rabelais went through several printings in the mid-sixteenth century. His books were generally printed singly, in pamphlet form; after mid-century, they began to appear in roman type, *as did most other French books. Le Tiers Livre*, appearing in 1546, is the first printed in roman type; it is thus occasionally seen as marking a transition of the more popular Rabelais to the 'humanist' Rabelais.[27] But this is not necessarily a shift from 'gothic' to 'humanist' sensibility. What happens is a shift in what might be called the 'zero degree of typography' from gothic to roman; with the growing use of roman fonts, the 'marked' form of type (once roman), becomes (at least for the printers) the older *bâtard*. A Rabelais in *bâtard* type at the end of the century would not, for its printers, be the same as a Rabelais in *bâtard* type at the beginning of the century.

Yet it is extremely difficult to generalize on such matters. To assume a shared interpretation among printers and readers (who doubtless had books printed at various periods on their shelves) involves a far more perfect communication of conventions than we ourselves generally experience. Again, readers did not choose their Rabelais; they simply took what printers offered them, and printers printed in the typefaces type cutters offered them. What to later historians appear to be obvious shifts in typefaces ('gothic' to 'roman') must be discussed in terms of specific cases. What these studies show is that printers' intentions, even when manifested in terms of format (the sheer size of the book) are not always represented by typography.[28] Unless there is convincing evidence to the contrary, it seems best to assume that the Rabelais pamphlet in roman (*Le Tiers Livre*, 1546) had roughly the same *destination propre* as the earlier pamphlets in bâtard (*Gargantua*, 1534; *Pantagruel*, 1532).

Le Livre and *le livre*

As in Eisenstein, the precise subject matter or field in *L'Apparition du livre* is named but not clearly defined; it is something that is at the centre of a number of historical changes: 'Thus the printed book played its part in a whole range of basic changes which were taking place at the time.' To Febvre and Martin, at the centre of these changes is 'le livre,' 'le livre imprimé,' or occasionally 'le Livre,' but these distinctions, real or not, are often lost or simply ignored in the English translation and transcription. Their 'Book/book' functions as does the English phrase 'print culture,' and changes its shape as quickly:

> Le Livre, ce nouveau venu au sein des sociétés occidentales; le Livre, qui a commencé sa carrière au milieu du XV siècle, et dont nous ne sommes pas assurés, au milieu du XXe, qu'il puisse longtemps encore continue à remplir son role.

'Le Livre' is something different from 'le livre,' although both blur quickly into 'le livre imprimé' (never capitalized, I believe), which itself is an abstraction, perhaps 'The Printed Book,' rather than any particular material printed book or group of them. Yet one of these (or all) is responsible for 'creat[ing] new habits of thought':

> We hope to establish how and why the printed book was something more than a triumph of technical ingenuity, but was also one of the most potent agents at the disposal of western civilisation in bringing together the scattered ideas of representative thinkers. (10)[29]

So is 'Le Livre' the institution surrounding particular books housed in libraries? *des livres imprimés?*

The French word 'livre' in 'histoire du livre' seems to provide a basis for discussion, but in so doing, becomes unassailable and apparently not subject to critical review. It generates instead a series of polemics and narratives that in turn lend an illusion of legitimacy to their originary concepts. Under the headings 'le livre' or 'le Livre' can be arranged all bibliographical works loosely related to such things (bibliographical works that Eisenstein, by contrast, seems to renounce).[30] And many of these studies define a level of 'Book-ness' involving the very statistics over which the grand narrative can be written. In much of the work of Annales historians, the connection between the two levels is logical or persuasive, but often the two levels are detached, as here. It is difficult to determine which notes provide the details of discussion on which the Annales narrative builds, and which serve as little more than decoration – documentation not for the narrative itself, but rather for Febvre and Martin's initial assertion of their own competence in the field.

2 Twenty Million Incunables Can't Be Wrong

2.1 The Calculus of Book-Copies

> The central importance of print-capitalism will be discussed below. It is
> sufficient to remind ourselves of its scale and pace. Febvre and Martin
> estimate that 77% of the books printed before 1500 were still in Latin
> (meaning nonetheless that 23% were already in vernaculars) [ref. Febvre
> and Martin, 248–9]. If of the 88 editions printed in Paris in 1510 all but 8
> were in Latin, after 1575 a majority were always in French. Despite a
> temporary come-back during the Counter-Reformation, Latin's hegemony
> was doomed.[1]

This quotation comes from one of the more influential books in cultural
studies of the last twenty years: Benedict Anderson's *Imagined Communities*. Anderson's political argument is often expressed in terms of empirical data. It is both the function and the foundation of this data that I will
examine here. I take as my starting point one of Anderson's specific
claims, one found in a number of standard book histories: that during
the fifteenth century, 20 million printed books were produced and
disseminated:

> It has been estimated that in the 40-odd years between the publication of
> the Gutenberg Bible and the close of the fifteenth century, more than
> 20,000,000 printed volumes were produced in Europe. (18)

The statement is repeated on p. 37: 'As already noted, at least 20,000,000
books had already been printed by 1500, signaling the onset of Benjamin's
"age of mechanical reproduction."'[2]

The source for this specific figure and for much other data on early book production is Febvre and Martin's *L'Apparition du livre*; the reference here is to the English edition, pp. 182–6. The figures provided by Febvre and Martin are as follows:

> This amounted to no less than 35,000 editions produced in no fewer than 236 towns. As early as 1480, presses existed in more than 110 towns, of which 5 were in today's Italy, 30 in Germany, 9 in France, 8 each in Holland and Spain, 5 each in Belgium and Switzerland, 4 in England, 2 in Bohemia, and 1 in Poland. From that date it may be said of Europe that the printed book was in universal use. (*Coming of the Book*, 182)

The later editions of *L'Apparition du livre* contain a series of often qualifying notes not included in the early versions of the French edition that I have seen. On this particular statement, note 271 of the English edition reads in part: 'These figures are intended only to give an idea of the scale of operations. They are based on an annotated copy of K. Burger, *The Printers and the Publishers of the XV. Century with Lists of their Works* (London, 1902).' (The 'annotated copy' of Burger is not identified.) Anderson's reference must be to p. 186 and its note 272, which reads cryptically 'cf. p. 248ff.' I assume the 'cf.' means that pages 248 and following provide some contradictory information. And indeed, p. 248 of *The Coming of the Book* states: 'Some 30,000–35,000 different editions printed between 1450 and 1500 have survived, representing 10,000–15,000 different texts, and if we were to take into account those which have not survived the figures would perhaps be much larger.' The Annales rhetoric is suddenly dizzying. What does it mean to say that if we were to take into account texts that have *not* survived the figures would *perhaps* be much larger? Febvre and Martin proceed:

> Assuming an average print run to be no greater than 500, then about 20 million books were printed *before 1500* [note 343], an impressive total even by 20th-century standards, and even more so when we remember that the Europe of that day was far less populous than now. There were certainly fewer than 100 million inhabitants in the countries where printing developed, and of them only a minority could read. (248–9)[3]

Contrary to what is implied here, the extremely problematic figures on population are not basic facts that anyone should know or remember. And the figures on print runs and book distribution are just as complex.

Twenty million books were *not* distributed among 100 million inhabitants, since those hypothetical 20 million (?) books would have been printed over, say, fifty years, and distributed among a population that *at any one time* might have been 100 million. The question should be: How many books were produced in fifty years in relation to the number of inhabitants in Europe during those fifty years? Are we talking about one book-copy per five persons? Is that a lot? Or do we have to consider how many persons of reading age there were at any given time? And if so, how many books were available at that same time? Human beings live and die and we obviously need to consider that in order to do any meaningful statistical work on them, but book-copies live and die as well, and in equally complex and unpredictable ways. Any claim about their numbers has to consider this as well. Obviously, these are irritating and complex questions, but the meaning of the particular terms must be dealt with before we can speak with any meaning about 'reading revolutions' of the fifteenth century.

Let us begin by looking at something bibliographers and incunabulists can deal with: note 343 to the English version of *L'Apparition du livre*:

> Of course we mean only to indicate some idea of scale. According to Vladimir Loublinsky, production would be somewhere between 12 and 20 million copies. Cf. the review of the first edition of the present book in *Vestnik Istorii Mirovoi Kultury*, Moscow, 1959, no. 4.

The reference, without page number, to a Russian journal not readily available in every library will be unhelpful for many readers. With no small difficulty I have found it, and Loublinsky does not quite say what Febvre and Martin claim.[4] Loublinsky is criticizing, as others have done, the dated scholarship on which Febvre and Martin base their claims and their careless attitude toward that scholarship. Following this criticism, in what I am told is a rather convoluted paragraph, Loublinsky notes that he himself had estimated this total at 12 million books some twenty years earlier. He concedes that that figure might be low, but asserts that Febvre and Martin's categorical statement that 20 million books existed (a statement found on pages 281, 377, and 396 of the first French edition) is careless and reckless.

Febvre and Martin offer no help on the question of why 20 million should be 'somewhere between 12 and 20 million.' What statistic has been revised? Is it the figure concerning average edition size? Should the estimate 500 be lowered to 300? Is it the number of estimated editions?

Has this number been lowered to 20,000? Or is it the very definition of 'edition'?

These are the questions I will address in the following sections. We should bear in mind things that we already know, the commonplaces of book history and social history: many people lived in the fifteenth century, and many read books; many books were produced; some have not survived, but some are now in libraries; books were produced in editions of various sizes; many books were in Latin; political institutions favour the rich. The difficulty, then, is not with such general conclusions, none of which would ever be seriously disputed. The difficulty is in associating such commonplaces with empirical evidence – evidence that everyone seems to agree will in some way support certain incontestable generalities. How do we get from that object in an archive – the catalogued book in the Rare Book room – to the 'things we know' about history and politics? This is a much more difficult process than many scholars seem to acknowledge, and it belittles the information contained within those archival objects to imply that they can provide easily accessible support for banalities generated by an entirely different set of political and cultural conditions.[5]

The Counting of Incunables

To understand the difficulties involved in a concept as basic to book history as 'the number of books printed in the fifteenth century,' we can consider the more detailed estimates of this figure; minimally, we need to find out what happened to some 8 million incunables, the difference between Febvre and Martin's often cited figure and the lower figure of Loublinsky. The most important modern survey of surviving incunables was begun by the Kommission für einem Gesamtkatalog der Wiegendrucke, established in 1904.[6] By the Second World War, seven volumes were completed (A-Federicis), enumerating 9729 presumed editions or *Inkunabelausgaben* and the principles of description continued to evolve. In 1935 Kurt Ohly claimed that the Kommission had considered some 425,000–450,000 exemplars (book-copies), and that another 100,000 were known, but not yet inventoried. Ohly claimed further that as of 1930, the Kommission had described some 37,639 separate editions.[7]

For incunabulists of the early twentieth century, the key question did not concern how many book-copies there might once have been, but rather how many editions (*Inkunabelausgaben*) these book-copies represented. The problems for this period concerned matters of cataloguing and inventory, and the basis for both was to be the notion or definition of *Ausgabe*. Because of the type of problem the Gesamtkatalog Kommission was attempting to solve, by *Ausgabe* was meant (tautologically) 'subject of particular entries in their catalogue, the *Gesamtkatalog der Wiegendrucke* (hereafter *GW*).' The Kommission intended to provide a catalogue base that would serve to organize all known copies of surviving fifteenth-century books. They were less interested in questions that were later to concern Anglo-American bibliographers such as Fredson Bowers – the definition of 'ideal copy' and consistent distinctions between 'issue,' 'state,' and 'variant' – all problems of descriptive bibliography.[8] Their early published fascicles did not even provide a complete inventory of copies; listed copies were rather representative of the editions implied by the catalogue entry. The published catalogue thus did not function, as does the ongoing *Incunabula Short Title Catalogue* or the earlier *Census of Incunabula in American Libraries* by Frederick Goff, as a survey of surviving book-copies. The Kommission was also not directly concerned with questions that might be posed by historians of 'print culture' – questions about popularity or the number of books distributed and in circulation among readers.

The Kommission's catalogue (*GW*) was not complete in 1935 when Ohly made these statements quoted above and it is still incomplete; to determine the number of entries (or editions) it would recognize when complete requires some calculation. Dachs and Schmidt in 1974 estimated the number of editions that would be included in *GW* if complete, and came up with a figure of about 27,500, some 8000 editions short of the figure proclaimed by Ohly in the 1930s. Independent calculations by Paul Needham confirmed this number. Dachs and Schmidt point out that this figure was in dispute among the Kommission workers themselves.[9] The calculations involved are not overly complicated now, and would not have been complicated in 1930, even though fewer volumes of *GW* were in print at the time. The *GW* is alphabetical. And by comparing it to other alphabetical incunable catalogues (catalogues that are, in their own terms, 'complete'), a percentage should be derived showing what *GW* might contain if completed according to the principles defined by its initial volumes. Among the difficulties noted by Dachs and Schmidt was that Hain's 1810 *Repertorium*, the most complete catalogue available, was itself incomplete, lacking the concluding entries (from the letter V). And all incunable catalogues produced between Hain's catalogue and the *GW* fascicles of 1932 are to some extent based on Hain (at least using it as a cross-reference or as a means to identify their own editions). By distinguishing what might be called 'Hain-based' catalogues (those produced prior to 1932), from those produced after this date (for example, Goff's American *Census*), Dachs and Schmidt came up with the following figures: based on incunable catalogues produced prior to 1932, the GW entries (A–Federicis) seemed to constitute a low of 34.9 per cent, a high of 41.0 per cent of recorded incunables (the high figure was obtained by comparing *GW* with Hain). When based on catalogues produced after 1932, the range of these figures was 36.5 per cent to 38.7 per cent.[10] The range was narrowing as the identification of editions became more accurate, and it was narrowing in a direction away from the figure one obtains by comparing GW to the incomplete Hain catalogue (41.0 per cent). Dachs and Schmidt finally estimate a 'known' number of incunable editions ('Gesamtzahl bekannter Inkunabelausgaben') as 'not much over 27000,' a figure which they say does not correspond in any way with what they claim is the figure of 'approximately 40,000' one finds in the scholarly literature.

But the story Dachs and Schmidt tell is not simply about numbers of editions. It is about a dispute between the spokesmen for the Kommission itself (primarily Kurt Ohly) and Konrad Haebler. Ohly claimed that in March 1930 the Gesamtkatalog Kommission manuscript had 37,639 descriptions, but gave no source for this, nor any clear statement as to the precise nature of those descriptions. This figure was at odds with the estimates by Haebler, in what was then, and to a large extent still is, the only single-volume treatment of the field of incunable study, his *Handbuch der Inkunabelkunde*. Here, Haebler estimated the number of editions as 'nearly 30,000.' Haebler's *Handbuch* is not lavishly produced, and Carl Wehmer, disputing this figure, claimed that the statement by Haebler must be a typographical error.[11] Haebler, however, repeated this figure in 1921.[12] Dachs and Schmidt note that Haebler was using the same evidence in reasserting his figure of 'nearly 30,000' as was the Gesamtkatalog Kommission in claiming 37,639 descriptions (91).[13] Meanwhile, most German scholars seemed to accept the figure of 40,000. Non-German incunabulists were somewhat less certain, and tended to use the lower figure of Haebler.[14]

Ohly's note says that the number 37,639 would be diminished by the discovery of doublets in the descriptions and by the number of sixteenth-century editions that were inaccurately listed in the preliminary descriptions as incunables. But he claims as well that such losses would be made up for by the discovery of early book fragments representing presently unrecorded editions: thus to the aid of this high estimate would come the field of *Makulaturforschung* (the study of fragments) (87). Yet what do such 'book fragments' mean in the context of a total 'number of editions' or 'number of book-copies'?

Clear distinctions must be made between several things that are often conflated: real book-copies that exist in the real world; real book-copies that existed in the fifteenth century; book-copies imagined to have existed in the fifteenth century; and descriptions of book-copies. These are all quite different things. And what Ohly seems to have been unwilling to consider with serious scepticism was how radically different are descriptions and actual book-copies. Descriptions of book-copies do not necessarily reflect the actual book-copies in the real world.

Furthermore, one must consider Ohly's reference to *Makulaturforschung* (see following chapter below). Ohly claims that any overestimates (for example, the existence of 'doublets' in the Gesamtkatalog Kommission's manuscript) would be compensated for by the continued discovery of fragments of previously unrecorded books and editions, that is, traces of, say, early grammar books (many from Mainz and the Netherlands are known only in fragments) that had been used, discarded, and cut up for use in bindings. In the early twentieth century, the numbers of such fragments recorded in scholarly literature was indeed increasing. But 10,000 hypothesized discoveries would tax even the most optimistic visions of the future of *Makulaturforschung*. Such fragments are only to be found in fifteenth-century and sixteenth-century bindings, and new ones could only be discovered in such bindings that had not been previously examined for them. Just how many unexamined early bindings are there? And how many were there when Ohly was writing?

Since 1932, very few of these fragments have been discovered, and most of those now recorded were already known to the Gesamtkatalog Kommission.[15] The holdings of libraries today show evidence of the work of early 'Makulaturists.' The Huntington Library, with the second largest collection of incunables in America, contains several thousand early bindings, and most seem to have been seriously examined, some perhaps by researchers at the Huntington, but most by dealers in the book trade well before the books arrived at the Huntington. I have found only one set of fragments representing an unrecorded edition, and these were already cut out of the binding and preserved loosely in the covers. The endpapers of numerous early bindings have been removed (and I assume catalogued and sold elsewhere); several bindings have had their paper boards removed from now limp and empty leather covers. If the missing pasteboard consisted of recycled leaves of early books, these too are now housed and probably catalogued as a group of fragments in some distant library. Where are unrecorded fragments in any significant numbers to be found?[16]

Furthermore, just what does a discovery of new fragments mean in terms of the entries in *GW*? To Ohly, these new fragments would increase the number of *GW* entries. That is certainly true, but the addition of such numbers would not necessarily increase the number of editions these numbers represent. For some entries (for example, 'Donatus'), the cataloguing rule is generally to supply a separate catalogue number for each discovered fragment (or set of fragments). The various catalogue entries and the book-copies they refer to might well represent the same edition, but this is something for later researchers to determine (see chapter 3 below).

This is different from the cataloguing rules for most other book-copies in *GW*, where the catalogue entry is close to what one would expect of a descriptive bibliography: the purpose is to distinguish editions and to describe ideal copy (individual owners and libraries can thus identify their own copies and match them up with particular catalogue entries). If one has, say, two leaves of the Gutenberg Bible in one library, those leaves are assigned the same *GW* number as the loose leaves of a Gutenberg Bible in any another library, whatever parts of the text those leaves come from and whether or not they happen to have come from the same book-copy. For Donatus fragments, comparable sets of leaves would in most cases be assigned an autonomous *GW* number; thus for Donatus, a single edition (and possibly even what was once a single book-copy) might be represented by several entry numbers. Thus, while Ohly's envisioned *Makulaturforschung* might well have increased the number of 'catalog entries,' this increase in catalogue entries would not necessarily result in an increase in 'numbers of editions.' In fact, the apparent increase of known editions implied by the actual increase in catalogue entries would be illusory.[17]

The estimate of 20 million given in Febvre and Martin seems to be based on the assumption of some 35,000 editions. According to the latest bibliographical statistics available to them, they were off by some 25 per cent on the number of editions. According to the note in the English edition, they were off by some 40 per cent on the number of book-copies. Do we say then that instead of 20 million, or their revised estimate of 12–20 million, this figure should be closer to 8 million?

There are still other factors affecting these estimates. Ohly claimed the Gesamtkatalog Kommission had examined 450,000 copies and knew about another 100,000. Are we to assume (for a figure of, say, 10,000,000) a survival rate of about 1 in 15? A survival rate that only includes inventoried copies, and not those lying in private libraries (something that would increase that percentage quite dramatically)? This figure may strike me as unsettling (perhaps it is too high; perhaps it is too low), but oddly, my anxieties over this can only be quieted by assuming things equally unsettling – uncomfortably high (or low) average edition sizes or an overly high (or low) estimate of total numbers of books. Without constant reference to the comforting 'things we know' (there is growing literacy; the rich oppress the poor) it is very difficult to know what to do with such figures.

Let us return to Dachs and Schmidt. What is all the fuss about anyway? Dachs and Schmidt note in their conclusion that this is not a purely 'academic' exercise. Libraries and owners have the right to know 'what portion of the entire book production of the fifteenth century their collection represents,'[18] since a higher or lower number will affect the value of each collection. This statement is somewhat misleading, because an accurate estimate of the number of fifteenth-century editions is not going to provide the basis for determining this figure. The problem it can solve is rather 'the portion of the number of editions of the fifteenth century a given library possesses in its collection,' a completely different matter.

Dachs and Schmidt go further: these figures are fundamental to all questions of literary-sociology; 'false premises can here lead to false conclusions' (94). But will they? Consider Schoenberg's statements in *Theory of Harmony*:

> In this sense, it is of little consequence whether one starts with a correct hypothesis or a false one. Sooner or later the one as well as the other will certainly be refuted. Thus, we can only base our thought on such conjectures as will satisfy our formal necessity for sense and coherence without their being considered natural laws ... [For] it is entirely possible that in spite of an observation falsely construed as fundamental we may, by inference or through intuition, arrive at correct results; whereas it is not at all a proven fact that more correct or better observation would necessarily yield more correct or better conclusions.[19]

We will see in a later chapter that many bibliographical conclusions, true or false, are not really the product of false premises nor of false logic, but rather are more accurately described as products of bibliographical assumptions. In the present case, there can be no separation of conclusions from assumptions. Ohly and Haebler will disagree not only about the number of editions, but also about the methods used to determine that figure, and about the assumptions that are required in order to determine it.

It is interesting that Needham does not enter this argument. In 1940 Dachs and Schmidt seemed compelled to offer a weak gesture in the direction of cultural history. Needham, however, sticks fast to the number itself, and even goes further, denying the legitimacy of certain tempting uses of the 1998 *ISTC*, the most complete and accurate enumerative catalogue of incunables now available:

> But the reader had better pause before starting to compose a little article on 'The Contraction of European Printing, 1477 to 1479.' The User's Guide warns that the Year of Publication field may enable 'rough statistical work' to be done, but that the uncertainties of assigning dates to undated editions means that the results 'are always likely to be in varying degrees imprecise' (p. 19). This remark is correct so far as it goes, but the warning should probably be stronger: the Year of Publication field is inadequate for even the roughest of statistical analysis.[20]

The implication here, if we take the statement in its strongest sense, is that the database can only be used for the very precise and limited purpose for which it was designed, and that is as a union catalogue; the primary work that will grow out of it is not 'literary-sociological,' but rather further refinements of the catalogue itself (see as an example Needham's own Appendix to the review). The gap between the material and the discussion remains insurmountable, and may even be a direct function of the precision with which the data and material are defined and refined. Thus the better the bibliographical tools, the less reliable they are in their general applications.

2.2 The Quantification of Evidence

A 1996 article by U. Neddermeyer addressing the possibilities of a 'quantitative' description of late fifteenth-century book production is more seriously documented than the casual estimates given by Febvre and Martin, but its implied method reveals the problems inherent in any such study. Neddermeyer's main interest is in late medieval manuscript production, and his discussion of fifteenth-century book production occupies only the opening pages.[21] If it is ever to be possible to determine exactly how many books were produced during a particular period, Neddermeyer claims, then the second half of the fifteenth century is the most valuable period for a book historian to study, since the number of editions involved does not reach unmanageable numbers. He accepts the figure of 27,000 (the lower of the Gesamtkatalog Kommission estimates), and defines the problem as the determination of average 'edition size' (*Auflagehöhe*); (one should say here more accurately that what is necessary is the number of book-copies per *GW* entry, which is not quite the same thing).

> Die zahlreichen erhaltend Einzelbelege (mir sind allein für den Zeitraum bis 1500 über 160 bekannt) erlauben es, den jeweiligen Durchschnitt sowie seine Veränderung recht präzise festzumachen und darüber hinaus sogar Unterschiede zwischen den einzelnen europäischen Ländern herauszuarbeiten. (24)

> [The numerous extant pieces of evidence (I know of over 160 for the period to 1500) permit us to make very precise each average as well as its modification and therefore to expose even differences between particular European countries.]

The notion that it is advantageous to use as a basis of study a period in which there is a 'manageable' number of books may well be an illusion; the low number of total books is matched by a paucity of external evidence concerning their numbers and the claim of precision ('recht präzise') is unsettling here. Neddermeyer does not give a catalogue of those 160+ references, but many apparently are the now familiar ones found in Haebler's *Handbuch der Inkunabelkunde* (I will return to this source below).

Neddermeyer points out that the notion of a generalized average edition size or print run for fifteenth-century books is misleading. The average number of copies per print run may vary over time (and does, based on the scattered data here). If the average edition size in the last decade of the fifteenth century is high, and the total number of editions in the same decade is also high, these figures will dominate and overwhelm the figures from the earliest decade in which the average size is much lower. The mathematics of this is complex, and Neddermeyer does not spend much time with it. The figures he arrives at are 6 million books for Germany, and for Europe generally, 18 million. Even with the lower estimate of number of editions, we are back to Febvre and Martin's estimate (at least, back to a moment before their note of retraction). Several million missing incunables have reappeared.

If we divide this number by the number of known editions (18 million divided by 27,000), we come up with a figure of 600. But this figure is, of course, misleading, since the estimate of the 'number of books in the fifteenth century' includes book-copies from unrecorded editions as well. If we assume, without any precision, a number of lost editions, that average edition size might be lowered: if half the editions are lost (is that what anyone claims?) and these lost editions are spread evenly through the period (unlikely), that average figure will lower to, say, 300.[22] This is also illusory, since one cannot correlate 'likelihood of survival' with 'size of print run' in any meaningful way.

No one, to my knowledge, has come up with a mathematical or even a convincing bibliographical model of how such figures might be computed. Estimates of particulars (size of print runs) will depend as much on the final figure (the '20 million books') as on any specific evidence; that is, any conclusions will inevitably beg the question, and the logic will run as follows: *given* 18 million incunables; *given* 27,000 known editions; *given* an average print run of 300 per edition, how many lost editions are there? Since some of these figures are so vague as to refer to no more than 'orders of magnitude' (is this what Febvre and Martin meant by 'some idea of scale'?) it is obvious why mathematics will not be of much assistance.

When we turn to the evidence itself, we find further difficulties. According to Neddermeyer's tabulation of his 160+ known pieces of evidence, for German regions, the average edition size in 1461 is 229; in 1500, the average is 1032. What these figures mean is 'the average figure cited among the recorded pieces of evidence for these dates' (as statements of historical edition size, they should obviously not be listed with three and four significant digits). Yet even if we assume that he is correct in his assertion of 160+ known pieces of evidence and assume further that each one of these pieces of evidence is reliable and the numbers incontrovertible, we still do not have a useful body of statistical evidence here. To so construe it, we need a series of even more problematic general assumptions.

First, those that deal specifically with the data itself:

1 that the average chosen for each decade is comparable, regardless of the specific evidence supporting it
2 that all figures are equally representative, that is, that the figures are not only reliable but representative, in 'precisely' the same way

Such assumptions are not valid and the precision of the figures is apparent only. We cannot plot the average for, say, 1461 (for which I assume only a dozen editions could provide evidence) against the average for 1500 (in which many more editions are obviously available for consideration) unless we assume that the figures for each are equally representative, that is, unless we can say that the figure 229 has the same relation to actual book-copies produced in the 1461 as does the figure 1032 for actual book-copies for books produced in 1500. There is no reason to assume this, and Neddermeyer does not address this question at all, but without it, the statistical base collapses.[23]

The pieces of evidence, which I assume include statements in books themselves and various inventories, are also not random, nor do they survive independently any more than book-copies themselves survive independently. A large firm has a greater chance of providing such an inventory and retaining its correspondence than does a small one.[24] Books with greater print runs are obviously in greater need of inventory (whether that inventory is used to track stock in a warehouse or to be the means for advertising) than books with small print runs. Some books were doubtless produced in extremely small print runs, but to my knowledge, no empirical evidence has been cited for books where this might apply (for example, early grammar books printed on vellum, and small pamphlets).[25] Furthermore, a reference in the 1490s cannot be said to be comparable to a reference in the 1460s. The book trade has become familiar and an inventory or advertisement will exist in the context of that everydayness of business – a quite different context from that in the 1460s. Whether the conventional everydayness of business will result in more accurate or less accurate references to print runs is of course something we also do not know.

Neddermeyer's 160+ pieces of evidence are not many when compared to the 27,000 recorded incunable editions they are supposed to represent. What is aberrant is the existence of any external evidence at all about edition size. All we can say with confidence is that 'any case whereby we can match a defined edition with external evidence about its edition size is a "non-representative" case.' The figures suggested by such nonrepresentative cases may or may not be representative of other figures, but there is no way of knowing that, and it requires a great leap of bibliographical faith to assume it.

Many of Neddermeyer's references seem to be from Haebler's *Handbuch der Inkunabulkunde*, a study that since its publication has provided incunabulists with something of a 'canon' of evidence. The quantitative use of this evidence by Neddermeyer depends absolutely on the assumption that 'all references to edition size are of equal reliability'; Haebler's own selection and presentation of the evidence in his *Handbuch*, however, show that Haebler himself does not accept that. Haebler's discussion, at least in his *Handbuch*, seems wedded to the notion of a high figure. Note how 'low' print runs are characterized by Haebler: 'Die bescheidensten Auflagen, von denen wir bestimmte Nachricht haben, belaufen sich auf 100 Exemplare' (*Handbuch*, 142). This becomes a means of rejecting smaller estimates: the 'modesty' of the 100 exemplar print run makes a smaller print run out of the question. Thus, when we have a reference to Schoeffer in 1480 producing forty-five exemplars, this number must refer not to the number of copies produced, but rather to the number a middleman (*Auftraggeber*) wanted for a particular purpose. Other small print runs are treated similarly. These were produced only during the 'timid beginnings' of the press (143); they indicate a lack of business experience, or a time 'when commercial interest is not in question' (143). In other words, small print runs are things to be excused – they are aberrant.

I close with a final note on the blurring of evidence and theory, showing how elements of the larger historical narrative (the *grand récit*) intrude upon the evaluation and definition of particular evidence, and this involves presumed cases of 'expanded editions,' that is, editions whose print runs are increased during production. Such cases are familiar in the sixteenth century, but earlier cases may well involve appeal to the abstract 'Expansion of Printing' motif as an explanation for bibliographical facts of single printing ventures: that is, printing as a fifteenth-century institution expands; during this time, the size of average print runs also expands; specific print runs increase during production. What I call the 'myth of expansion' pertains to cases where an edition exists in part in two settings – a common and perfectly reasonable explanation of that is an increase in print run during printing. One argues that *during* the print run, the printer decided to produce more book-copies than he had originally planned; all later sheets were printed in these increased numbers, but sheets already printed had to be reset and as many additional copies printed as were necessary to make up the increase in total planned edition size.[26] However, the specific internal evidence (parts of an edition exist in two settings) does not necessarily mean extended print runs. There are many other explanations possible. Nor, oddly, does the assumption of print runs extended during production yield more fifteenth-century book-copies than would otherwise be estimated by bibliographers or social historians calculating, say, 'total numbers of books.' In the cases I have examined, such books are often classified as separate editions. For cataloguing purposes, an incunable with two colophons is regarded as two editions; an incunable with two preliminaries is two editions.[27] A scholar committed to the myth of expansion might construe these as evidence of increased production of an edition, implying one edition rather than two, but if we accept this, such bibliographically documented 'increased production' results in an equally well-documented decrease in what are called editions, or GW's Auflagen) – the basis for estimating total book-copies (that is 'average print-run' × 'total number of editions' = 'total number of book copies'). The total number of hypothesized book-copies must paradoxically decrease if such presumed cases of expanded print runs are accepted.

Examples

The external evidence bearing on edition sizes is of various kinds – book lists, inventories, and statements by printers in the books themselves. Collectively, when deployed in studies such as Neddermeyer's, this evidence is impressive, but let us look at a few of the better-known examples.

Probably the best known and most often cited single piece of external evidence is printed by Sweynheim and Pannartz – a letter of Ioannes Antoninus de Buxiis to Sixtus IV appealing for support for printing, prefaced to Nicolas of Lyra, *Postilla* (1471–2; Goff N-131). The letter gives a list of books by Sweynheim and Pannartz, including with each the number of 'volumes' printed:

> Donati pro puerulis ut inde principium dicendi sumamus: unde imprimendi initium sumpsimus: numero trecenti CCC.
> Lactantius ... volumina octinginta vigintiquinque DCCC.XXV.
> Epistolarum familiarium Ciceronis volumina quingenta quinquaginta. DL

The preface is often reprinted, and was included among the thirty-two examples in Konrad Burger's *Buchhändleranzeigen* (1907), Tafel 10, (most of Burger's examples do not give edition sizes). The lists of Burger and the additions made by Voulliéme were included in Haebler's own lists of evidence in *Handbuch*, 142–5.[28]

Each of what we would call editions in the Sweynheim and Pannartz letter is said to be printed in runs of 275 or 300 (the number 825 in the

Lactantius refers to the total number of volumes of a three-volume edition). Yet the very detail of the list has been given a sceptical reading by Rudolf Hirsch:

> The size of editions remains monotonously stated at 275, with only four exceptions. I have come to the conclusion that neither the venerable cardinal Bussin ... nor the printers themselves remembered the size of the editions in most cases, but thought that the figure of 275 was about right.[29]

Hirsch is similarly sceptical about the evidence from other such lists, for example, the list by Schoeffer (1469–70) listing twenty titles printed between 1458 and 1469.[30]

> It is difficult to say what conclusions we may draw from such lists on the sales appeal of books. We know practically nothing of the size of editions, and small editions had obviously a much bigger chance of being sold out. All three grammars published in Mainz before the printing of the advertisement are missing from the list. (64, n. 10)

Each piece of evidence, according to Hirsch's implications, must be examined in its own peculiar context. But often, those very contexts are lacking or grossly incomplete. The evidence from particular lists is simply not generalizable. There is a final and somewhat unnerving paradox here, one Hirsch implies but does not state directly: the more apparently corroborative evidence we have, the less reliable it may be in any particular case. Contemporary authorities cited the figure 200–300 not because that reflected a particular print run, but rather because that was the figure traditionally cited.

Another type of evidence is in direct statements by printers. The most famous of these are two early colophons by da Spira, often quoted. Again, that 'monotonous' figure of 300 recurs.[31] Cicero, *Epistolae ad familiares* (1469; *BMC* 5:153; Goff C-505):

Hesperie quondam Germanus quosque libellos
   Abstulit: En plures ipse daturus adest.
Nanque uir ingenio mirandus & arte Ioannes
   Exscribi docuit clarius ere libros.
Spira fauet Venctis: quarto nam mense peregit
   Hoc tercentenum bis Ciceronis opus.

[The German once took his books from the north, and now he is here about to give many. For Ioannes, a man marvellous for his genius and art, learned to write books more clearly with bronze. Speyer favours Venice. For in the fourth month, he completed this work of Cicero twice in 300 copies.]

If I read this colophon correctly, it claims that the book was produced twice in issues of 300 copies each – the same figure given in the Pannartz and Sweynheim inventory.[32]

The traditional nature of this figure is further suggested when we look at the later variant of that colophon, where the word 'three' seems to be required but is not necessarily attached to the number of hundreds of volumes produced (*tercentenum*); this, the colophon for Augustine, *De civitate dei*, completed by Vindelinus da Spira (1470; *BMC* 5:153; Goff A-1233):

Qui docuit Venetos exscribi posse Ioannes
Mense fere trino Centena volumina plini
Et totidem Magni Ciceronis Spira libellos:
Ceperat Aureli: subita sed morte perentus
Non potuit Ceptem Venetis finire volumen
Vindelinus adest eiusdem frater: & arte
Non minor: hadriacaque morabitur urbe

[Ioannes, who taught the Venetians how a hundred volumes of Pliny and the same number of books of Great Cicero could be copied in about three months; he began the Augustine, but suddenly died, and was not able to finish the volumes begun for the Venetians. His brother Vindelinus came, no less skilled: he was delayed in an Adriatic city.]

I believe this means 100 volumes of each in three months, since 'three hundred in a month' could have been expressed metrically, following the exact scansion for 'tercentenum' as in 1469, as 'Mense fere tercentenum volumina plini.'

And finally, from the same press, the colophon of Sallust (1470; *BMC* 5:155; Goff S-51):

Quadringenta dedit formata volumina Crispi
Nunc, lector, venetis spirea vindelinus.
Et calamo libros audes spectare notatos
Aere magis quando littera ducta nitet.

[To Venice Wendelin, who from Speier comes,
Has given of Sallust twice two hundred tomes.
And who dare glorify the pen-made book,
When so much fairer brass-stamped letters look?][33]

Compare the later version of this in the second Sallust edition (1471; *BMC* 5:158; Goff S-54):

Quadringenta iterum formata uolumina nuper
Crispi: dedit venetis spirea vindelinus.
Sed meliora quidem lector: mihi crede: secundo
Et reprobata minus: antea quam dederat.

Did the second edition contain the same number of books? Or was the word 'quadringenta' too good to pass up?[34] See also, from a different printer, the colophon to Cicero, *Epistolae ad familiares* (Foligno: Neumeister, [1471]; *BMC* 6:599; Goff C-507), and the figure of 200 volumes:

Emilianus auctor fulginas: & fratres una
Ignenio prestante uiri. Numeister & auctor
Iohannes almanus recte qui plura peregit
Tulli ducenta nuper pressere uolumina recte
Que uiserat probus episcopus aleriensis
Fulginei acta uides & laribus Emiliani.

These colophons suggest the evidentiary paradox implied by Hirsch. The more such pieces of evidence we have that give these rough figures, the *less reliable* any one of them becomes. Evidence, thus, is reliable to the extent it is singular. But that same evidence, in that it maintains its singularity, becomes less generalizable.

In English, there are few clear pieces of evidence regarding edition sizes. For the late fifteenth century, a lawsuit involving Pynson supplies some evidence.[35] The earliest and most often cited reference to book production is by Caxton, in the 1475 *Recuyell of the Historyes of Troye*, the epilogue to Book III. It is perhaps possible to translate this into numbers of book-copies similar to those derived from continental sources, but only by introducing those numbers by way of an assumption. Caxton seems to claim that all books are begun and finished on the same day, which must mean, if anything, that the press can print an entire run of single sheets (or pages?) in one day:

> Also be cause I haue promysid to dyuerce gentilmen and to my frendes to
> adresse to hem as hastely as I myght this sayd book / Therfore I haue
> practysed & lerned at my grete charge and dispense to ordeyne this said
> book in prynte after the maner & forme as ye may here see / and is not
> wreton with penne and ynke as other bokes ben / to thende that euery
> man may haue them attones / ffor all the bookes of this storye named the
> recule of the historyes of troyes thus empryntid as ye here see were
> begonne in oon day / and also fynyshid in oon day / whiche book I haue
> presented to my sayd redoubtid lady as a fore is sayd.[36]

In order to produce an edition size acceptable to modern myths of the
expansion of printing, one must assume that he means, 'I began each
book on a single day; I finished each book on [another] single day.' The
logic of interpretation here might run as follows: the number of sheets
an individual press might produce in a day is generally estimated at 1000
for 'classical' presses in the sixteenth and seventeenth centuries. Caxton
doubtless did not achieve that efficiency. Assuming that his statement
makes sense, we can assume again a print run of 300. But the question
remains, does such a statement have to make sense at all? Or are we
equally to trust printers' statements that goose quills are no longer
necessary?[37] Hirsch's scepticism is well taken. All of these pieces of
evidence make sense if we assume beforehand we know what conclusion
they are all tending toward: those '20 million' books.

I conclude with a quick look at the rhetoric of J.M. Lenhart – a scholar
whose 1930 monograph, *Pre-Reformation Printed Books*, is used without
critical comment by Hirsch, even though Lenhart appears to share
none of Hirsch's scepticism. In it, we find again the familiar figure of
20 million, although here increased by an additional 47,000 volumes:

> The editions of the early incunabula were not large. As a rule no more than
> one hundred or one hundred and fifty copies were struck off the press by
> the printers. Before long, however, the number of copies printed was raised
> to 300. By the year 1480 editions of 400 and 500 copies had become the
> rule ... In 1478, 930 copies of the Bible in Latin were printed. Seven years
> before (1471), 1000 copies of the voluminous commentary of Panormitanus
> on canon law was printed ... In view of these facts bibliographers agree now
> in establishing 500 copies as the average of editions issued during the

fifteenth century ... These calculations establish the fact that the book-production of the latter part of the fifteenth century exceeded twenty millions; from 1445 to December 31, 1500, were printed 40,095 editions comprising 20,047,000 copies.[38]

What Lenhart gives as facts are generalizations from very small pieces of evidence – the evidence that appears in Haebler and that seems to be the basis for nearly all these estimates. Lenhart's calculations also violate one of the basic principles of such estimates, as the final figure (20,047,000) contains the five significant digits of one of its components (the dubious figure of 40,095), rather than the single significant digit of another (the even more speculative 500 copies per edition). Hirsch was sceptical of bibliographical conclusions based on these estimates; Lenhart, by contrast, chides incunabulists for their timidity.

Finally bibliographers have always shown a tendency to under-estimate the productions of the press of former ages. (14)

We notice the striking fact that the estimates of bibliographers were always understatements. (184)

These statements are simply false, as Dachs and Schmidt's study shows. Nor is there any real evidence (or even possible evidence) for the following statistic: 'In view of the fact that as high as 98, 99, and 99.5 percent of the copies of many editions have perished, we will not marvel that the loss of whole editions constitutes ten percent of the entire output' (15).

We are back again to our 20 million incunables, a figure that even Hirsch, through his tacit reliance on Lenhart, might be forced to accept. Again, we must consider: exactly what question are we asking? What does it mean to say there are X number of books? Why are we interested in that figure? The mathematician might have one answer; the descriptive bibliographer another. A cultural historian might be interested in the distribution and influence of the book, the Idea of the Book, or perhaps the contemporary idea of the distribution of the book. Then, again paradoxically, the soft evidence of the verse colophon, Caxton's claim, and even the rejoicing of the geese who no longer have to give up their feathers, might take precedence over any extant book list, or even the physical objects housed in our libraries.

2.3 Note on the Relative Popularity of Juvenal and Persius

I have noted above Paul Needham's warning about a specific search field (the Date of Publication) of the 1998 CD-ROM *ISTC*; it cannot be used even for the 'roughest of statistical analysis' ('Counting Incunables,' 489). Such a caveat could apply to more than the specific search field of this catalogue, and the following pages provide a case of why that might be so, or why this, the most complete and versatile of all enumerative catalogues of fifteenth-century printing, does not provide us with firm support for levels of discussion beyond those specifically articulated by the database itself. The case here involves some very familiar classical texts, and statements as to the popularity of these texts. Febvre and Martin (255), relying for the most part on Hain's 1810 *Repertorium*, give the following figures as indicative of the popularity of classical authors during the fifteenth century (the numbers refer to 'number of editions,' or more precisely 'entries in Hain,' and, when available, 'entries in *GW*'):

Juvenal – 61 editions listed by Hain
Persius – 33
Lucian – 19
Plautus – 13
Terence – 'no fewer than 67'
Sallust – 57
Livy – 23
Vegetius – 99 (!)
Caesar – 16 (source here is *GW*)

These figures can be compared with those given by the second edition of *ISTC*. I have attempted to filter out what *ISTC* lists as 'post-incunables':

Juvenal – 55
Persius – 43
Lucian – 28
Plautus – 9 ('comoediae' only)
Terence – 116 ('comoediae' only)
Sallust – 66
Livy – 22
Vegetius – 7 (a search including extracts yields 15)
Caesar – 17

Now let us examine what these figures mean. Suppose one were to ask: Which dramatist was more popular, Terence or Plautus? The answer seems to be Terence (an answer one probably knew before seeing any of the figures). But suppose one were to ask what enumerative bibliography has to say about the relative popularity of Juvenal and Persius?

When we consider such individual authors, the results of *ISTC* searches are murkier. For 'Decimus Junius Juvenalis,' the number is fifty-six of which one is a post-incunable. For Persius, under an Author search, one finds fifty, of which seven seem to be post-incunables. The ratio seems to be 55:43. But this is not quite true. *ISTC*, in an Author search, functions as does Hain or *GW*, and defines 'author' as the main entry author. The 1471 edition of Juvenal and Persius by Da Spira is listed: 'Juvenalis, *Satyrae*'; the notes include the statement 'Add.: Persius.' That is, each book can appear under one author and one author only, except in the case of a text jointly authored. Many editions listed by *ISTC* under Juvenal contain the full text of Persius. One finds these by searching in an 'All Fields' search 'Add: Persius,' and for these, one finds nineteen; all of these are included within the fifty-five incunable editions attributed to Juvenal, and none is listed under Persius.[39] So the ratio should perhaps be in favour of Persius – 62:55 – a ratio that seems suspiciously unlike the result one would get from a strict reading of the figures in Hain as recorded by Febvre and Martin.[40]

At this point, we must ask what sort of information we are expecting here? Do the physical books have much to say about whether Persius was a mere add-on, unread, while buyers, like the *ISTC* cataloguers, concentrated on Juvenal? The book-copies I have seen are variously annotated, but those annotations almost without exception follow the rule that the first texts in any book are annotated more heavily than the concluding texts. Was the text of Persius in these copies ignored because it was the second item printed or bound in a composite volume or *Sammelband*? Is this 'accident' to be considered an index of popularity not in spite of but rather because of the possibility that it is itself a cause of that popularity? Does this bear on the question asked earlier concerning 'number of book-copies' or the popularity of books expressed as a function of those book-copies?

What we are more likely interested in are questions such as the following: How popular were these authors? How many copies were produced? Is production a measure of demand? Were the texts read together? How many of the separate editions are really the same edition? How many editions of Juvenal and Persius are bibliographically 'the same' or in some way part of the same 'printing venture'?

Let us take as an example some of the earliest editions, those of Juvenal and Persius by Han (Rome, 1469–78), and use only the resources provided by enumerative bibliography. There are four Han editions: 1469 (Juvenal), 1470 (Persius), 1471 (Juvenal), 1478 (Juvenal and Persius).[41] None of these provides a date; only the 1471 Juvenal has a colophon, and this gives neither date nor place, but only the printer, Han, who is mentioned in a verse colophon often found in Han books.[42] The 1478 edition is bibliographically one book, although of the surviving eight copies listed in *ISTC*, only four have both Juvenal and Persius; three others have Juvenal only, one has Persius only.

The 1478 edition, with the colophon naming Han, seems to be bibliographically distinct in its production and structure from the 1469 and 1471 Juvenals, and the 1470 Persius. Why? It will take a detailed survey of these copies to determine whether the printer intended *all* copies coming from the press to contain both texts. Without such a survey, is it reasonable to suppose, as those who wish to calculate the number of book-copies produced in the fifteenth-century must, that the three editions of 1469–71 are to be counted as, say, 600–900 book-copies (assuming 200–300 copies per print run), and the 1478 edition, say, one-third that number of book-copies? To what extent does our definition of 'edition' reflect facts of production and demand in the fifteenth century? Are these Han editions not all part of the same 'printer's venture,' the printing of Juvenal and Persius to meet imagined demand?

As a comparison, we can look at what *ISTC* lists under Han for Cicero (1469). Here *ISTC* lists five separate editions: *De amicitia*, *De officiis*, *Paradoxica Stoicorum*, *De senectute* and *Somnium*, and *Tusculanae disputationes*. Only the last includes a colophon. According to *ISTC*, the first four are 'often with' each other, and that seems to be the case with about half the copies listed in *ISTC*.[43] Of the last, *Tusculanae disputationes*, there are twelve copies (its slightly higher survival perhaps a function of the existence of the colophon) and of these, at least one is bound with other 1469 Cicero texts by Han. These are standard works by Cicero, often printed together or bound together in the fifteenth century. If we search 'Cicero, De Officiis Add:' in *ISTC*, we get fifty-three editions (that is, fifty-three editions contain roughly the same works listed as separate works in the Han editions above, but are listed as single editions containing these multiple texts).

For printers in the fifteenth century, these are not problematic cases:

one could print Cicero alone or as a composite text, and one could combine Cicero texts in various ways for sale, whatever the facts of their printing. For the modern bibliographer or print historian, however, they present difficulties. If we were to pose the question discussed in the chapter here, that is, if we wished to say something about the number of book-copies represented by the Han editions as defined in *ISTC* or *GW*, and we began with an arbitrary but rather modest number – say, average print runs of 200 copies – we would immediately run into a problem. Do these titles represent 200 books? (a single printing venture), or should we separate the titles and speak of something on the order of '1000 books'? Can we simply dismiss these differences as barely rising to the level of an 'order of magnitude'?

Books, in their later histories, obviously did not obey the strictures of descriptive bibliographies. Bibliographically unrelated books were often bound together as *Sammelbände,* and were often taken apart by later dealers, at times in an apparent attempt to increase the number of titles in their inventories. Thousands of the incunables in the Huntington and in the Library of Congress, the two largest American collections of incunables, came from the twentieth-century German dealer Otto Vollbehr, and very few Vollbehr 'items' are composite volumes. A book that can be defined as an autonomous unit with a single title and coherent set of printing signatures is generally bound as a single unit; many such single volumes often have modern bindings with covers constructed of pages from disbound incunables. It is obvious that Vollbehr routinely separated books bound together in *Sammelband,* even composite books clearly intended as single editions by their print-ers and so listed in bibliographies; this was doubtless an attempt to produce artificially high numbers when computing the number of books sold.[44] But are those bibliographical boundaries any less artificial or unhistorical than the physical boundaries as remade by a twentieth-century dealer?

The case points out the difference between an edition in the biblio-graphical sense, an edition in the textual critical sense, and what I call somewhat loosely a 'printer's venture,' involving editions in both senses. The individual book-copy that results from such a venture and is the basis of our knowledge of all these things is an object in a library, whose history may show that its 'book-copy-hood' changed over time through binding decisions – decisions that had little to do with its origin. The technical terms of bibliography ('edition,' 'issue,' 'state') are not the same as the perhaps unnamable historical units or ideas that respond to the question: What was the printer attempting to produce and put on the market as a unit?

As we look at this information, which I have attempted to make no less bewildering than it is, we eventually must pull back: What is the information these book-copies provide? What are the conclusions we could draw? To what extent do these copies provide us any general information? To ask bibliographers to provide answers or solutions here is not reasonable, since the enumerative bibliographers have done a fine job for their own purposes (in *ISTC*), and the descriptive bibliographers (whose work is recorded in the individual entries of *GW*) have done a fine job for theirs. What the print culturists make of the information recorded in either of these resources will be determined by the conventions and needs of discussions of print culture.

There are any number of general conclusions that book historians might make: Juvenal and Persius were popular authors: their popularity was about the same. There were many editions of each. They were associated. The same printers printed each. Not one of these questions could not have been answered before we looked at the evidence. In this case, a detailed analysis of the evidence provides answers to none of the questions one might have asked. The information provided by bibliographies is again a function of the questions bibliographers wish to ask, and bibliographical databases such as the 1810 Hain *Repertorium* or the 1998 *ISTC* foresee and to some extent determine all the questions they could be used to answer. When asked more abstract questions, these resources do little more than reproduce the banalities of book history and classical histories that could be written almost without regard to detailed study of individual books.

3 What Is a Book? Classification and Representation of Early Books

3.1 The Cataloguing of Early Book Fragments

All discussions of books or the idea of books have some tacit definition or understanding of the nature of the material objects that constitute or initiate the matter under discussion. Even such abstract topics as The Book depend to some extent on objects in libraries and how those objects are defined and catalogued. To generalize about The Book requires (does it not?) that we be able to recognize and point to a book when we confront it; when our basic cataloguing systems refer to particular books or classes of books, we can form some general idea about what they are even if the books themselves are not ready to hand (that is, we have some minimal familiarity with the conventions of how information about these objects is disseminated). But do we? The following chapter is directed at particular items that show how difficult it is to arrive at any clear understanding or agreement as to what the objects at the foundation of these discussions are.

Histories of the book, both popular and scholarly, have been disproportionately concerned with what historians refer to as 'monuments.' For those interested in fifteenth-century books, this might mean items in exhibition catalogues, presumed rarities such as the Gutenberg Bible, Polifilo's *Hypnerotomachia* printed by Aldus, the Nuremburg Chronicles. Paradoxically, what these histories consider a book to be is something that most closely resembles these special and often unique kinds of books – the books valued by the book trade, and thus promoted by scholars who, until recently, necessarily have had very close relations with that book trade.[1] My focus here is on more modest objects – fragments of books, particularly grammar books – things that are no less 'bookish' to cataloguers and the book histories based on the evidence from these catalogues, but things that also demonumentalize the objects of history. How are such objects organized as categories of knowledge? How are they represented? How do we know anything about them? The questions here deal with minutiae, and although some of us find the perplexities of book description at worst amusing, readers willing to feign contentment with the notion that our discussions of books are baseless might wish to skip some of the doubtless irritating detail. The first section deals with the nature and source of these fragments and the cataloguing problems such books pose; the second section deals with type measurement and facsimile representation, two things basic to the classification of these books.

Many of the studies cited in the previous chapter (those attempting to estimate the number of books produced in the fifteenth century) rely on the unstated assumption that products of press = objects of catalogue entries = books. One finds in these studies little discussion of what these catalogue descriptions refer to, even though the conclusions many studies of early printing and print culture promote (for example, conclusions about the rise in literacy) are only meaningful in terms of the specific referents of such catalogue entries. Some of these entries refer to codices, others to pamphlets; some refer to broadsheets, and some even to scraps with only a few lines of print. These are not all things we normally consider books, nor do they all bear on an abstract topic such as literacy in the same way. The question addressed in the previous chapter – 'How many books were there, or how many books were distributed, in the fifteenth century?' – depends entirely on the specific cases. If a catalogue entry means 'an edition of 500 book-copies,' then our statistical evaluation of a union catalogue such as *ISTC* or *GW* might be able to generate numbers of '20 million.' If a catalogue entry means only 'a fragment of a book copy,' then for these entries, the ratio of book-copies to catalogue entries may be, instead of 500:1, as low as 1:1; and if that physical fragment represents a trial edition only, or if it is, say, an indulgence, the number of fifteenth-century book-copies represented by its corresponding catalogue entry is 0.

Among the earliest products of the printing press are grammar books (the Donatus *Ars minor*), and hundreds of presumed editions of these books are represented only by fragments of particular book-copies. In discussions of early printing, such elementary grammar books are conceded to be the most popular product of the press – a staple. They are also surely one of the best indices of literacy: as long as there are numerous well-used grammar books circulating, there must be what is called 'growing literacy.' Yet these grammar books, central as they are to questions about early print culture and literacy,[2] are as evidence extremely difficult to quantify or even to describe in any coherent way.

Let us look at some comments by Hirsch, who is again following and somewhat misled by J.M. Lenhart:

> Considering the new emphasis on reading it is surprising that so few primers (or other tools used in teaching the rudiments of reading) are known. (*Printing, Selling and Reading*, 152)

It is rather striking to see this statement so near the conclusion to Hirsch's study, unless, by some oversight, by 'known' Hirsch means 'extant.' *GW*, well underway by the time Hirsch wrote this, has nearly 1000 entries under authors who wrote what we would consider primers: 'Donatus,' 'pseudo-Donatus,' and 'Alexander of Villa Dei.' What has happened to these thousands of books and fragments in the discussion here?

Lenhart's classification of early books seems to hide such elementary books, relying on categories (from Robert Steele's earlier estimates) descriptive of the monumental book: theology, literature, law, science. These account respectively for 45.5 per cent, 36.06 per cent, 10.93 per cent, and 8.51 per cent of fifteenth-century editions.[3] Such editions are essentially print runs, not what we would call 'titles' or 'book-copies,' and so the relation to popularity is not a simple one. The percentages are further misleading in that they are based on a seemingly monumentalist notion of what books are. If we go into a modern book store, we can see quickly the kinds of books that the categories here do not clearly define: dictionaries, cookbooks, self-help books. Fifteenth-century books of this sort do not fit into the four categories well, because they are not the kinds of books that literary scholars are much concerned with as books. Many of them are included within (and swell) the category 'literature' (schoolbooks such as the Donatus grammar, the elementary *Lucidarius*, and perhaps even cookbooks), but as Hirsch's statement quoted above suggests, they seem to disappear from view.

The disappearance of these books from the discussion of 'percentages of book production' is related to facts of their survival. Most of the earliest of these grammar books do not survive as anything we could call books: they are, rather, books in books – fragments that survive as binding material – owing their existence to the value of the books for which they supplied raw material. Everyone who has examined early books is aware of the way fragments of other books appear in early book-bindings. Early bindings in their structure provide a number of uses for waste paper and scraps from earlier books: the boards, usually of wood, are often constructed of paper, the scraps, sometimes printed, pressed together as in cardboard. Strips of paper or vellum are also used as backing strips along the spine; vellum strips can serve as hinges to support the connection of board to the book itself; paper and vellum can be used as pastedowns (leaves pasted to the inside of the board, covering the wood and hinges) or flyleaves (extra leaves bound between the text page and the board itself). The main source of such material is earlier books, both manuscript books and printed books.

The less early books and their bindings have been sophisticated (that is, 'meddled with') by collectors or the book trade, the more likely they are to contain scraps of early printing. By the late nineteenth century, well before most of the major American collections were formed, it was well known that some of the earliest examples of printing were repre-sented by such fragments, but it was also felt that such fragments (valu-able though they might be in and of themselves) did not enhance the value of the books in which they were contained. Fragments were thus removed and sold separately. In a collection such as the Huntington, whose books were in large part channelled through the late nineteenth- and early twentieth-century book trades, few of these fragments survive. I have already mentioned the propensities of one major twentieth-century dealer, Vollbehr, who clearly sacrificed original bindings to increase the number of items or 'lots' he could sell to Huntington and the Library of Congress.[4]

Such fragments (the subject of *Makulaturforschung*, noted in a previous chapter) are generally dealt with as evidence of typographical history. The initial question studied by collectors of these fragments was never, Do these fragments represent books? but rather, What do they tell us about the early history of printing? and in particular, the 'hoary old question' that so tested the patience of Febvre and Martin – What region could claim primacy in printing history?[5] More recently, the value of these fragments has been seen as evidence of the early book trade, or of the noncommercial distribution of books.[6] In this section, I examine this from a different perspective. The question that concerns me is not, How do those fragments add to the typographical evidence contained in a particular collection? but rather, What is the status of those fragments as 'books' when catalogued in union catalogues? – a somewhat different question from the questions the earliest cataloguing of these fragments intended to answer.[7]

Printer's Waste/Binding Waste

A basic distinction in binding history is the difference between what is called 'binder's waste' and 'printer's waste.' I am not certain where this distinction was first articulated, but the earliest clear distinction I have seen is in Henry Bradshaw's essay on early Dutch typefonts (1871):

> Such fragments in the binder's hands are either sheets of books which have been used up and thrown away, and may be called *binder's waste*; or else they are spoiled sheets or unused proofs from a printer's office, and may be called *printer's waste*.

A similar distinction appears in E.P. Goldschmidt without reference to Bradshaw, although Goldschmidt adds a third category: 'bookseller's waste.'[8] It may be that the more closely we try to apply any general, universalized formula to what we actually find in the bindings of real books in the real world, the more we need to multiply categories to account for the individual cases. I am concerned here only with the distinction between 'books in use' and 'materials produced by a press' and for that, the binary distinction is serviceable.

Bradshaw made this distinction while wrestling with a much more irritating question: What is a book?

> It may be said that mere specimens of woodcut printing, as the Biblia pauperum, and other such books, having nothing typographical about them, should not have been included ... Where however they are actual books, I have admitted them into my list, while excluding all single wood-cut sheets, pictures, etc. The latter belong rather to a history of engraving. (260)[9]

The main phrase here is, 'Where however they are actual books ...,' a phrase Bradshaw never defines. The only possible meaning this can have, however, is that a book is 'something bound' and ready for use.

Paul Needham has argued that even something collated and sitting in a press warehouse is not a book. What makes a book is the 'binding.' I believe what Needham means by 'binding' is, however, not real binding, and I do not think the distinction between book and nonbook can be made on the basis of internal evidence (something Needham's definition attempts to do). What distinguishes a book from a nonbook involves something external to the book itself – its actual use and potential for use – something contained less in the book itself than in the institution of book distribution. A book, that is to say a book-copy, thus must be defined as a book functionally, not essentially.

An example of this is the much-repeated anecdote concerning Politian's *Miscellanea*, found in a letter from Jacobus Antiquarius to Politian. Antiquarius claims he first saw a copy of Politian's book in the hands of youths, distributed in individual quires among them ('ad legendum dispertitum quem in manibus habebant inter se librum'). Grafton describes this book-copy as having been 'taken apart,' although it is more likely that the book was never 'together.' Early books were ordinarily purchased in loose quires, and in this case, it is these quires that are dispersed. A book such as this, in autonomous sections and of some notoriety, could be read most quickly by not having it bound at all.[10] This book-copy was not only 'ready for binding,' but it was clearly much used. It had, however, no particular value as a material object, but only as the repository of a text. Yet this particular book-copy, of which no physical trace remains, is no less a book than the bound, and in some cases signed, copies presently housed in libraries.[11] It is that 'potentiality for use' that is at the heart of the distinction between printer's waste and binder's waste, a distinction that in turn defines what a book is, as opposed to what one might find defined in a book catalogue or a catalogue of holdings for a library catalogue of holdings.

The Huntington Library has several sets of fragments of early grammars, the two most important in my view being the vellum fragments of the Donatus *Ars minor* (Dutch prototypography) and the set of paper fragments of the pseudo-Donatus *Rudimenta grammatices* (Augsburg: J. Zainer).[12] They are a good example of the difference between the two types of waste found in bindings, and thus of the problems Bradshaw was dealing with in defining 'bookness' of such things; they also point out the difficulties involved in relating particular book fragments to our notion of 'edition.' The first set, of the Donatus *Ars minor*, consists of binding strips contained in an early South German *Sammelband* of two fifteenth-century editions. They are of an early Netherlands edition of the *Ars minor*, printed in what is known as Pontanus type (for one of the early texts printed in this type) or 144G (i.e., a Gothic typeface measuring or measurable as 144 mm for 20 lines; problems with this particular form of identification will be discussed below). There are twenty-one surviving sets of fragments of the Donatus printed in this same type, but it is not possible to say whether the Huntington fragments belong to any of the editions represented by them. The fragments are rubricated, and obviously come from a book that was 'read to pieces' before ending up in the binder's shop.

The second set is of the pseudo-Donatus *Rudimenta*, purchased by the Huntington after the fragments were catalogued in *GW*; it consists of ten paper sheets, including one that is clearly a proofsheet. Each is a bifolium (one potentially folded sheet = one bifolium = two leaves or folia = four pages of text). The proofsheet consists of apparent trial impressions of various pages; on one side, the two pages are printed with opposing orientation (one appears upside down); on the other, each page impression is overprinted with a page impression from a different page of text (see fig. 2). Not only was this proofsheet not bound in a book, it seems never to have been intended to be bound in (and *as*) a book. One of the bifolia in this set prints the same text found in another bifolia, but the two do not have the same page breaks; in fact, they are not even close. There is simply no way to collate these ten bifolia as a book, even if we disregard the proofsheet. And there is no sign on any of these bifolia that they were ever used as a book. There is no marginalia; there are no holes indicating sewing into quires. The physical appearance of the proofsheet (which could not have been in a distributed book) does not differ in any significant way from the appearance of any other sheet. Do these fragments then represent one book (with various proofsheets), two separate books, or no book at all?

What we have here is a *possible allusion to* a book (or books) but *not an example of one*. The leaves were recorded in *GW*, but there is no record of their provenance or record of the binding from which they were apparently ripped. In *GW* they are catalogued immediately next to a three-leaf set of fragments at the Pierpont Morgan Library set in the same type. And curiously, the coherent sections of the Huntington set of fragments collate more easily with sections of the Morgan fragments than they do with other fragments in the Huntington set. The Morgan fragments also show no sign of use: there is no sign that they were ever part of a book – no marginalia, no evidence of binding, and no evidence of their origin. Again, a possible allusion to a book; or rather, an allusion to an imagined or once intended book, but like the nearly contemporary Huntington fragments of this text, not an example of one.

A catalogue, however, can do no more than what *GW* does: each is assigned a number. Each, thus, has the bibliographical status of a 'book-

2. Proofsheet, pseudo-Donatus, *Rudimenta Grammatices* (Ulm: Joannes Zainer, 1480–90), Goff D342. Photo courtesy of the Henry E. Huntington Library, San Marino, CA.

copy' that itself is presumably representative of an edition for which some ideal-copy description is desirable. Yet strictly speaking, it could be argued that these provide 'external evidence' for a book only; they are no more deserving of a catalogue number or entry than an external reference to other books for which no copy is extant (for example, a reference in a contemporary inventory to an otherwise unrecorded edition would not get a catalogue entry).

Fragments such as this have a peculiar status in bibliographical catalogues. An entry in a catalogue generally means an edition, or issue, although there are various ways in which the distinction between edition, issue, and state might be worked out in any catalogue.[13] For these fragments, however, the entry means something entirely different. Each entry refers to a particular unit of fragments housed in a particular library; that is, one of the organizing principles of classification is *present location* – certainly an element of certain kinds of bibliographies (enumerative bibliographies, for example), but not an element of most descriptive bibliographies. When these hundreds of fragments are finally listed according to type, press, and other physical features, then it is the job of the bibliographer to speculate on how many editions these constitute.

The *Gesamtkatalog* and the Treatment of Early Grammars

The following section deals in more detail with the conflicting ways *GW* handles two of these early grammars, the Donatus *Ars minor* and the *Doctrinale* of Alexander of Villa Dei, books which in some union catalogues (*ISTC*, for example) seem to constitute 3–4 per cent of the total number of fifteenth-century editions. For Donatus, *GW* provides an initial outline of entries; first under 'Ars minor' (GW 8674–9029):

A. late medieval normal text (GW 8674–8986)
   I. without commentary;
   II. with German interlinear gloss
   III. with Commentary of Florentius Diel (Etymologia Donatia)
B. Donatus melior (GW 8987–9029)

This is followed by editions of the *Ars maior* and other works by Donatus (GW 9030–8). What I am concerned with here is what is described under section A.I.: *Ars minor,* 'late medieval normal text, without commentary.' For these, *GW* has entries GW 8674–8971, slightly under 300 apparent editions. These are divided into two groups: (A.I.a.) – early Mainz editions and early Netherlands editions (GW 8674–813) (all of these exist only in fragments); (A.I.b.) – 'various editions' (GW 8814–971).

GW subdivides the first group according to the typefont used, two for Mainz and five for the Netherlands: (1) Mainz: type of 36–line Bible (DK type, named for the 'Donatus' and 'Kalendar' which are printed in this type) (GW 8674–97); type of the 42-line Bible (the Gutenberg Bible) (GW 8698–722); (2) Netherlands: Pontanus or Donatus type (GW 8723–38); Saliceto or *Doctrinale* type (GW 8739–80); *Speculum* Type (GW 8781–806); *Abecedarium* type (GW 8807); type of the Donatus printer (GW 8808–13).[14]

Mainz:

DK type	24 editions
Gutenberg Bible type	25
Total	49 editions

Netherlands:

Pontanus type	16 editions
Saliceto type	42
Speculum type	26
Abecedarium type	1
Donatus type	6
Total	91 editions

The *GW* entries that follow these 140 entries – what *GW* categorizes as 'various editions' (GW 8814–971) – are more like what we consider 'books'; they are represented largely by material books containing complete texts. The 140 entries above (GW 8674–813) refer to something else entirely. What these entries represent are not 'books' or 'editions,' but rather sets of fragments located and catalogued in various libraries. Different sets of these fragments are categorized together under the same number only in special cases, as when the extant fragments were once physically part of the same leaf or bifolium (as in GW 8687 and 8689). But *GW* provides other organizing systems as well. Preceding the entries themselves, *GW* provides an outline organizing the fragments as textual units; these units are defined by the only critical edition of the *Ars minor* available, one constructed by Paul Schwenke as an aid in organizing these fragments. Here, there are thirty-seven units, corresponding to the thirty-seven chapters of Schwenke's reference edition. The text on Schwenke, chapter 1, can be found in twelve copies; the text on chapter 2, in nine copies, etc.[15] The two organizing schemata (the textual one based on Schwenke, and the one based on present location of sets of fragments) of course do not in any way correspond.

Neither of these organizing frames defines the normal bibliographical category of 'edition'; the discussion of edition is contained in specific entries, although the entry numbers themselves do not reflect the conclusions. The first twenty-four *GW* entries refer to fragments in the type of the 36-line Bible. Those twenty-four entries are said to exist in four editions (*Ausgaben*) according to the number of lines printed on each page: the 26-line edition, the 27-line edition, the 28-line edition, and the 30-line edition. The implied definition of 'edition' is very problematic, for it suggests that such things are uniform throughout in terms of format (lines per page). Any two leaves printed in the same typefont with the same number of lines per page (given that they can be collated) are considered parts of the same edition. This is a reasonable principle for organizing evidence, but it is not an accurate statement about editions or print runs in any early printing shop.

GW 8674 and GW 8675

Let us consider the descriptions of GW 8674 and GW 8675, the first two entries. These are fragments in DK type of the earliest Mainz editions. The description and collation formula for GW 8674 is as follows:

18 Bl. [a^{10} b^8] 26 Z. Typ. 1:164G.

This means that the presumed edition contained 18 leaves in two quires of 10 and 8 leaves respectively; there are 26 lines per page and the type is type 1, measuring 164mm for 20 lines. There follow descriptions of the text on individual pages (what I have underlined below is a truncated version of the black-letter text printed in the description):

Bl. 1a *[^{6}]A[rtes] or* ... Bricht ab Bl. 10b Z. 25 ... *futuro amator* ... Bl. 11ff. unbekannt.

That is, the recto of leaf 1 begins with space for a 6-line initial, the first letter of the text 'Partes'; leaf 10 breaks off on the verso with the quoted text. And no further leaves are known.

The first line is an ideal copy description; the phrase '18 Bl.' (18 leaves) should perhaps be in brackets, since those 18 leaves are simply a hypothesis, as is the inferred collation a^{10} b^8. What exists materially are only fragments, somewhat cryptically described as follows: 'Berlin *SB (Perg., 2 Doppelbl. = 1/9 u. 2/10 z.T. def.)'; that is, in the Berlin Staatsbibliothek, there are two bifolia (4 leaves = 8 pages) in part defective, from the initial and final pages of signature *a* (leaf 1 is obviously conjugate with leaf 10, and the description should be corrected to read 1/10 and 2/9).[16]

GW 8675 is from the same type of edition (or from what *GW* calls a 26-line edition):

18 Bl. [a^{10} b^8] 26 Z. Typ. 1:164G

Bl. 1–13 unbekannt. Bl. 14a Z. 5 *Imperativo modo* ... Bricht ab Bl. 14b Z. 25 ...
  quod conjuga | ... Bl. 15ff. unbekannt ...

Krakau *UB. (2 eins. bedr. Bl. [=*Korrekturabzüge*] Z. 5–26, bzw. 3–26 = Bl. 14a
  u. b).

This begins with the same ideal copy description as in GW 8674. In the preceding description for GW 8674 we were told that leaves 11 and following are unknown ('Bl. 11ff. unbekannt'). Here we are told leaves 1–13 and 15ff. are unknown. The description is correct but unsettling, insofar as the number '14' is defined as *1–13 and 15ff. unknown.* The implication is of course that these 'unknown' leaves are to be inferred – precisely what is said in the collation formula, where the bracketed collation means 'inferred' but the number of leaves reads out magisterially '18 Bl.' What we have here are two 'leaves printed on single sides [=proofsheets] lines 5–26 and some of 3–26 = leaves [in this case 'pages'] 14a and b.' That is to say, we have no evidence that this is a book at all, were it not for GW 8674, which possibly belongs to the same print run.

A logical conclusion might be that GW 8674 and GW 8675 should be catalogued together – just as *STC* classifies all copies of the Shakespeare 1623 folio under the same entry, whether they are fragmentary, sophisticated, or full of press variants. That is, they should (ideally) be catalogued together under ordinary cataloguing rules – those rules that apply to all books except books that have survived in the manner peculiar to early copies of the Donatus *Ars minor.* But ordinary cataloguing rules are difficult to apply to these fragments.

The *GW* bibliographers have done what is quite rational to do. Their entry provides the basis for a descriptive bibliography of these fragments and the books they imply; it includes a preliminary essay on that subject and a system of organization that provides the sketch for any future descriptive bibliography (the organization of fragments by typefont and inferred printer). But *GW* has stopped short of hardening those preliminary decisions through the assignment of catalogue numbers that would reflect them, and has maintained the principle that one *GW* number shall refer in this case to single sets of fragments catalogued together in one individual library; other sets can be included within the same number only when they are materially joined to these.[17]

Alexander of Villa Dei, *Doctrinale*

A second popular grammar is Alexander of Villa Dei's *Doctrinale* in Latin verse. As is the case with the Donatus, there are hundreds of known editions, and the earliest examples are fragmentary (although more of these consist of full leaves than do the earliest Donatus examples). The earliest extensive survey of these was by Theodor Reichling in 1894, who considered over 250 manuscripts and 300 printed books; these printed books he believed constituted twenty-six separate editions. Reichling was unable to examine all of the earliest printed fragments, and claimed that these numbers of estimated editions would have been much higher 'had I followed the librarians of our day and placed separately the single parts of different impressions of the same editions.'[18] As a grammar, the *Doctrinale* serves different pedagogical purposes; these purposes affect both its later survival and subsequently its treatment by bibliographers. Donatus's *Ars minor* gives basic grammatical paradigms that are to be committed to memory. Obviously, copies were well used and read to pieces (this is a claim one hears made for many books, but one for which only these early grammars provide a great deal of material evidence). Alexander of Villa Dei's *Doctrinale* is in verse, and is concerned with matters of prosody. Its hexameters are not elegant, but they are easy for beginning Latin students to construe and more important they can be easily scanned (modern readers with a few years of Latin can confirm this by reading through a selection of them). The hexameters thus serve as a memory device for the rules and generalizations that apply to the difference between long and short syllables – the basis for Latin verse. It provides an alternative to the piecemeal memorization of prosodic rules and illustrative word lists. The *Doctrinale* drives these long and short vowels into the memory by placing them in a line with sometimes forced but nonetheless unambiguous hexameter scansion, the one verse form familiar to all beginning Latin students through their experience with Vergil and Ovid. If you memorize a few lines from Alexander, you will have in your memory all the correct prosodic quantities for the vowels contained there – no small accomplishment! This is a welcome comple- ment to Donatus, which locates, say, the proper form of the future perfect second person singular as directly following the first person singular future perfect of the same verb. The *Doctrinale* cannot be used as a reference book as Donatus can; it needs to be memorized to be of use, and thus, individual copies were not subject to constant use and abuse. Copies thus survived the fifteenth century in better condition than did contemporary grammars of Donatus. Once in the book trade, its verse form doubtless added to its specious 'literariness,' further enhancing its chances of survival among collectors.[19]

In the *GW* entry, the *Doctrinale* reflects different cataloguing prin- ciples. The main entry begins with a long introduction, cols 470–83, in which the surviving fragments are organized according to edition, and it is these editions that are assigned *GW* numbers. The total number of such editions is 236 (GW 933–1169); sets of fragments are classified according to the editions to which they belong.[20] The editions them- selves are divided into two groups: straight-text editions and editions with commentary. The text editions are divided into 'early Dutch frag- ments' and 'various text-editions' (*sonstige Textausgaben*) (GW 937–81). The early Dutch fragments are given only four entries, GW 933–6 based on the typefont used: editions in *Saliceto* type are divided into a 28-line edition (GW 933) and a 29-line edition (GW 934, 935); GW 936 includes fragments in *Speculum* type (a 32-line edition). More than four editions in the ordinary sense of 'edition' may be involved here.

GW 933 has three subentries: 933 I, 933 II, and 933 III. These suben- tries refer to the fragment sets in three different locations; each of these sets contains two leaves. The main entry for GW 933 is in two parts; the first appears to be an ideal copy description, one that organizes the particular leaves in the subentries:

46–48 Bl. etwa 174 x 96 mm (Perg.) Lagen: [a⁸ ...]. 28 Z. Type: 5.

Bl. 1 night erhalten. Bl 2 = 933 I Bl. 1. Bl 3 nicht erhalten. Bl. 4 = 933 II Bl. 1 ...

That is, this edition has between 46 and 48 leaves of vellum, measuring about 174 × 96 mm. Its first quire contains 8 leaves. It has 28 lines per page, and is printed in type 5. The first leaf is missing; the second leaf is represented by leaf 1 of GW 933 I. In each of the subentries (933 I–III), the extant leaves are identified according to copy-specific criteria (that is, each set is numbered 1a, 1b, 2a, 2b regardless of how they collate and regardless of where they appear in the hypothesized edition). Cross-references are provided for the text to Reichling's edition. There are several apparent contradictions built into this description, having to do with the conflation of edition-specific and copy-specific details. But most of these (for example, the reference to size) could be found in any *GW* entry.

GW descriptions for the most part are what English bibliographers call 'ideal-copy' descriptions: they refer to an idealized book-copy (not a text) that corresponds to what the printer may have had in mind when producing the individual copies still extant. For GW 933, all the extant evidence tells us is that the first quire must be an 8. Beyond this, GW 933 is little more than a generalized inventory of fragments, whose very title is problematic: 'Alexander de Villa Dei: Doctrinale. P. 1–4'; the unqualified statement 'P[artes] 1–4' means that this is an ideal copy description, that one can infer a complete copy containing those parts, yet no physical evidence of those parts is extant.

GW 934 is much better represented. *GW* gives the collation '[$a^8b^8c^{11}d^{10}e^9$?]' this is what the printer intended to produce. Twenty-two sets of fragments survive, all examples of the same text printed in the same apparent format, in the same typefont. They are classified as the first of two entries with the heading '29 zeilige' (that is, there are two separate 29-line [editions]; the word *Ausgabe* appears in the general heading). In what sense, bibliographical or otherwise, do these sets of fragments represent a single *edition*?

The general introduction for entry GW 934 lists each of the presumed 46 leaves of this edition with the surviving copies that contain them (the reference is to the page of text in the ideal copy; subheadings contain cross-references to the line number in Reichling). Many of these leaves are represented by more than one copy, for example, 6, 14, 18, 31, 32, 34, 38, 39, 40, 43, 44, and 45. I assume that all the fragments listed as containing the text on any one such leaf are similar in format and will collate with other fragments from other sections, that is, page breaks of individual fragments containing the same text correspond (they do in the truncated examples given in the *GW* descriptions); the *GW* bibliographers assume that a printer would have produced all these sheets together, planning to bind indifferently any of the examples of one bifolium with any of the particular examples of another bifolium. However, even though these bifolia differ from those classified under GW 935 ('alle weichen von Nr 935 ab'), are they necessarily from the same edition? That is, are the settings the same? Are the differences slight enough to be considered 'press-variants'? Or is what we have more akin to 'page-for-page reprint' – an extremely common practice in early printing, every example of which would or should be considered bibliographically a new edition?

Because *GW* provides incipits and explicits of the leaves in each fragment group, texts can often be compared. And in none of the cases where *GW* provides actual text do these texts correspond exactly (I accept *GW*'s statements that in cases where text is not transcribed, the text is identical to that in other examples). Differences are obvious even in textual reproduction of the texts in the conventions of *GW* typesetting. In some cases this is simply a matter of an abbreviation: leaf 18, 'futurum/futu[rum]' (IV/4b and IX/1b). In others entire lines seem to have been reset.[21] Leaf 38 is represented in four fragments: I/3, XIX/1, XX/1, and XXI/1, and the beginning and ending lines are represented as follows (Reichling lines 2127, 2154, 2155, and 2184). It is difficult to give a full sense of this within the limitations of my keyboard and how my own keyboard strokes are represented in print; I transcribe in roman what *GW* transcribes from the originals according to its own conventions of black-letter typesorts:

934/I, leaf 3:
Agnitus esto breuis societ[ur] cognit[us] illi
Asopu[m] retrahas europa[m] siue piropu[m]

Ut plac[et] e[sse] canoph[us] ysop[us] q[uo]q[ue] iu[n]ge[re] debes
U sup[er] r' lo[n]ga sed purpura ponit[ur] extra

934/XIX/1:
Agnitus esto breuis [...]
Asopu[m] retrahas eu[...]

Vt plac[et] e[sse] conoph[us] ysoph[us] q[uoque] iu[n]ge[re] debes
V sup[er] r longa sed purpura ponit[ur] extra

934/XX/1:
(1a is unreadable [*unleserlich*])
Ut placet [...] canoph[us] ysoph[us] q[uoque]
V super r longa sed purpura ponit[ur] extra

XXI/1:
[agnitus] esto breuis societ[ur] cognitus illi
Asopum retrahis europa[m] siue pyropum

Vt plac[et] e[sse] canoph[us] ysoph[us] q[uoque] iu[n]ge[re] debes
V sup[er] r longa sed purpura ponit[ur] extra

Even if *GW* transcriptions include errors, errors doubtless multiplied in my own transcriptions, these versions of the lines are not typographically or textually the same. It is not clear that any one set is an obvious correction of errors in another, and without optical collation, it is not possible to say whether they are even variants of the same setting (that is, what appears to be the same text when transcribed is not necessarily the same setting at press). There is thus no way from the *GW* description to determine how many editions these represent. There is further, because of the limitation of description to matters of location and text, no way to determine the 'bookness' of the various examples. There is no reference to marginalia, ownership marks, annotation, or indications of binding – all evidence that would be crucial in determining the bibliographical status of those numbers that *GW* assigns.

The treatment of Alexander's *Doctrinale* is quite different from the treatment of Donatus's *Ars minor*. Sets of fragments are assigned to potential editions, and the number of editions implied by the *GW* numbered entries is, by the standard of Donatus, artificially low – more in accordance with what one defines as an edition elsewhere in the work. Yet can either of these highly problematic cases be generalized? And has the more sophisticated and detailed cataloguing of modern reference works made such generalizations easier?

Let us look finally at the Hain catalogue from the early nineteenth century, the basis of the *GW* catalogue and during its day the most complete reference work for incunables available. Hain has about two-thirds of the editions known and catalogued in the mid-twentieth century. In the entry under Donatus, the number of Donatus editions (the *Ars minor*) is roughly the same as the number of the Donatus variant editions (the *Rudimenta*, the *Ars minor* with commentary, translations into the vernacular, the *Ars melior*). Of the texts that seem to translate into what *GW* means by the 'normal text without commentary,' I count thirty-five, about one-eighth of what are now in *GW*. There are roughly the same number of others. For Alexander of Villa Dei, Hain has entries 662–774, that is to say, 112 entries; *GW* has 344 entries; *ISTC* has 393.

Hain was of course interested in text, not in fragments. And

Makulaturforschung had barely begun when he was compiling his catalogue. What Hain meant by a book was what we mean by a book, and an entry in his catalogue was a means of identifying that book – a book represented by a printing of a text. The discovery of fragments, however, threw this system in disarray. Hain's thirty-five editions of Donatus increased eightfold in *GW*, whereas for Alexander de Villa Dei, a book represented by somewhat larger units (full-page fragments or even complete books), the ratio of Hain to *GW* entries is closer to what it is with other books.

Conclusion

So now let us return to the questions that generated this discussion in a previous chapter. On what basis does one determine such things as the popularity and number of books in the fifteenth century? Hain's definition of a book is clearly much closer to what we mean by books when we discuss such things in anything but bibliographical contexts. Does this mean we should use the less sophisticated and accurate of bibliographical aids to make our estimates of numbers of books within an abstract context such as 'print culture'? If so, are we not simply reproducing in the late twentieth century the assumptions brought to scholarship in the early nineteenth century? In that case, wouldn't we do better, as many scholars have, simply to ignore the entire problem of evidence and cite instead the sentiments of a real nineteenth-century scholar, Burkhardt, for example, who had the advantage we do not enjoy of a body of evidence that was compiled and built roughly around the same intellectual suppositions he himself used to analyse it?

The specific things or objects that we have been discussing here are fragments – not books, but parts of books; not parts of book-texts, but material parts of extratextual features of books. They are things that are central to all questions of book production, reception, and reading practices in the fifteenth century, but things that are at the same time oddly elided in discussions. It is difficult to know where to place them according to some of the more gross cataloguing categories of the nineteenth century: theology, literature, science, medicine. It is difficult to determine how to count them. It is difficult to determine to what extent what we call ordinary press practices – those Printers of the Mind products, coming off the press at regular intervals in their 300-copy packets – applied to them. It is hard to dismiss such cases (involving hundreds of defined editions) as mere exceptions, since similar exceptions appear wherever our attention falls, whether on monumental printing projects or on presumably routine ones. That the Gutenberg Bible is exceptional goes without saying. English bibliographers would doubtless say the same of the earliest productions of Caxton. Other examples from early printing would be the two unique copies of the *Canon Missae*, one of the great classics (bibliographically) in two-colour printing. One is at the Bodleian; there is a partial copy at Columbia. The printing procedures for its multi-coloured initials are complex, and no one imagines the elaborate printing procedures for each page could have been repeated in a press run of 300. Another such book is the *Book of Hawking* from St Albans (1486; GW 4932), an example of three-colour printing. There are thirteen surviving copies, doubtless a significant percentage of the entire print run. More common books also pose problems for anyone wishing to quantify evidence, or even to use the evidence that seems to be available. Breviaries, like grammar books, are a staple of early printing, but organizational peculiarities of such books make it impossible to equate 'print run' with 'edition.' In breviaries planned as two-volume editions, one run of the psalter was printed for both the winter and summer volumes, and catalogues deal with such books variously. Just as bothersome are the works of Cicero – printed separately, but destined to be bound together as *Sammelbände*, as are nearly all early printings of Cicero found at the Huntington. To what extent does the individual entry found in an incunable catalogue (referring, say, to one of the bibliographically defined editions included in such a composite volume) respond to any unit that might have been circulating or was intended to circulate in the fifteenth century? Problematic examples show up whenever one looks for them, and there are examples in all genres of incunables.[22] How many such exceptions can our abstract conclusions and assertions about print culture in the fifteenth century accommodate? And if such exceptions pose no threat to our theories, how strongly can those theories relate to the material evidence that is presumed to lie at their base?

3.2 Type Measurement and Facsimile Representation

In the following sections, I examine another aspect of early book identification, taking as a starting point some of the early grammatical fragments discussed above. The subject here is the measurement and facsimile representation of type. Type measurement is an important aspect of type identification, which in turn is the basis for assigning books to printers and for charting the careers of those printers. The most important studies are, in English, Robert Proctor's *An Index to the Early Printed Books in the British Museum* (1898) and the *Catalogue of Books Printed in the Fifteenth Century Now in the British Museum* (1908–) (*BMC*), and, in German, the sometimes unwieldy survey of typefonts by Haebler, *Typenrepertorium der Wiegendrucke* (1905–24). These are supplemented and supported by several series of facsimiles: the 'Woolley' photographs; publications of the Type Facsimile Society; Konrad Burger's *Deutsche und italienische Inkunabeln in getreuen Nachbildungen* (Leipzig, 1913 –); and the large and often crumbling boxes of plates in *Veröffentlichungen der Gesellschaft für Typenkunde des XV. Jahrhunderts* (Berlin, 1907–39) (*VGT*).[23] The first part of the following section examines some of the inevitable problems involved in the quantification of typographical evidence. The second part deals with the problem of facsimilization itself, taking as its subject one of the earliest attempts to describe a printer's career in terms of a history of typefonts: Blades, *Life and Typography of William Caxton* (1861–3).

My interest in the subject of facsimile representation is an accident. Some years ago I noted that the title-page engraving of Chaucer's tomb in the 1721 Chaucer edition by John Urry was a copy and a tracing of a similar engraving in Elias Ashmole, *Theatrum Chemicum* of 1653; the measurements were identical, as was the general disposition of detail. Obviously, publishing images of these side-by-side would provide far more convincing visual proof than my simple assertion, and so I had photos taken of each, and checked the 'actual size' box in the photo order. In one of the photo orders, this instruction was overlooked, and the two images seemed to have little direct relation. I asked the photographer for another image; it would be better and probably easier, I suggested naively, simply to reshoot actual size rather than manipulate the image – something I felt must be unworthy of true scholarship. The photographer did not hesitate: 'What are your conclusions?' I told him. 'Fine,' he said. 'I'll just adjust the image size in order to support that. No need to reshoot.'

Aside from what this says about my naivety, it illustrates a problem with facsimile reproduction itself and with what could be called the reproduction of that reproduction – the publication of visual evidence. For the Chaucer engravings, what I pretended to want was proof – a demonstration, not a decorative illustration for an essentially verbal argument. What I got was what I really wanted – a convincing illustration, professionally and perfectly manipulated.

My first of two case studies deals with the facsimile representations of Dutch prototypography – facsimiles produced by various technologies from 1868 to the present: Holtrop, *Monuments typographiques des pays-bas au quinzième siècle* (1868); Zedler, *Von Coster zu Gutenberg* (1921); and Hellinga and Hellinga, *The Fifteenth-Century Printing Types of the Low Countries* (1966). Based on the plates in Holtrop, Henry Bradshaw organized the types as follows (I include what is now given as the standard measurement for 20 lines):[24]

Types 1 and 2 – *Speculum* (Holtrop, plates 17 and 19) (110 mm, 103 mm)
Type 3 Valla type (*Facetiae morales*) (Holtrop, plate 25) (113 mm)
Type 4 Pontanus type (Holtrop, plate 23a) (144 mm)
Type 5 *Pii Secundum Tractatus de mulieribus pravis* (Holtrop, plate 23b) (123 mm)[25]
Type 6 Donatus fragments, BRH 556 (Holtrop, plate 31a) (123 mm)
Type 7 Donatus fragments at Uden (Holtrop, plate 32a) (120 mm)

Examples of these types were not available in England, and Proctor in his 1898 *Index* did not even describe the types themselves (as he did for most printers) but simply referred to Bradshaw's study. Bradshaw's distinctions became the basis for all other classifications of these types, including the most recent and detailed catalogue by Hellinga.[26]

Before proceeding, it is important to note the difficulties prototypography posed for Proctor. For most books, Proctor enjoyed an advantage over other incunabulists: he had a wheelbarrow, and on the British Museum shelves, he was able to isolate the fifteenth-century books, and physically locate them according to the towns and dates named in their colophons.[27] He could then match up visually and physically any undated or unidentified book by the typeface, of which his shelves contained as complete a repertory as then existed. The material result was the physical arrangement of books at the British Museum, an arrangement followed by several other libraries. The textual result was the single-volume *Index* cataloguing British Museum incunables; in the introductions to each printer, Proctor provided brief quantifiable details about many types, but many of his identifications are, for the reader, vague, and it is difficult to know what, say, 'Koelhoff type 2' is or looks like unless one has a series of Koelhoff types, already identified, at hand.[28]

The *British Museum Catalogue* (*BMC*) built on Proctor, but supplemented his descriptions with facsimiles and provided summary headings making type identification more practical; it also used a more useful system of measurement (*BMC* measures 20 lines from the bottom of line 1 to the bottom of line 21, whereas Proctor measured from the top of line 1 to the bottom of line 20; only the *BMC* system can give useful measurements for units of less than 20 lines). The user can therefore identify a typefont in a number of cases simply by 'ballparking' it (German? French?), and scanning the introduction to the presses of this volume for typefont numbers that match (for example '98G' – a gothic typefont measuring 98 mm for 20 lines). One then checks the facsimile plates for these, and finally the entry itself. Since the British Library has examples of about a third of the incunable editions extant (these include of course the most popular ones), there is a good chance of success.

Prototypography presents several practical problems here: few libraries contain more than a few examples;[29] many of the examples exist in fragments only; many of these are on vellum and subject to shrinkage. Information about prototypography now must be transmitted textually through the two means of identification provided by *BMC*, both reproducible: measurement and facsimile. In the terms I have defined in this study, that involves the translation of the typeface (something that produces specific marks in specific books) into something abstract – text. Such a means of transmitting information works for many fifteenth-century books, but for the fragmentary booklike objects we are dealing with here, these two classes of information, facsimile and measurement, do not always correspond.

For prototypography, Bradshaw and Proctor relied largely on Holtrop's lithographic facsimiles and organized these without explicit reference to quantifiable type measurements (there is no easy way to translate the measurement of a 4- or 5-line fragment into the '20-line' unit as defined in the Proctor system). A typefont essentially means their abstract categorization of these images, and somewhat paradoxically, such implied mental images of unmeasured typefonts may be more accurate than the quantifiable information found in later catalogues.

In 1921 Zedler provided alternative, photographic facsimiles to Holtrop's 1868 lithographic facsimiles. In 1966 an even more systematic series of facsimiles was provided by Wytze and Lotte Hellinga in their catalogue of fifteenth-century Dutch types. Fragments should be (and in fact are) more easily identifiable to incunabulists but they do not necessarily match the facsimiles that provide the basis of their identification and organization.

Part of the reason for this concerns fifteenth-century materials them-selves: vellum shrinks; paper (presumably) shrinks less. This fact is noted in a number of bibliographies, including the introductions in *BMC*, although I am not certain anyone has actually quantified this in a study of early book-copies surviving in vellum and paper.[30] Another concerns modern technology, one I have alluded to above: photographs are not easily and reliably reproducible and disseminated in actual size, at least, not through techniques used in the production of ordinary scholarly monographs or studies (*BMC* facsimiles are exceptional in this regard).

My example here is Bradshaw's type 4 (Pontanus type). The sole fragmentary example of that type from the Huntington contains only 5 lines, and multiplying these in various ways produces figures within the ranges given for this type in the Zedler and Hellinga facsimiles (2 lines = 14 mm; 4 lines = 28 mm, etc.).[31] All catalogue descriptions agree that there is only one type to fit this description, called variously 142G or 144G. Nonetheless, a systematic comparison with the published facsimi-les of Holtrop, Zedler, and Hellinga is disturbing, since for this particu-lar type, the various facsimile images are quite different. While our example corresponds perfectly to one of these facsimiles (in this case, Zedler's), that same example does not seem to correspond at all to the other two (Hellinga's in particular).[32]

Holtrop has three relevant plates illustrating this type: Planche 13 [49] abc; Pl. 24 [37]; and Planche 23 [9] (Pontanus).[33] The examples in Holtrop's plate 13 [49] abc are only fragments, which measure 13–14 mm for 2 lines. The two Donatus full leaves shown in Planche 24 [37] have 20-line measurements of 139 mm and 140 mm; the Pontanus shown in Planche 23 [9] measures 142 mm. Hellinga's plates 9 and 10 are from pages of the Pontanus in Cambridge University Library (Inc.3.E.1.1); the plates show the type measurement as 143 mm+, closer to the *GW* description of this type as 144G than to Hellinga's own measurement of 142. The actual pages from the Cambridge University Library copy of Pontanus used in this reproduction (fols 2^r and 2^v) measure 142 mm for 20 lines.[34] The most striking variation comes in Zedler. Zedler's black and white figure (Abb. 4) shows this type (also from a Pontanus) as measuring a whopping 148 mm/20 lines. All of Zedler's photographic plates and the figures that use Donatus fragments to illustrate this same type, however, show the type as much smaller. In Zedler's photographic plates (the basis for my own identification of the Huntington fragments and I assume the basis for identifying other such fragments), this type is shown as measuring 139 mm.

Such variation may be due to the systematic shrinkage of vellum, which overall makes type impressions for the Pontanus (on paper) seem larger than those for the Donatus (on vellum). But one has to assume a fairly systematic shrinkage of 3–5 per cent to account for the variation here. There seems also a tendency on the part of facsimiles to overemphasize such historical differences.

Zedler was the first to describe differences in the various examples of these types; Zedler's own conclusions were that the two books found printed in this type (the Donatus and the Pontanus) represent two states of the type. The type has been misnamed: according to Zedler, the Pontanus is a late use of the type cut originally for the Donatus grammars, grammars that themselves, somewhat confusingly, provide the name for a different variety of early Dutch type.[35] What Zedler called 'states' of this typefont consisted only of differences in particular typesorts or the presence of particular typesorts (ligatures). The later typefont state did not involve a recasting of the type body itself, and Zedler said nothing about the apparent variation in size in particular examples; nonetheless, his illustrations make such differences even more pronounced than they had been in Holtrop. In Zedler's Abb. 4 (Pontanus) 10 lines = 74 mm; 20 lines would be 148 mm. In Zedler's Tafellen I–III (all of Donatus), 20 lines = 138 mm. Yet bibliographically, following Zedler, one must say that a type that matches his Tafel I (and measuring 138 mm) is by definition an example of Pontanus type, which measures 142–4 mm.[36]

In GW the type is defined as measuring 144 mm, and all examples of that are so identified. The GW listing is particularly interesting, because of the principles that operate in the cataloguing of such grammatical fragments – principles we have discussed in the sections above. Entries for these fragments are copy-specific, or at least *tend toward* becoming copy-specific. However, the GW type description remains completely idealized. What the identification '144G' means here is not 'a gothic type face that in this example measures 144 mm for 20 lines (or would measure that if there were 20 lines)' but rather 'a type that is "the same" as that normally described as "144G."' In fact, if a GW bibliographer had examined the type, measured it at, say, 138 mm, and found it similar to Zedler's Tafel I, measuring 139 mm, such a result would be recorded, even in the copy-specific context of the Donatus entries, as '144G.'

What is now 'old technology' (a Xerox machine with a reducing option) is generally sufficient to manipulate the various facsimile reproductions and even real-world examples so that they correspond. Any example of this type on vellum that appeared to measure, say, 138 mm, could be easily rationalized by a scholar as a shrinkage of an originally 144 mm type. The more individuals one has to account for as exceptions, the less one might wish to think of these *as* exceptions. Why do all but a few examples of '144G' have 20-line measurements of 138–40 mm?

All these facsimiles are reproductions, and we read them as pictures of the original, representations of the original, copies of the original. Because of the conventions of such reproduction, others, as I do, may tend to read Zedler's photographic reproductions as more reliable than, say, Holtrop's lithographic ones. I judge their accuracy not by size but by appearance (I am trained to believe photographs in scholarly articles do not misrepresent evidence). My thinking of them in terms of accuracy, however, indicates that such facsimiles are finally not reproductions at all; they are rather visual descriptions. Images such as these become descriptions because of the unreliability of printing technology when reproducing images in actual size.[37]

The type measurements are supposed to respond, not to marks on a piece of paper or vellum, but rather to the matrices – the mould for the type sorts that eventually produced these images. Measurements assume, to some extent, a classic form of type production, involving punches, matrices, and multiple type sorts. The matrices, if any were extant, would be the physical counterpart of the bibliographer's 'ideal copy,' with one difference: ideal copy is a pure abstraction, even in historical terms; the matrices are (or were) physical. Each embodies the intention of a producer. Because early matrices no longer exist, however, a historical matrix is as ideal as the bibliographers' ideal copy of a book. For an ideal copy, we give the description that the extant books allow us to imagine the printer intended. But what does a matrix size mean? Isn't this entire complex of assumptions challenged by recent studies denying the classic theory of type production on which it may well depend?

All of the early grammar books printed with these types are in vellum, and since vellum is more susceptible to shrinkage than is the paper on which such works as the Pontanus are printed, the paper measurements should be more accurate; that is, they better retain the intended size of the type manifested in the hypothesized matrix. Yet it seems absurd to have as a rule that type measurement should follow the largest copy – in this case, as Zedler argues, this is the least representative copy and the least responsive to the type of product (Donatus grammars) that the printers and type cutters intended to be printed with this typeface.

The catalogues are caught between attempting to give 'ideal copy' information and 'copy-specific' information, and in the present case, such information is extremely difficult to sort out. Their classificatory numbering – whether arbitrary and based on recent scholarly history ('Hellinga type 4'), or quantifiable and based on material evidence (*GW*'s '144G') – refers to potential products of idealized matrices, whose actual products do not correspond either to these idealized matrices or to each other. The material world, with its shrinking vellum and erratic photographic images, keeps getting in the way of the textual world of descriptive and enumerative bibliography. A bibliographer could, as earlier cataloguers, opt for simple accuracy: the phrase 'Type #4' is sufficiently abstract to allow for all the shrinking vellum and erratic photography possible, but to one unfamiliar with the typefaces themselves, such a description is almost useless. *GW*'s '144G' is better, even if '144' really means (in the real world) '138.' The rule in bibliography is no different from the rule in other endeavours: 'inaccurate information is always superior to no information.'

William Blades, *Life and Typography of William Caxton*

The second problem I will deal with involving facsimile production of early type is from the mid-nineteenth century – the lithographic facsimile plates and the block-print 'imitations' in William Blades, *The Life and Typography of William Caxton* (1861–3).[38] Adrian Johns has rightly noted the importance of this project in his *The Nature of the Book*, but his interpretation misrepresents the precise problem faced by Blades and his facsimilists; Johns, as a modern scholar, seems to have projected onto late nineteenth-century facsimile production the same goals and conventions that might apply to late twentieth-century facsimile production:[39]

> [Blades] was arguing that Caxton had been the first English printer, and that he had learned his craft from Colard Mansion – an unorthodox candidate. Blades did so on the basis of their type. His representations of Caxton's and Mansion's typographical characters were therefore intended to be compared exactly, in precisely the same way as handwriting would be compared by a paleographer. Readers were encouraged to examine their facsimiles 'through a magnifying glass.' The irony was that no printing technique practiced in early modern Europe itself could ever have permitted such minute comparison. In its very 'accuracy of form,' Blades admitted, the lithographic art falsified its subject. In its very fixity it misrep-

resented the impressions being reproduced, which had themselves *not* been uniform. It seemed that Caxton could be secured only by a new, different technique. (375)

Johns's characterization of Blades is part of his general polemic against notions of typographical fixity and the association of printing with textual stability. Johns is arguing here that lithography 'misrepresents' early printing by presenting type images as fixed, and thus attributes to early printing a fixity that was never there. As a general characteristic of visual reproduction, this may be true, but my concerns here are with the association of that general claim with the images in Blades. The paragraph oversimplifies both the facsimile process (the Caxton and Mansion facsimiles, as we will see, were produced by two completely different methods) and the complex and often contradictory goals of both Blades and his facsimilist, G.I.F. Tupper. I am not certain Blades ever admitted what Johns claims he does; while Blades's own statements at times reveal a naive view of the facsimile process, the notes by Tupper suggest that the naive view of facsimile production (accurate representation) may never have been included in the work that goes under his name.

Tupper's notes have been studied in detail by Robin Myers.[40] These notes show that Tupper did not conceive his work, as Johns inadvertently implies, as merely dilettantish. He was not attempting to provide a 'pretty picture' or an 'accurate picture' of Caxton's types. His illustrations are not really pictures at all. Blades's *Life and Typography* is a history of Caxton publications based in large part on a history of the typefaces and typefonts used by Caxton. That history and the very conception of such a history requires an accurate description of Caxton's types, and this is what facsimiles offer. What Blades needed from his facsimilist and what Tupper provided (Tupper himself was somewhat clearer on the nature of the problem than was Blades) was exactly that: not a picture, but a *description*.

BLADES AND THE LITHOGRAPHIC PROCESS

Tupper's images were produced by transfer; the pages were traced by hand on transparent paper in contact with the original, and these images were in turn transferred to the stone for reprinting.[41] Even in 1860 there were alternative methods for producing lithographic images of printed pages; one involved 'charging' the ink on the printed page, and transferring its image directly onto the stone. Such a method, one known to the earliest lithographers, could not be used for Caxton, since it meant the destruction of very expensive originals.[42] Although all these methods have been called 'crude,'[43] the seemingly more accurate photographic methods, once available, were rejected by many facsimilists for reproducing too much of the extraneous material which was of no interest to press classification and history. Note what such 'extraneous material' is: ink marks on paper, that is, the actual impressions of ink on the pages of a book.[44]

Blades seems to have understood the process, although in the end, he interprets it somewhat differently from his facsimilist Tupper:

> A few words on the Plates. Only those who have endeavoured to obtain a real facsimile, – one which, for identity of types and exactness of measurement will bear the closest examination by the side of the original, – know the excessive difficulty of producing an Artist clever and patient enough to execute the tracing, and the workmen skillful enough to print it. (1: ix–x)

This indicates a fairly secure grasp on the lithographic process itself, but Blades seemed to believe that the quality of a facsimile is a matter of its accuracy, its indistinguishability from the original.

> This method [transferring a tracing to the stone], however, is liable to two sources of error – the stretching of the tracing paper in the act of being transferred to the stone, and the gradual clogging of the letters in working ... Both these difficulties have been successfully surmounted in those Plates described as 'Facsimile,' and the Reader may not only depend upon the accuracy of form, but may be sure that the width and depth of the page do not vary from the original ... As no two copies of the same work are in all respects exactly alike, the particular book from which each plate is taken is noted. (1: x)

This led Blades into the view that there were essentially two kinds of reproduction, which he distinguished in his plates as 'Facsimile' and 'Imitation.' For a Facsimile (produced by lithographic tracing and transfer), the primary goal was 'accuracy'; a good Facsimile was indistinguishable from the original:

> I have just seen the progress made with the facsimile illustration of No. 1 Type and am delighted with it ... Given a paper similar in appearance to Caxton's and I would defy Old Caxton himself to have repudiated it as one of his own offspring.[45]

By contast, what Blades labels 'Imitations' are printed not from lithography but from blocks. Although one can easily imagine the transfer of an image from an original to a block with each step involving physical contact between an original and a copy, these were obviously regarded by Blades as less accurate than what he called a 'Facsimile.' The 'Imitations' in *Life and Typography* are on the whole slightly cleaner; there is no attempt in them to reproduce copy-specific details such as wormholes and raised quads (all shown in the 'Facsimiles'). Furthermore, because they are printed with letterpress blocks and not a flat stone, the impression of each mark on that block is visible and can be felt on the reverse sides of the page. Apparently, Blades felt the differences between the Facsimiles and Imitations were crucial enough to distinguish these two types of copies even in the captions of the plates themselves. A modern reader, however, would be hard pressed to distinguish these at a glance; they are not distinguishable in the recent (and reduced!) photographic reprint of Blades by Burt Franklin,[46] and probably would not be distinguishable if I risked the confusion and frustration involved in attempting to reproduce them here.

When we look at these images under a glass, as Blades himself invites us to do, the lithographic plates appear flatter, and much less 'like' an original than the three-dimensional 'Imitations.' In this sense, the Imitations are a better representation of the early type than are the Facsimiles, produced by direct contact with the original. In another sense, however, the Imitations are completely idealized, with no imperfections in the paper (wormholes), and no stray ink marks – two qualities that Tupper represented in his 'Facsimiles.' To Blades, however, the key distinction between these was not in their appearance but in the process involved in their production, a process that itself was somewhat idealized in his description, since Tupper's lithographic method required the same free-hand tracing of an original that would be required in block reproduction.

To Tupper, the distinction between these two processes does not seem to have been paramount, but the often competing goals of the facsimilist were a good deal more complicated than they were admitted to be by Blades. Tupper's notes prove he struggled with many of the theoretical problems involved in facsimile production. What should be the object of reproduction? the ink marks on a page of a particular book copy? a generalized image of the ink marks of a repeated type sort? the physical face of a particular type sort? or the faces of the hypothesized matrices and punches that created those sorts? In his 'Notes on the Peculiarities of Caxton's Types' (MS St Bride 22508), Tupper calls his work 'tracings' and notes the particular questions facsimile making involves:

> The object has been to show the true face of the type as nearly as possible from a printed example ... without idealizing – but I confess I am by no means satisfied with this plan and trust that if any one should ever go over the ground again (which there is no chance of my doing – once in a lifetime being sufficient) he will, as I at first intended, give 2 representations of each character – one showing the true face of the type – discarding the surplus ink round the edges – the other an exact facsimile of an *average* impression as it appears.[47]

Tupper tries to distinguish 'truth' from 'idealizing,' but comes to no solution. The goals of facsimile making are not simple, and according to Tupper, these various and often competing goals should perhaps be separated and embodied in different types of images.[48] When Tupper notes the various goals of the facsimilist, he is quite different from Blades. His phrase 'true face of the type' (the goal of a facsimile representation) refers not to a type impression but to the piece of type itself; the 'exact facsimile' is the representation of the ink on the paper produced by an 'average' typesort (particular sorts, of course, will differ slightly).[49] What Blades cites as the main goal of the facsimilist (accuracy) is not even noted here: to Tupper, the competing goals do not seem to include this one.

Bibliographically, the question is central to the history of early printing. Blades's contemporary incunabulists (Campbell and Bradshaw) were moving to the conclusion that the identification of a printer meant the identification of a typefont, and a typefont is the product of the matrices that produced the particular type sorts in a case of type. What appears to be an idealization in Tupper's images is actually a historicization – the identification of the type case in the possession of a particular printer (the distinction between Caxton 2 and 2* is one that can be attributed to Tupper himself). To the nineteenth-century bibliographer, type identification meant the historical classification of books and thus the recovery of fifteenth-century printing history.

Although Blades might have considered his facsimiles to be copies or reproductions of an original, Tupper was interested in recording something else about that original. Tupper's plates include an 'Alphabet' of each typefont, which Blades describes as follows: 'a complete synopsis of every fount of letter used by Caxton, with an Alphabet of each, including all the single, double, and triple letters, signs, contractions, &c. – ' (2: v). Tupper's Alphabets include also accidentally printed quads – things never intended to appear on the page.[50] These quads show that Tupper's images never completely textualize the evidence; they never make it completely reproducible. Those quad impressions, however much they may appear to be the same in each copy of *Life and Typography*, are a clear reminder to the reader that every type impression is finally unique.

When Blades invites his readers to examine his facsimiles under glass, this is an examination that will take place within the conventions of nineteenth-century facsimile production. Compared to, say, pen facsimiles, Tupper's plates are certainly noteworthy for their accuracy.[51] But the term 'accuracy,' finally, does not give a fair description of what Tupper is doing. Under a magnifying glass (despite what modern theorists of difference may claim), any two examples of printing, whatever their texts, will appear far more similar to each other than either will to any photo, pen facsimile, or even the most accurate lithograph. Tupper, unlike other facsimilists in the book trade, is not trying to produce a substitute for a printing page. Tupper's lithographs are *descriptions,* and when Blades asks his reader to examine their details under a glass, what that reader will find is not a convincing illusion (the indistinguishability of the facsimile from the original), but rather the minute details of Tupper's visual description.

Such descriptions are the same sort of stylized drawings one might find in an early twentieth-century bird book. Tastes in such things change: compare, for example, early editions of Roger Tory Peterson's *Birds of North America* to later editions, or to alternative editions. The more recent the edition, the more closely the illustrations resemble colour photographs (and perhaps birds as well). Yet Peterson was not trying to produce and market pictures of birds, beautiful or otherwise. He was giving systematic and stylized visual descriptions of them. To say that such descriptions are less convincing ersatz birds than are modern photographs may be true, but such thinking will not get you far in a cloud of fall warblers.

4 The Notion of Variant and the Zen of Collation

4.1 Charlton Hinman and the Optical Collator

The following chapter deals with the definition of 'variant' in early printing: in the first section (4.1) I discuss some of the early machines designed to detect press variants, that is, changes introduced into individual sheets and pages during the course of a print run; in the second (4.2) I discuss the definitions of press variants as found in recent editions. The way modern bibliographers discover differences in the corresponding pages of book-copies of the same edition – differences that will define such things as edition, issue, and state or variant – is through the optical collator, a device that allows images of pages of different copies to be superimposed. Such collation was presumably done earlier in the century by eye, through what Gordon Lindstrand describes as the 'head-wagging, finger-pointing method of individual sight collation,' or what Randall McLeod refers to as the 'Wimbledon' method.[1]

According to its inventor, Charlton Hinman, the machine was inspired by stories he had heard about efforts by military intelligence to determine the success of bombing runs; photographs taken before and after bombing runs were superimposed and compared (because of the difficulty of reaching the same precise point to take such pictures, Hinman felt these stories, however inspirational, were false).[2] Optical collators of various designs involve superimposition of two similar images. Specific differences will appear in various ways, either in the viewer's brain (as in the mirrored or stereoscopic versions), or as a projected image of some kind (as in all versions of the Hinman). In the simplest collator (similar to the hand-held stereoscope), superimposition takes place in the brain, and minute differences in two similar images appear as three-dimensional areas on the conflated image; where these differences occur on backgrounds that are identical, the background will appear in two dimensions. In Hinman's collator, and in modified versions of it, two images are projected and superimposed onto an external surface, and differences are highlighted by alternately illuminating each image; differences appear as moving areas against an otherwise still background.[3] The earliest detailed discussion of these effects is found in Hinman, who describes less what is done than what is seen. The operator must first make the adjustments to 'superimpose very precisely the images of the two objects' (132). Then the lights flash:

> The operator therefore seems to see, when the two objects are in fact identical, only a single motionless exemplar. But of course he is actually seeing first one object and then the other; and if they are *not* the same, his attention is immediately caught by apparent motion at the points of difference – where his eye is being presented alternately, first with one thing and then with something else.[4]

In practice, Hinman's machine and the more recent designs that replace it depend on a version of binarism (located either in the machine itself or in some cases in the viewer's perception). Although in theory that principle should not restrict the design of any such machine, it does affect and has affected the tabulation of evidence collected by these machines: something is either 'variant' or it is 'invariant.' As a result, what scholars claim is a 'full collation' of all copies is often something less than that – a comparison of each copy with a selected base copy.

For Hinman's mythical bombing runs, this would present no problem; what is required is information regarding 'before and after'; damage is progressive and the sequence of states is known in advance. But differences in printed sheets involve both correction and damage, and the sequence is not known in advance. What is required is not simply a comparison of pairs of sheets but a comparison of all sheets. I will argue here that this fundamental aspect of the collator has led to a 'textualization' of the results of collation, and that what scholars have thus far described as evidence bearing on printing procedures (historical events in a printing house) are rather textual abstractions (logical manipulations of evidence by textual critics).

The Method of Optical Collation

There are several descriptions (often very amusing) of how various collators work. Those who use collators apparently assume they are doing the same thing, or roughly the same thing. But are they? Collators apparently have been tested against each other,[5] but as far as I know, there are no detailed published records of the results. There is no detailed description available of how the differences between various collators and the improvement in design specifically bears on results. Nor, most important, is there a standard account of how the results obtained from any collator should be tabulated; even if one assumes that specific and articulable standards are applied for the collection of information in any one editorial project, there are no accepted guidelines on how to apply those same standards to any other editorial or collating project.

I have used three types of what would now be considered early or even primitive collators, and these, for me, produce more or less the same results. The first is the Hinman collator (those at the Folger Library and the William Andrews Clark Memorial Library in Los Angeles). The second type is the mirrored collator, in two of its designs: the McLeod collator (one I have never been able to use properly), and a simpler version of it, the Hailey's Comet, which I believe I can use as efficiently as it was designed to be used. The third collator type I use is my own eyes.

These collators all pose their separate and special problems, and I begin with the Hinman. The Hinman collator is large and cumbersome, with extremely heavy plates for holding the books; in the model at the Clark Library, the various lights function correctly about half the time. For books of small format (the basis of the Dryden edition, or for the quartos used in the Beaumont and Fletcher edition edited by Bowers), it may have worked well. For large folios it is almost impossible to get the books in place without risking some damage. To go through a folio page by page requires constant adjustment, not only for each page, but for sections of each page. As every user of these collators must know, the lenses will not focus on an entire page at once. One cannot see a variant at the top of a folio page and one at the bottom of the folio page without refocusing; in other words, one cannot find a variant in a specific location unless one intentionally and purposefully looks for and suspects a variant in that particular location (a principle that I am certain has an effect on the results, or at least, always has had such an effect in my own results). To scan each page with the care required to find (or to suspect) a variant in each section takes time. One either succumbs to what I have heard described as the 'Zen of collation,' which I assume means a serene indifference to that time, or one imagines that the time could be better spent doing something else in those Rare Book rooms with their limited hours.

In his early articles, Hinman estimates that the mechanical collator will increase collating speeds from forty to fifty times. He does not describe the alternative methods he has in mind here,[6] and it is impossible to know what is being compared. He must be referring to a line-by-line, letter-by-letter comparison of two texts – the 'head-wagging, finger-pointing' method. This method will find textual differences, even minute ones, but not differences in line-by-line re-settings at press. For that, one might use the equally laborious method noted in McKerrow:

> Take any page of the book and find in it two full stops at a distance of some ten or a dozen lines apart ... Now lay a ruler on the page from one of these stops to the other and note the letters or parts of letters that it cuts. If a rule placed in a similar position in the other copy cuts the same letters, the chances are many hundreds to one that the two pages were printed from the same setting-up of type. (*Introduction to Bibliography*, 183)

But this method, laborious as it is, will very likely not find substituted letters, broken sorts, etc., that do not alter in some way the physical placement of *other* letters, and, although early studies on press variation are generally silent about the methods used, I assume most used some form of the first method, that of literal transcription or comparison.[7] Hinman himself never attained the speeds he estimated in 1954, and his one specific note concerning his procedures in his 1963 *Printing and Proof-Reading of the First Folio of Shakespeare* comes close to despair. This note has apparently been overlooked by those scholars, and there are many of them, who have praised Hinman for his thoroughness:

> Having spent more than two full years collating Folger Folios, I speak feelingly on this subject. The great bulk of the variants I ever found I had of course found by the time I had gone through some 20 or 25 copies. Thereafter the going was very tedious, and almost no new variants were turned up during the last six months I devoted to full-time collation. And morale suffers as returns diminish – especially when such further returns as there may be cannot reasonably be expected to add much to our understanding of the problem in hand. Long before I had collated fifty copies, moreover, it had become apparent that a great deal *was* to be learned about the printing of the Folio by a study of its types. After searching for evidence of proof-correction throughout only two-thirds of the Folger Folios, therefore, I turned my attention to types – and not, I trust, too soon. But I should perhaps record here, for the benefit of anyone who may wish to continue

the hunt for variant readings, what work remains to be done on the Folger collection. Except in quires ss–vv in the Tragedies, and in all the pages throughout the book that are hereafter listed as variant, the following Folger copies have *not* been collated by me: Nos. 39–41, 43, 46–47, 51–52, 56, 58, 61–64, 66, 69–70, 72–74, 77–79, and the various fragments that are not numbered as separate whole copies. About a year would be required to collate these copies, given the aid of the 'machine' now available at the Folger Library.[8]

For large books, I cannot see how anyone using a Hinman collator can obtain the speeds first estimated by Hinman.[9] In my own use of the Hinman, I have always limited my use to the search for specific variants in specific sections of books.

My experience with other mechanical collators is similar. Both the McLeod collator and the Comet designed by Carter Hailey consist of mirrors; they are simpler versions of the Lindstrand comparator, which employs adjustable lenses. With one eye, one looks directly at a page in copy 1; with the other eye, one looks at the same page in copy 2 through a pair of adjustable mirrors. If the mirrors are properly adjusted, the images are superimposed in some way (at least, they are superimposed in the brain). Since the apparent distance of one of these books from the eye is independently adjustable, it is not necessary that both copies be identical in size. For both collators, the books sit on angled wooden stands, much like those one finds designed to support books in English libraries. The backrests are flat but can be tilted about 30 degrees. Prof. McLeod's work has been on Ariosto and Hollinshed's Chronicles. To balance two folios on these stands must be a remarkable feat. I have never seen him do it, and I assume there are librarians who wish they could say the same thing. Mr Hailey has worked primarily on the 1550 Crowley edition of *Piers Plowman*, a small volume, one which does not test the limits of the stand. McLeod and Hailey obviously use Xeroxes when possible.

Although individual users' experiences will differ, I admit to having had many difficulties with these devices despite my enthusiasm for them. Some of these were incidental and not the direct result of the design of the collators themselves. My difficulties with the McLeod collator were due largely to the inaccurate set-up and bad instructions by an overly proprietary reader at the Huntington. No one using the collator in that set-up (one completely at odds with Prof. McLeod's clear instructions) could possibly obtain reliable results; several readers did use it that way, however, and I assume their results are now published. My difficulties with the Comet were due largely to a recalcitrant adjustment screw, and to attempt to describe this problem in detail would cause almost as much aggravation as the problem itself.[10]

Other difficulties were the result of the essential nature of these devices. Mirrors do not actually superimpose two images; for these particular machines, there is no 'hard copy' of the results with the variants neatly highlighted in three dimensions (no photograph of what everyone who has used such a collator successfully experiences, or claims to experience). What superimposes the images are certain very complicated processes in the nervous system and the brain. The process is the same as in the stereoscope; the mirrors force the eyes to see one set of images, which some part of the brain apparently (and stupidly) interprets as the same object. Another part of the brain sorts out the conflict by interpreting minor differences as implying three-dimensionality.[11]

To attain this illusion, however, requires some preliminary adjustment. One adjusts the two mirrors controlling the image for one eye until that image is the same size and orientation as the image viewed directly with the other eye; the two images thus will (or may) seem to be superimposed. To explain the aggravation this involves to anyone who has not experienced it is difficult. Exact superimposition is possible, but impracticable. Furthermore, one cannot do with the mirrored collators what one does with the Hinman versions: isolate the process of superimposition from the process of detecting variants. Both designers, McLeod and Hailey, recommend doing this: the user should concentrate first on superimposing the images exactly before examining the results (that is, before allowing the brain to process and interpret the illusory superimposed image). This is not at all easy or straightforward. The eyes and the mind 'leap ahead,' adjusting sight lines and refocusing so as to superimpose the two images even when the mirrors are completely out of adjustment.

Once I had the mirrors properly adjusted (or thought so), I faced the same problem I faced with the Hinman, a problem all those who have designed these collators acknowledge. The collator can only superimpose small images: perhaps a few lines, perhaps as much as a small page.[12] Folio pages inevitably require readjustment: one looks for variants at the top of the page, readjusts the mirrors, then looks for variants at the bottom of the page. I have often found that when no variants appear, it is not because they are not there; it is rather because I have misadjusted the mirror. I can spend an afternoon on the Hinman. The maximum time I have ever managed to spend on either of the mirrored collators is two hours. The maximum time I believe I have ever worked efficiently on it is one hour.

Because of the practical difficulties presented by these two forms of collation, I generally have used a third method, which I describe as the Human Hinman. It is essentially a sight collation (or 'crossed-line-of-sight' collation) involving superimposition of images, and I believe it is the fastest and most efficient method available. Here, the two books are placed side-by-side in bookstands, in whatever way is most convenient. For folios, the easiest way seems to be to lay them flat on the desk, with the fore-edge facing the reader. Open them like two desktop computers, and face the set of pages as one would face the screen of the computer (the lines on the pages will read vertically). Stare at the two pages, and cross your eyes. The images will double; on a good day, after a deep breath, two of the now four images will superimpose magically as a third image. And on this superimposed image (or perceptual illusion), variants in the two copies stand out in three-dimensionality, just as they do in the McLeod, Hailey, or Lindstrand collators. You record them. It is possible (but no one knows for sure) that the variants recorded this way are the same ones that might be discovered and recorded by using a machine. The advantages are speed and convenience. There is no special equipment, and one can use whatever bookrests a Special Collections library supplies or requires. One can turn pages quickly, and one can view an entire page with far less readjustment of focus than is required with the machines. The drawbacks are similar to those associated with other collators. If you require reading glasses of any kind, you need a slightly lower magnification in order to read a page in that middle distance of bookshelves and computer screens. And here, more than with the Hinman, the *entire* process and interpretation of what one sees takes place in the brain, and there is no assurance that others will perceive the collated pages in the same way. Try to describe precisely what you see in a stereoscope. Are you certain that is what everyone sees? In other words, are the results you as an individual get looking through a stereoscope repeatable in all their details?

There are obviously major methodological problems with the use of such machines and methods. One must assume that the indescribable processes of the human eye or the interpretation of specific details on a screen can be the basis for detecting evidence of historical processes and events at press. For detecting resettings and clearly isolated differences (the resetting of entire words and phrases), any of the methods and machines will work and produce reasonable results. On the level of the minutiae scholars often deal with here, however, I am sceptical.[13] The actual evidence one gets is not quantifiable; yet not only is that evidence tabulated and quantified, it is also presented as units of text that exist in discrete packets. There are opposing states: variant and nonvariant. There is no middle ground. In the collator, what one detects is an opposition, one between, say, uniformity and difference – an area of apparent three-dimensionality (itself illusory) against a two-dimensional background, or the Hinman's apparent 'flickering movement' against the unmoving background. The scholar then records this, but the process at press is never so simple.[14]

Let us consider what this evidence is supposed to mean. There is a locked forme at press. A sheet is printed. Forces are placed on the forme. The paper is wet, and will dry. Another sheet is placed on the tympan. The forme is reinked. The ink is not the same as earlier. The tympan is pressed onto the forme. More extreme forces. Another sheet is hung to dry. When operations are considered in this way, there can be no question of absolute identity. All the word 'identity' suggests here is 'the maintenance of the textual integrity of the locked forme.' All copies are physically distinct; the visual sameness is to some extent illusory.

The interest, of course, comes when the forme is unlocked. If a conscious change is made, then the two sheets will be different (textually). However, if no specific change is made, then it is not clear what a collator of any kind will make of this. It is quite possible that physical changes can take place (type can break, a line can work loose, a line set too loose can move). The Hinman might well create some 'flickering movement'; the eye or the mirrored collator might well detect 'three-dimensionality'; the computer superimposition might produce red and blue traces for certain sections of text. Yet what will the scholar do? What is the difference between negligible difference and recordable variation?

The utility of the collator for textual criticism is not the issue here. The problem I am concerned with is the projection of the textual-critical evidence onto printing history: textual variants (evidence the scholar tabulates) are seen as evidence of specific processes at press. Hinman's much-praised *Printing and Proof-reading* was qualified by Hinman himself, and its purpose placed on an increasingly abstract level: note in the following statement how the subject moves from actual events at press to abstract objectives (called 'real objectives') of those making corrections:

Thus it would be hollow to assume that all the variant readings that will ever be found in the Folio must be brought to light by the collation of fifty copies – or, indeed, by the collation of the entire Folger collection. Without doubt the record is not yet absolutely complete. But it is nearly enough so, I believe, to show us approximately how much proof-reading was done, and also to make quite plain what the real objectives of this proof-reading were. (1: 245)

Let us consider now the way in which evidence is gathered by those using collators. The method scholars use seems to involve a control copy of some sort, although some descriptions of collation suggest (wrongly, I think) that one can use multiple bases for collation without affecting results.[15] Since one cannot get the physical books together (the copies of the First Folio available to Hinman at the Folger are of course exceptional), one obtains photos of whatever copy can be most conveniently reproduced; these images are then taken from library to library or used as a basis for comparing other images of these additional copies.

The analogy with textual criticism (or, say, one of the earlier forms of textual criticism) is transparent. To determine variation, one tabulates all variants against an arbitrarily chosen 'basis of collation' using, I assume, one of the various methods described in textual-critical contexts (see chapter 5.1 below). All textual variants are thus recorded, and there is no obvious flaw in this method as long as we limit its application to textual matters. When we know the textual relation of text A to the basis of collation, and text B to that same basis of collation, then we also know the textual relation of text A to text B. We will find all textual variants no matter what we use as a basis of collation.

But when we extend this method to the history of printing, there are problems. If we use the collator purely as a text collator, the only advantage over manual collation is speed. Its methodological advantage seems rather to be in its ability to detect nontextual relations, that is, full or partial resettings at press, changes, not all of them textual, that show manipulation of a printed forme. Yet to use the optical collator for this purpose is to inquire into a different level of evidence, one not of text but rather of material impressions of text. And if we do so define the purpose of the method, then the normal method of using one base text against which to collate all other texts is no longer adequate to gather the information we need.

In order to gather evidence regarding printing procedures, it is not enough to collate copy A against copies B and C. One has to collate copy

B against copy C. Suppose one were looking at three copies of a single printed sheet and wished to know the sequence in which they went through press. A reads *text*; B reads *texht*; C reads *tex t*. Textually, the relations among these copies seems to be AC|B. But an optical collation might reveal different relations: if copy A were the basis of optical collation, the investigator would note that neither B nor C collates; since the readings in B and C differ, the various readings would be grouped A|B|C. If B were the basis of collation, somewhat different results obtain. One might note only that each has a reading that differs from the base text and organize B | AC (recording base text *texht* vs alternative reading *text*). Or, if B and C collate visually, one might assume an uninked letter in C and group BC | A. Unless we are dealing solely with matters of text, there is no way to determine the relationship between B and C (*texht* | *tex t*) or between A and C (*text* | *tex t*) unless one collates them directly, and no way to determine whether what we are dealing with here is type movement, misinking, or a press variant.

Again, if what we are concerned with is textual criticism, then none of this matters: we have only two variants: *text* and *texht*. We know *text* is correct; *texht* is an error, and based on other factors, we might also determine the direction of variation (whether toward correctness or error). However, if we are interested in the workings of a press (which is one of the reasons to gather such information), then we need to go further. We cannot assume that because B and C show the same apparent variant against A, then B and C will necessarily collate. Even further, given minute differences in all copies that investigators must ignore as indifferent 'clutter,' we cannot assume that if both B and C are defined as 'invariant' against A, then B and C will necessarily be 'invariant' in terms of each other; the apparent 'clutter' distinguishing these copies from the base text might well evolve into 'variation' when the two are viewed against each other. We must collate every copy against every other copy. If there are three copies, we will need to do three complete collations, not two, and the numbers increase at an alarming rate: four copies require six collations; five copies require ten.

4.2 The Logic and Description of Press Variation

A single erratum may knock the brains out of a whole passage ... Add to this, that now and then there is to be found in a printing house a presumptuous intermeddler, who will fancy himself a poet too, and what is still worse a better than he that employs him. The consequence is, that with cobbling, and tinkering, and patching on here and there a shred of his own, he makes such a difference between the original and the copy, that an author cannot know his own work again. (William Cowper to William Unwin, on press corrections)[16]

The second problem related to collation has less to do with the collators and the procedures for using them than with the very definition of press variation (what the collator is looking for) and the means for recording that variation. To what extent is the evidence a scholar records the result of, say, Cowper's 'presumptuous intermeddler,' and are these results simply a projection of the methods used to detect and record them?

The most important early descriptions of press variation in English are by McKerrow in 1927 and by Greg in 1940.[17] The study of such processes was clearly in the interest of textual criticism. Press variants have the same textual-critical status as manuscript variants:

> The ultimate end of these inquiries is, of course, the establishment of the true text, and it follows that the press reader's emendations in the quarto can only be of consequence either where the more authoritative folio omits the passage or where its reading is on some ground or other open to suspicion. (Greg, *Variants in King Lear*, 183)

> There is no disguising the fact that editors have left the textual criticism of *King Lear* in a thoroughly unsatisfactory state ... This is hardly surprising seeing that the necessary apparatus was not available. I believe that now the whole of the information needed is at the disposal of editors, and it appears to be high time that they set about the job of preparing a text of the play that shall be based upon a properly reasoned estimate of the evidence. (Ibid., 190)

Peter Blayney's critique of Greg changes the terms of the argument and the relationship between textual criticism and bibliography.[18] Blayney, however, reiterates the statements of McKerrow and Greg regarding the subordination of the bibliographical to the textual-critical: 'The controlling factor throughout this investigation has been the need for information which can be applied – however obliquely – to the study of *Lear*' (10); 'The scope of the bibliographical investigation has been defined by its purpose as the foundation for a textual study' (11). The same distinctions and hierarchy are implied by Greetham:

The last stage in the strictly bibliographical process is textual bibliography, the employment of the technical information derived from analytical or descriptive bibliography in charting and evaluating the effect of he technical history on the text itself. Some bibliographers would regard this as an end in itself, but most textual scholars see paleography, codicology, analytical and descriptive bibliography as merely a prelude to the 'real' business of textual scholarship: the reconstruction of an author's intended text.[19]

The word 'real' is well placed in inverted commas, since the 'real' here is similar to the referent of the medieval philosophical term *res* – the abstract thing that organizes the world of material; it is somehow more real than the material that provides a witness to it.

Fredson Bowers was the most outspoken proponent for bibliography as an autonomous discipline:

> Analytical bibliography deals with books and their relations solely as material objects, and in a strict sense has nothing to do with the historical or literary considerations of their subject matter or content. (*Principles of Bibliographical Description*, 31)[20]

Even Bowers, however, seemed to subordinate material bibliography to textual bibliography in his discussion of 'ideal copy':

> Thus an ideal copy is a book which is complete in all its leaves as it ultimately left the printer's shop in perfect condition and in the complete state that he considered to represent the final and most perfect state of the book. (113)

The goal of the descriptive bibliographer – the book's 'final and most perfect state' – is similar to the goal Fredson Bowers defined in other contexts for the textual critic – the text incorporating the author's 'final intentions.'[21]

An interesting variant of these assumptions, subordinating bibliography to the more important work of textual criticism, is found in Gaskell:

> Bibliographers, like other scholars, have to be able to think logically, to judge critically, and to persevere in tediously repetitive tasks; but in addition they must understand the history of book production. The study of printed books as material objects and the right interpretation of the printed

documents of the past will be based primarily on a knowledge of how authors' manuscripts were transcribed in type, printed, distributed, and sold.[22]

The statement is curious, because it seems to say that we must know what most of us would regard as conclusions ('how authors' manuscripts were transmitted') before we can develop the methods to arrive at those conclusions (the 'study of printed books as material objects').

The thesis I am arguing here is that Gaskell's unintended paradox has literal force, and that the subordination of analytical bibliography to textual criticism has seriously affected the methodology of and the evidence derived from study of processes at press. Rather than provide information that could serve as the basis for progress in other fields, bibliography has simply repeated on a less convincing material level fallacies that are already endemic to the textual-critical field itself.

What is press variation? In principle, the process is simple. Type is set, locked in a forme, and placed in a press, and a number of sheets are run off. Before the print run is complete, changes occur. Some are deliberate (stop-press corrections: the press is stopped, the forme is unlocked, and changes are made in the type). Others are accidental (type moves; type sorts break). The cause of others is indeterminate. The result is that the sheets printed from that forme are different, and sometimes they may be grouped systematically (as embodying 'uncorrected' and 'corrected' states). In the section above, I dealt with the problem of discovery. Here I will deal with the problem of organization and presentation.

To make any bibliographical (rather than textual-critical) progress, one must make a series of assumptions. First, one must define the unit of printing. For the books that are generally the object of these studies, the unit of printing is the 'forme,' that is to say, one side of a complete sheet. For a quarto, this contains four pages; for a folio, it contains two. Sheets that are the products of any given forme (the basic unit of printing) give evidence of a series of corrections, and these corrections may be related in some systematic way. If, for example, changes are made early in the press run, most copies in the print run will show the later state. If further changes are made on the same forme later in the press run, fewer copies will show them.[23] Extant copies of course constitute only a small portion of the entire historical print run, and this complicates matters. These copies will in some way reflect the procedures at press, but there is no guarantee that they are representative copies (that is, that they contain examples of all states, or that they are distributed evenly in the press run).

Let us begin with a few examples from Blayney's *Texts of King Lear*, whose chapters include some of the most detailed studies of press variation available. A simple case is from #41 (Ariosto, *Satyres*, 1608–9, *STC* 744–44.5). Pages from the outer forme of sheet A show two variants. These are probably deliberate corrections and in part the distinguishing features of *STC* entries: 'Schoolmastrs | Schoolmasters' and '1608 | 1609.' Of the nine extant copies, six show *Schoolmastrs* and *1608* (uncorrected states of variants *a* and *b*; this could be written '*a*[u]' '*b*[u]'); two show *Schoolmasters* and *1608* (*a*[c] and *b*[u]); one shows *Schoolmasters* and *1609* (*a*[c] and *b*[c]). There are thus three states, representing three of the four possible combinations of these two variants. Since these corrections are sequential, there will be no copy that shows the fourth combination *a*[u] and *b*[c], that is, the uncorrected state of variant *a* (*Schoolmasters*) with corrected state of variant *b* (*1608*).

A similar case is Blayney #37, Thomas Sparke, *A Brotherly Persuuasion to Unitie* (1607, *STC* 23020). The outer forme of sheet B has two sets of variants:

thgings | things
yealded | yeelded

These distinguish state 1 from state 2. A second set of variants distinguishes states 2 and 3:

Reader | Reader (swash R)

stronger, | stronger

surplesse | surplesse (replaces defective -ss-)

some men spetially | some men speeially

Of the eight fully collated copies, seven show corrected states of each set (*a*[c] and *b*[c]), one shows uncorrected variants of each (*a*[u] and *b*[u]), and with only these copies, one would assume two states. Evidence for three states comes from a partially collated copy showing *a*(c) and *b*(u) (readings include *things, yeelded, ... stronger ... some men speeially*). No copy, thus, will be found that combines *a*(u) with *b*(c).

The case highlights several principles. The first involves the meaning of the term 'correction' as conventionally used to describe these situations. In cases such as this, one determines 'direction of variation' the same way one determines it in textual criticism (Blayney assumes 'thgings' was corrected to 'things'). But the word 'correction' in these contexts is potentially nothing more than a metaphor; what we are really talking about are early and late states. Moreover even cases of deliberate corrections do not necessarily result in a correct text: the later variant *speeially* is clearly incorrect, even though it is technically 'corrected.'

A second point concerns the way early and late states are combined. This principle, simple as it is, has caused even experienced bibliographers difficulties in more complicated cases, and it is worth risking some redundancy to ensure that it is completely understood. A simple, but clearly invalid, way of expressing the relation between early and late states might seem to be the following: if a forme has multiple sets of variants, copies with early states of one variant will have early states of the other. This tempting formulation applies only to cases where all those variants are created at the same time. If the corrections are made at different times, such that a printed page involves two processes of correction, then the principle must be stated negatively: if a copy exhibits an early state for variant *a*, and a late variant for variant *b*, *no copy* will exhibit a late state for variant *a* and an early state for variant *b*. There is no way around this simple principle as long as the historical relation of these variants is represented by the distinction of states. A textual-critical decision regarding one of the variants has implications for the other (in a way that textual-critical decisions of manuscript variants, which behave like individuals, do not).

I will give one final illustration. Let us suppose corrections are made to variant *a* in a sheet, with copies distributed according to states as follows:

1 2 3 4 5 | 6 7 8 9 10

Five copies show the early state, five show the late state. At some time in the process, another variant is introduced, in this case, after seven copies are printed:

1 2 3 4 5 6 7 | 8 9 10

The evidence a bibliographer will have is of three apparent states.

1 2 3 4 5 | 6 7 | 8 9 10

Copies 1–5 show the early state of both variants; copies 8–10 show the late state of both variants. Copies 6 and 7 show the late state of variant *b* and the early state of variant *a*. No copies will show the early state of *b* and the late state of *a*. This fairly obvious point must be understood completely. The fact that there are copies with such 'mixed' states (the early state of *a* combined with the late state of *b*) is a perfectly predictable state of affairs. This indicates no disorder or anomaly in the correcting process: it only shows that the two changes on this page were made at different times. As long as there are no copies exhibiting late state *a* combined with early state *b*, there is nothing anomalous or remarkable about the correcting process implied by these variants.

The reason for dwelling on this rather obvious point is that a parallel principle applies to dealing with printed variants on opposite sides of the sheet. Bibliographers are rarely bothered by the existence of 'mixed' states on a single page or forme – in cases involving multiple variants, some copies will combine an uncorrected form of one with a corrected form of another. Yet when this situation involves different sides of printed sheet (inner and outer formes), bibliographers are less untroubled.

The question bears on what is called the 'perfecting process' – the way sheets already printed on one side are run through the press for printing the reverse side. Some bibliographers have stated categorically that sheets are perfected in precisely the same order in which they are originally printed.[24] Other bibliographers believe that sheets are perfected in no particular order, and cite as evidence for this apparent chaos the existence of sheets showing 'mixed' variants (an uncorrected state on one side of a sheet combined with a corrected state of another variant on the other). McKerrow seems to assume that because early printed books often contain sheets with corrected variants on one side and uncorrected variants on the other, the order of sheets must have been routinely disturbed prior to the perfecting process:

> It results from this [the hypothesized drying process] that the order in which the sheets are perfected is undetermined, and if during printing, corrections are made in the *outer* forme, as they were in the *inner*, there is no reason for assuming that the sheets which were printed from the uncorrected inner forme will be perfected from the outer forme while that also is in its incorrect state. (*Introduction to Bibliography*, 210–11)[25]

McKerrow is incorrect; no principle of disorder is necessary to explain the existence of sheets with mixed variants. If a sheet shows variation on both sides, there will likely be copies that have early states on each side;

there will be copies that have late states on each side; and there will be sheets that show one of the two possible 'mixed' states. This is precisely what happens when there are multiple variants on the single side of a sheet. Even if the sheets are perfected in the same order as first printed, there is no reason to expect that a sheet that has late variants on one side will also have late variants on the other, any more than one should be surprised to find early and late variants combined on the same side of a single sheet.

We can represent this hypothetically with the same notation used above for variants on a single forme. Again, let us assume a case of absolute regularity: sheets are perfected in exactly the same order that they were originally printed (that is, after being printed on one side, the sheets are printed on the other side in the same order). A sheet goes through press, and is corrected once. The copies exhibit two states:

(outer forme): 1 2 3 4 5 | 6 7 8 9 10

That sheet then goes through press again for perfecting (printing on the second side) and is, say, corrected once, this time later in the press run. The copies exhibit two states on the inner forme:

(inner forme): 1 2 3 4 5 6 7 | 8 9 10

Even if the sheets go through the press in precisely the same order for each printing, the result of course is that there will appear to be three states: there will be copies that show early variants on both outer and inner formes (in this instance, copies 1–5), copies that show late variants on both outer and inner formes (in this case, copies 8–10), and copies that are *mixed* (here 6 and 7). But only one of the two possible mixed states should occur. If one of these mixed copies shows early variant *a* and late variant *b*, then so will the other one. As long as we are dealing with a case where each side of the sheet exists in two states, there will be no mixed copy that shows late *b* and early *a*.

So far, I have only been addressing the logic of this problem. But the real world raises other problems: one involves anomalies – bits of evidence that result from processes in the real world more complex than what scholarly methods are designed to explain. In an earlier study of press variation, I showed that such anomalies do in fact exist, but they exist in a fairly predictable proportion. I referred to these as 'irreducible anomalies' since they were not consistent with the controlling assumption of regular perfection (what could be called a 'Printer of the Mind' perfecting process, whereby sheets always go through press in the same order). My conclusion there was that there might be ordinary and definable elements of the perfecting process that could account for them. I argued specifically against the opposing thesis, the thesis of despair: that in human endeavours, there are always anomalies that are beyond human understanding.[26]

In this book, however, I am not concerned with irrational historical human endeavours, or even rational and discoverable processes and procedures at press. I am concerned only with presumably rational scholarly endeavours and bibliographical and editorial methods, and the way in which scholarly argument has misrepresented and confused the evidence it presents.

McKenzie's Printers of the Mind act in regular fashion, but certain material things are beyond their control.[27] They are perfect, but their materials are not. Thus type can break; ink can fail to take; the ink ball can miss a piece of type; the forme can loosen. These two classes of events must be kept distinct; they are exactly parallel to the other problem I am addressing here, the one that distinguishes textual from material matters: textual matters are always perfectly reproducible; material matters are absolute in their singularity.

Let us now look at a few examples. These concern the tabulation of evidence.[28]

Case #1: correction | state | accident

The case comes from Bowers's Beaumont and Fletcher edition; it involves the first quarto of *The Tragedy of Thierry and Theodoret* and the recording of its press variants by Robert K. Turner, Jr.[29] For Sheet I(o), Turner records the following variant:

to part with't] to   with't

According to Turner, among extant copies, only BM1 has the 'uncorrected' variant with the blank space: *to   with't.* If we look at the variants of the inner forme on this same sheet, however, we realize that Turner's analysis cannot be right. BM1 is included by Turner among copies showing the late states for the inner forme. And for unique variants, we can apply the following rule: any copy with a unique early variant on one side must be among the group having early variants on the other; any copy having a unique late variant on one side must be among the group having late variants on the other. The variant *to   with't* cannot be early (what Turner describes as 'uncorrected') if the variants on the reverse side are late.

The problem is obvious. Turner has committed himself to textual-critical language, whereby an erroneous reading is defined as 'uncorrected.'[30] Intended corrections, of course, can result in error (something Turner would acknowledge), but from a textual-critical standpoint, it is hard to describe a compositor 'correcting' *to part with't* to *to   with't*. Part of the solution is simply to give up the language of correction.

But the reading in BM1 may be even more extreme; it may well be copy-specific, the result of a unrepeatable event, and if so, it would not constitute evidence of a sequential state at all (where 'state' refers to a state of the type in a forme, not to the copy-specific ink on a particular page). The word may, for example, have been misinked. Turner's explanation requires that there be 'something else there' in the locked forme – a blank, a quad – something for the compositor to manipulate and attempt to correct. What happens, however, is more easily explained as a material accident that occurs apart from intentionality. An ink ball fails to ink. A piece of paper falls across the inked type sort and blots it out (the precise thing that happens to all of us when Xeroxing fragile paper).

What obscures the bibliographical process is the imposition of textual-critical language – language that in this case makes the bibliographical solution unattainable. To repeat, with Blayney: what the bibliographer finds in his copies are, if repeatable, evidence only of states, not of their sequence. That sequence, or direction of variation, is generally suggested by the application of textual-critical assumptions. But textual-critical language and even ordinary bibliographical language can be misleading. Late states in printing are not always the result of acts of correction. In addition, there are some cases where we will need to distinguish even the seemingly neutral terminology 'variant' and 'state': a recorded variant is a material and possibly unique thing; it is not necessarily evidence of an abstract repeatable 'state.'

Case #2: Hidden states

The most careful scholar, the one most obsessed with detail, is likely to find the most variants. Case #2 comes from Blayney, #34, [Sarpi], *Apology* (1607) (*STC* 21757). On the outer forme of sheet (o)I, Blayney quite rightly organizes the variants in three states. The difference between states 1 and 2 involves the catchword *babi-* (state 1), corrected in state 2 to *I.* A second group of corrections, also involving this catchword, distinguishes states 2 and 3:

onely vyage | only voyage

wihi | *mihi*

Catchword: I | In

lney ther | neyt her

y | ly

The direction of variation for this group seems clear. (Copies with the catchword *babi-* obviously have the first of these variants.)

The inner forme of this sheet contains only one variant: *ouhgt* | *ought.* And only one copy, HN, has the obvious error *ouhgt.* If HN is alone here, and if the Printers of the Mind are doing their work, then for HN's *ouhgt* to represent the earlier of two states, HN would have to be included among those copies showing the earlier of the states in the outer forme. But this is not the case. Copies are organized as follows (vertical lines represent differences of state):

(outer): C C2 | HN | L O F

(inner): HN | C C2 L O F

HN is the sole witness to Blayney's state 2 of the outer forme, combining the catchword *I* with the early group of variants listed above. Apparently the two states *ouhgt* | *ought* are actually a hidden series of three states: *ought* | *ouhgt* | *ought.* An error occurs producing state 2. It is corrected to produce state 3, which is to all appearance identical to state 1. Textual-critical language can do no more than tabulate two states.

Case #3: The Separation of sheap and goets

Case #3 comes from a book collated by Gabler in the Bowers Beaumont and Fletcher edition, the 1639 quarto edition of *Monsieur Thomas.* Gabler:

There are forty-one extant known copies of *Monsieur Thomas* (1639) and two of *Fathers own Son* (n.d., 1661/2?). Of these, twelve have been machine collated, another fifteen have been seen and checked for the press-variants revealed in the first twelve. The remaining sixteen copies have not been inspected.[31]

What those sixteen uninspected copies have to do with the edition is not at all clear to me, unless Gabler expects those with access to them to collate them. Let us consider only those 'machine collated' and those 'seen and checked.'[32] The head title of the outer forme of sheet B has one variant (a comma vs a period) defining two states: *Thomas.* | *Thomas,*. Gabler groups these copies as follows (the semicolon distinguishes copies 'machine collated' from those 'seen and checked'; the vertical line again demarcates the two states):

3 6 11; 15 21 | 1 2 4 5 7–10 12; 13 14 16–20 22–7

A distinction between a comma and a period should give pause. That there were in the original formes two different type sorts representing these marks and that such type sorts account for Gabler's two states seems clear, but that each copy prints its individual type sort in such a way that it can be convincingly defined as belonging to one or the other state is another matter entirely.[33] Gabler's textualizing of the results (recognizing only the difference comma vs period) cannot deal with the possibility of a badly printed comma that appears to be a period (a possibility that is very real). That is, what appears on the page (an ink mark) does not always represent what is in the forme (the type sort that is the basis for our notion of state).

The inner forme of this sheet, B(i), also has two states, defined as follows: 'catchword I (present though gradually dropping out) | catchword (disappeared).'[34] Gabler organizes the copies as follows:

1 2 4 5 8–10 12; 14 16–19 21 24–7 | 3 6 7 11; 13 15 20 22 23.

Something is wrong. Most copies containing late states on one side seem here to contain early states on the other.[35] This is so unlikely that the first thing one ought to do is reverse the proposed sequence of states on one of them. The textual-critical assumption that the comma (textually correct) must be a later correction seems to be bibliographically in error.

We should rearrange the evidence as follows:

B(o): 1 2 4 5 7 8–10 12; 13 14 16–19 20 22 23 24–7 | 3 6 11; 15 21

B(i): 1 2 4 5 8–10 12; 14 16–19 21 24–7 | 3 6 7 11; 13 15 20 22 23

Things are now less mystifying. We have rid the scheme of its absurdities and left only its anomalies. Let us identify these by getting rid of unproblematic copies: those that contain both early or both late states (that is, copies 1–5, 14, 16–19, etc.). We now have the following irreducible anomaly:

outer forme: 7 13 20 22 23 | 21

inner forme: 21 | 7 13 20 22 23

There is no assumption of regularity that can account for this: copies 7, 13, 20, 22, and 23 have the early variant in the outer forme, the later variant in the inner forme, but copy 21 seems to have the late variant in the outer forme, the early variant in the inner forme. This might indicate a disorder in the perfecting process (this is the working assumption of my earlier study). It is also possible, however, that the evidence has been misread, or, more strongly, that the evidence is rather unreadable: there is an inherent flaw in transcribing bibliographical evidence in textual-critical terms.

The study of press variants is not a study of 'what is on the page' – something that is entirely copy-specific, and of no more textual-critical or bibliographical interest than, say, annotation by an owner. It is rather a study of what type sorts are in the forme. Not only do we need to know whether that mark after 'Thomas' is made by a comma type sort or a period type sort, we also need to know whether that type sort for the catchword has itself 'disappeared,' or if it is perhaps there but not leaving a visible mark on the page.

The first problem is difficult, but the second problem is the more intractable. I have no doubt that Gabler is correct about a catchword (in this case a single type sort) 'gradually disappearing.' I can even imagine how this takes place, although it would be desirable to have it explained: does the *I* simply fade fade fade until no longer visible? or does it drift, ever so slightly, until finally disappearing into the margin? In neither case does such a gradual process, even if perfectly regular, produce an obvious difference of two discrete states. At what point, at what exact point, does the catchword 'disappear'? And what basis do we have for assuming that such a process is regular? The assumption that type disappears implies to me either a poorly locked forme, or, minimally, a piece of type (in this case a single sort) that is not locked in place. The pressing of the tympan puts great strain on this loose type. Why should it move in any regular or predictable way? Type sorts, material as they are, move according to forces no one fully understands.

The copies I have access to here are the Huntington Library copy (17), the uninspected Clark Library copy (34), and the three Folger copies (14–16). Of the Folger copies, copies 1 and 3 have *I*. In Folger copy 2, this catchword is classified as 'disappeared,' but it has disappeared because there is a fold in the paper, eliminating as well the 't' in the word 'heart' above (or reducing it to an unreadable vertical line). The impression of the presumably 'disappeared' *I* is still visible to my eye. How this would fit a sequence involving more than two dozen other copies, I have no idea.

In Gabler's tabulation, however, not only do we now have 'Materials of the Mind' (that is to say, type behaves in an absolutely regular and predictable fashion and the *I* in the Folger copy 2 is enmeshed in this regularity), we also have 'Materials of the Mind that behave in a discrete fashion.' That is to say, they are in one state, or they are in another state; the *I* in the Folger copy, whatever traces may be visible, is 'disappeared.'

There is no valid way to distinguish states in a case such as this involving capricious movement of a piece of type, and no way, in addition, to speak with any certainty of *disappearance*, since the word 'disappearance' seems to apply to the inked impression on the page rather than to the sort itself. Have all the copies been checked with a raking light to see whether the type still leaves an impression? Are there any blind impressions? Are the pages washed and cleaned in such a way that this evidence does not exist? And, one might ask, is any of this laborious work worth doing or recording?

Press Variation and the Methods of Textual Criticism

As we talk about materials, we are involved in matters of evidence in specific copies that the study of press variation grossly oversimplifies. The study of press variation has always been a study of press correction, which in turn is based on the assumption of intentionality. A sheet was printed. The press was stopped. Someone, of great or limited intelligence, then did *something*, and another sheet was pulled. That *something* is what causes the variant. The researcher is interested in the intellectual source of these two variants: which one is earlier? and which one is more closely related to the copy-text?

This is a well-known textual-critical problem, and it has now been projected, by analogy, onto the press. Each pull of the press becomes analogous to the copy produced by the scribe. Then something even more problematic occurs: the scholar/textual-critic writes his display, and in that display, there is no room for different states with the same apparent reading (ought | ouhgt | ought), or the gradual movement described by Gabler. Variants must be arranged. They must be quantified. Even contamination must be something based on discrete and articulable anomalies. Textual-critical results must in turn be printed; they must be reproducible according to the changing limits and conventions of the Western alphabet, keyboard, or word-processing system. As such, this most materially based of literary studies (what was in the physical forme at press?) becomes as abstract as any text-based literary study: evidence representing historical processes at press is presented as pure text.

Let us consider what is at issue here. No one cares, from a textual critical point of view, what most of these variants are. In the example from *Monsieur Thomas*, neither the punctuation of a title nor the catchword is even part of the literary text of Beaumont and Fletcher. They are interesting only in illuminating processes at press (the subject of analytical bibliography). Yet in this case, analytical bibliography has been completely reduced to textual criticism: processes at press are described in textual-critical terms. The irony is that this particular variety of textual criticism is almost pointless. It is as if at this state in the Beaumont and Fletcher edition, everyone realized that no one gives a hang what Beaumont and Fletcher actually wrote.

Toward a Printing History

This chapter argues that optical collation has never provided the detailed information about printing history the method seems to promise. The method of optical collation, interesting as it is, is based on a fundamental contradiction that is itself a product of its own history. The earliest interest in these matters seems to be found in Anglo-American bibliography, the work of the so-called New Bibliographers – Greg, McKerrow, and later, Bowers. The reason for this interest was purely belletristic and textual: Shakespeare wrote nothing in vain, and it was a matter of supreme importance to determine what he wrote. Since the earliest witnesses to what Shakespeare wrote are products of the printing press, it was of fundamental literary importance to examine the workings and techniques of the press. Only in this way could one distinguish a reading that might have originated in Shakespeare from one that was a product of accidents or mechanical processes in the press room itself. It was this assumption that led to the tabulation of results, and these results were always presented in textual-critical form – a form that was a product of the medium of presentation (written critical arguments) as well as textual-critical assumptions (the primary interest was thoroughly literary).

Bibliographical work, in the service of textual work, always pretended to move from the material levels to more abstract textual ones. Bibliography was, to McKerrow, the foundation of textual-critical work. However, in this case, the reverse process has occurred. A fundamentally textual activity, itself a belletristic one in many senses, has been reimposed onto the material level of analytical bibliography, and has served to organize and thus to distort its results.

Optical collation, then, has not achieved either of its stated goals: it has not in any sense got us closer to, say, 'what Shakespeare wrote' or what anyone else wrote. Textual production, particularly literary textual production, remains recalcitrantly abstract, not material. In addition, the methods of collation have got us little closer to the material workings at press, since so much of the evidence tabulated bears on textual matters only. It has provided us first with what I call the Zen of collation – a state that anyone willing to spend any time with this can, with effort, attain. This is that state of sublimity one can achieve when typing up footnotes, checking punctuation, or alphabetizing the Mc- entries in a Works Cited list. This is not scholarship, but it is academic and it is work, and through it, one can end the day feeling that one has accomplished something.

It has also posed for consideration an interesting methodological problem that I am examining here. It is another example of the two fundamental principles articulated in this study – 1) the absolute singularity of material phenomena, and 2) the difficulty, if not the impossibility, of organizing evidence about that material into any sort of coherence without assuming the very conclusions that can be drawn from it. Even my critique of the results of such collation in the final sections above requires abstract assumptions: *because* of the anomalous nature of some of the results I find in the literature, there must be something wrong with the tabulation of those results; *because* the variant states as defined in a particular study seem problematic, there is something wrong with the definition of those states. Bibliographical methods are as much a product of the conclusions to which they purportedly lead as they are a means of articulating them.

5 Two Studies in Chaucer Editing

The issues discussed in chapter 4 developed historically in the context of editing, and the next group of studies (chapters 5 and 6) deal directly with editing. This chapter takes as subject matter Chaucer editing. The first section in this chapter is methodological; it deals with the definition of a term 'basis of collation' and how this seemingly technical term has been used in the service of particular editorial assumptions and predilections. The second tests the editorial claims of the new electronic edition with the two earliest printed witnesses included within it. These two sections focus on two editing projects now underway: one, the Variorum Chaucer, now almost two decades in progress, may well be the last ambitious Chaucer edition produced under classical editing assumptions. The other, the Cambridge CD-ROM, is the first that announces itself as produced under new technology.[1] Both have attacked earlier editorial efforts, particularly the critical edition of Skeat (1899), and the still widely used edition of F.N. Robinson (1933, 1957, rev. 1987) against which modern editorial projects on Chaucer inevitably must compete.[2] This attempt to define themselves against a particular tradition, however, has also led to a series of dubious assumptions, in part related to the promotion of a particular manuscript undervalued by Skeat and Robinson (the Hengwrt MS), and in part related to sometimes overstated differences in editing methods.

5.1 The Presumed Influence of Skeat's *Student's Chaucer* on Manly and Rickert's *Text of the Canterbury Tales*

This first section contests a myth of textual-critical methodology that gained some currency among Chaucer editors of the 1980s – the editorial effect of the text chosen as what is called the 'basis of collation.' The issues involved are basic to edition making, and concern the difference between the presumably disinterested gathering of evidence, and the directed organization of that evidence. I will discuss specifically criticism directed against Manly and Rickert's 1940 edition of the *Canterbury Tales* and their choice of Skeat's 1894 *Student's Chaucer* as the basis for collation, criticism based on the assumption that readings in the basis for collation exert a significant influence on editorial choices; both Manly and Rickert's critics as well as their supporters have seized on this aspect of the edition as significant. To George Kane, Manly and Rickert's use of Skeat is simply an indication of their flawed methods; to the editors of the Variorum Chaucer, who draw heavily on Manly and Rickert's authority, the difference between Skeat's text and that of Manly and Rickert is evidence of the superiority of manuscripts other than Ellesmere, specifically the Hengwrt manuscript. I will provide a test case to determine whether the assumption underlying these arguments has any validity.[3]

Basis for Collation

In textual criticism, a basis for collation is a preliminary text used to collect variants; in the editing process that follows collation, these variants are then used to create a final edited text. There are other types of textual-critical entities, real and theoretical, that are involved in the editorial process, for example, *base text*, a *best text*, or a *copy-text*, and these generally involve and imply specific editorial procedures. A base text is generally associated with eclectic editing (Skeat's *Canterbury Tales*, based largely on the Ellesmere manuscript, is one example; Robinson's 1933 edition is another); editorial reference to best text implies just that – best-text or single-text editing, whereby a single witness is considered the primary witness and followed to various degrees of slavishness (the 1845 edition by Thomas Wright, the Variorum Chaucer, and the 1980 edition by Norman Blake are examples in Chaucer editing); a copy-text in a strict sense (the sense used by W.W. Greg, who is generally cited when the term is used) implies recension editing: a copy-text is used for accidentals, but has no presumptive authority for substantives. The example from Chaucer is here the Manly-Rickert edition.[4]

A basis for collation, by contrast, need be nothing more than a preliminary text selected to organize the readings of various manuscripts. Obviously, in any editorial project, a single text could serve more than one of these functions, but the two processes of collating and editing are at least theoretically distinct.

In their introduction, during a lengthy and detailed summary of their methods of collation, Manly and Rickert state without comment: 'As the basis for collation we chose Skeat's "Student's Edition"' (2: 5).[5] That is, they used this text as a basis for coordinating various manuscripts and as a guide in constructing the various lemmata that would comprise the card files recording all variants of all manuscripts. George Kane, who has offered the most serious critique of Manly and Rickert in recent years, cites this directly as an example of their flawed method:

> The editors tell us that their basis of collation was 'Skeat's "Student's Edition"' (2: 5), but not whether they took into account the extent to which that is an edited text. ('Manly and Rickert,' 208)

> Manly and Rickert were aware that agreement in original readings is 'non-classificatory' (2: 24), but the edition does not show that they were troubled by the indeterminate originality of their base for collation, 'Skeat's "Student's Edition"' (ibid., 209)

Although Kane is unspecific here, he implies that a basis for collation will exert influence on substantive choices made in the editorial process.

The Variorum editors have also seized on this feature of the Manly and Rickert edition. Somewhat paradoxically, what appears in Kane as a criticism of Manly and Rickert's method, here seems to be used to support the validity of their results:

> MR [the Manly-Rickert edition] is different from all other editions in that its aim is not to present the text as corrected to accord with what Chaucer is presumed to have written but rather to reconstruct through recension the Archetype (O') of all extant written copies. It is noteworthy, therefore, that MR, though they use no base manuscript (the copy-text is SK), draw frequently toward Hg and away from El in their choice of readings. (Pearsall, *Nun's Priest's Tale*, 122)

> This reliance [of the Variorum edition on Hg] is not unreasonable, given its freedom from accidental error and from editorial improvement, and given too that the text that MR print, as established by the processes of recension, moves consistently from the text used as the basis for collation, Skeat's Student's Edition (MR, 2: 5), that is, a text based predominantly on El, toward Hg. (Pearsall, *Nun's Priest's Tale*, 97)

MR (who used SK as their copy-text); their great edition arrived by the recension method at a text consistently closer to Hg than to El, including the incidentals of spelling. (Baker, *Manciple's Tale*, 72)[6]

Although the vagueness of their argument here is exasperating, the underlying assumption is the same one found in Kane: the edition of Skeat somehow exerted an influence on Manly and Rickert on substantive matters. To Kane, this influence was pernicious (part of their flawed methodology); to Pearsall and Baker, this influence was overcome by the virtues of Hg; thus Manly and Rickert's text 'moves consistently' from Skeat's edition (itself close to El) *toward* Hg.

Now on the face of it, this argument is absurd. For it to have any validity concerning Chaucer's text, we have to assume several things: (1) that Manly and Rickert were right (their text is closer to Chaucer's than is Skeat's); (2) that the Variorum Chaucer committee is right (that Hg is as close to Chaucer as human beings can get).[7] That should be enough to discount the argument. But here, I am only concerned with the underlying assumption: (3) that Skeat's text is the base from which the text of Manly and Rickert 'moves.'

This last step involves the assumption that Manly and Rickert, like Skeat, were producing an eclectic edition, one with a base text, from which they departed more or less as evidence and fancy moved. This is why the technical distinctions outlined above are so important: a basis for collation is not a base text. A basis for collation is a material text used to organize variant readings, perhaps all variant readings. Its own readings are of no authority, and, if unsupported by actual authorities, would not even be included among the variants. Whatever one thinks of Manly and Rickert's results, I do not see how one can argue in good faith that they judged the readings of a student text to be as authoritative as those of the actual manuscripts they examined and collated.

Let me reemphasize here that in Manly and Rickert's edition, collating procedures are distinct from editorial procedures. I agree entirely with Kane that editorial procedures are never explained by Manly and Rickert: 'From the theoretical information supplied it is impossible to establish what the editorial procedures were, and thus also how effectively they were applied' (Kane, 'Manly and Rickert,' 208). However, their collating procedures (flawed though they may be) are described in great detail. Manly and Rickert describe, for example, the exact method of cutting the tabs at the top of the cardboard filing cards: 'Such things are minutiae, but they are not trifles; nothing is more wasteful of time and temper than a misplaced card without a guide ...' (2: 3–4). It is in the context of this detailed description that the single statement concerning their basis for collation appears: a statement simply tacked on to a paragraph describing the way in which lines can be located from photostat sheets: 'As the basis for collation we chose Skeat's "Student's Edition"' (2: 5). There is no further explanation and no justification for this choice. Rightly or wrongly, Manly and Rickert assumed that the particular readings of a basis for collation were not of any editorial consequence. The specific choice, then, did not in their minds even rise to the level of 'minutiae.'

Before proceeding, it is wise to consider what alternatives Manly and Rickert had. Pearsall and Baker criticize them for using an eclectic text of no authority as their basis for collation. In their own Variorum edition, by contrast, the basis for collation and base text (itself a best text) are the same: Hg. In other words, the editors decide first what the best text is (a close version of the final printed text), and *subsequently* utilize that text as the basis for collation for other selected manuscripts. Before collation even begins, the Variorum editors have chosen their base text and best text. The two processes of collating and editing are thus collapsed into one, with all major editorial decisions complete before collation even begins. As long as these editors know that only a few changes in the final text are to be made, there is nothing impractical or even theoretically unsound about this solution. It assumes, of course, that editorial results are known prior to the collection and collation of evidence. For Manly and Rickert, collating and editing were two separate processes: one first collated the variants, and *subsequently* began to edit.

That much is obvious, and why it has been ignored in Chaucer studies, I do not know. The question now is whether the choice of that basis for collation has any necessary and predictable effect on editorial decisions. Let me make it clear that I am not talking about any psychological effect: that is a different issue entirely. I am talking only about a technical effect of method.

A Test Case

As a matter of methodological principle, the particular basis for collation is irrelevant. You can use any variant, a translation, even the text of a different work. The results (the information made available for the editing process) will be identical. I will try to demonstrate that here. I recently had occasion to look at several early versions of the epitaph on Chaucer's tomb in Westminster Abbey. This is a text about which I hope no Chaucerian cares enough to cloud the issues its consideration can raise. There are a number of early versions, involving substantive variants, grammatical variants, and spelling variants. For the purposes of this exercise, I will consider versions by Foxe, Speght, Camden, Pits, Ashmole, and Dart, all produced from the late sixteenth to early eighteenth centuries.[8] I will collate first using the text of Foxe. Note that what follows, a collation, has *all the appearance* of a printed critical edition.

> Qui fuit Anglorum ter maximus olim,
> Galfridus Chaucer conditur hoc tumulo:
> Annum si quaeras Domini, si tempora mortis,
> Ecce nota subsunt, quae tibi cuncta notent.
> 　25 Octob. An. 1400

> 1.
> 2. Galfridus] Gaufredus (Sp); Galfredus (P)
> 3. mortis] vitae (Sp, A)
> 4. nota] notae (Sp, C, P, A, D); *notent*] notant (Sp, C, A, D)
> 5. 25 Octob. An. 1400] Anno Domini 1400, die mensis Octob. 25
> 　(Sp); 25 Octobris 1400 (C, P, A, D)

Or we can use Speght as the basis of collation:

> Qui fuit Anglorum ter maximus olim,
> Gaufredus Chaucer conditur hoc tumulo:
> Annum si quaeras Domini, si tempora vitae,
> Ecce notae subsunt, quae tibi cuncta notant.
> 　Anno Domini 1400, die mensis Octob. 25.

> 1.
> 2. Gaufredus] Galfridus (F, C, A); Galfredus (P)
> 3. vitae] mortis (F, C, P, D)
> 4. notae] nota (F); notant] notent (F, P)
> 5. Anno Domini 1400, die mensis Octob. 25] 25 Octob. An. 1400
> 　(F); 25 Octobris 1400 (C, P, A, D)

Or Camden:

> Qui fuit Anglorum ter maximus olim,
> Galfridus Chaucer conditur hoc tumulo:

Annum si quaeras Domini, si tempora mortis,
Ecce notae subsunt, quae tibi cuncta notant.
   25 Octobris 1400.

1.
2. Galfridus] Gaufredus (Sp); Galfredus (P)
3. mortis] vitae (Sp, A)
4. notae] nota (F); notant] notent (F, P)
5. 25 Octobris 1400] 25 Octob. An. 1400 (F); Anno Domini 1400,
   die mensis Octob. 25 (Sp)

Or a somewhat better known text compiled by Sarah Hale:

Mary had a little lamb,
Her fleece was white as snow.
And everywhere that Mary went
The lamb was sure to go.

1. Mary had a little lamb] Qui fuit Anglorum ter maximus olim (F,
   Sp, C, P, A, D)
2. Her] Galfridus (F, C, A, D), Gaufredus (Sp), Galfredus (P); fleece
   was white as snow] Chaucer conditur hoc tumulo (F, Sp, C, P, A, D)
3. And] Annum (F, Sp, C, A, P, D); everywhere that Mary] si quaeras
   Domini, si tempora (F, Sp, C, A, P, D); went] mortis (F, C, P, D);
   vitae (Sp, A)
4. The lamb] Ecce nota (F), Ecce notae (Sp, C, P, A, D); was sure]
   subsunt, quae tibi cuncta (F, Sp, C, P, A, D); to go] notent (F, P);
   notant (Sp, C, A, D)
5. 25 Octob. An. 1400 (F); Anno Domini 1400, die mensis Octob.
   25 (Sp); 25 Octobris 1400 (C, A, P, D)

Now we should in all fairness collate this variant with the others. Adding
these variants to those in the first example (based on Foxe), we might
have:

1. Qui ... olim] Mary had a little lamb (H)
2. Galfridus] Gaufredus (Sp), Galfredus (P), Her (H); Chaucer ...
   tumulo] fleece was white as snow (H)
3. Annum] And (H); si ... tempora] everywhere that Mary (H);
   mortis] vitae (Sp, A); went (H)

4. nota] notae (Sp, C, P, A, D); notent] notant (Sp, C, A, D); Ecce ...
   notent] The lamb was sure to go (H)
5. 25 Octob. An. 1400] Anno Domini 1400, die mensis Octob. 25
   (Sp); 25 Octobris 1400 (C, P, A, D); out: H

Or, given the eccentric nature of the Hale variants, we might construct
the apparatus for lines 2 and 3 as follows:

2. Galfridus] Gaufredus (Sp), Galfredus (P); Galfridus ... tumulo]
   Her fleece was white as snow (H)
3. Annum ... mortis] And everywhere that Mary went (H); mortis]
   vitae (Sp, A)

Or perhaps the H variants are so radical they should be simply listed
separately from all other variants with some statement such as: 'Instead
of lines 1–4, H has ... etc.' We might also choose (as did Manly and
Rickert on their collation cards) to indicate explicitly agreement with
the lemma; for example, for line 1 we might add in our collation 'So F,
C, P, A, D.' But such decisions concern only matters of convenience;
they do not affect results. All of the above collations provide the same
information.

There are then two questions: (1) an editorial question: What is the
critical text? (2) a methodological one: What specific effect will the
choice of basis for collation have on the process of constructing this text?

What is immediately apparent from the above is that none of the
collations provides in and of itself an answer to either of these questions.
We cannot construct, from the basis of collation alone, the critical text;
that is, the collation itself does not determine editorial procedures. The
information provided concerns only variant groups: for example, D is
identical to C; A and Sp are together on certain substantive variants.
Without further information or further editorial principles, we can do
little more. Among the editorial principles we might follow are the
selection of a copy-text; this might decide for us how to deal with pure
spelling variants (for example, *Galfridus/Gaufredus*). We might also choose
to correct obvious grammatical and metrical errors (for example, *nota*).
We might also decide that the variants in H are so radical as to constitute
a *different text*. None of these editorial decisions requires us to recollate
the variants, since all accurate collations provide the same information.
If a basis for collation affects the edited text, that has nothing to do with
editorial method per se; it rather has to do with editorial psychology or

specific and flawed editorial decisions (for example, the decision that a basis for collation is an authority).

So what does one choose as a basis for collation? In economic terms, the ideal basis of collation in such a situation would be a text (perhaps a constructed one) that for each variant used the one contained in a majority of witnesses. The more manuscript readings that the basis for collation contains, the fewer variants must be laboriously recorded. The closer the basis of collation is to the readings of the majority of manuscripts, the easier it is to determine lemmata, that is, the basis against which one defines variation. The only consideration should be one of convenience: you might just as well choose a vulgate text, and hope it contains the variant (whether original or absurd) that appears in the greatest number of manuscripts. The more ordinary variants contained in this text, the easier the process of collation becomes.

Look at the above examples again: suppose the editorial task were defined as the production of a text of a well-known nursery rhyme, and we decided that these were the six extant versions. Now there would be very good reasons for selecting the Hale variants as obviously superior, and each one might appear in the final edited text. But as far as matters of collation are concerned, *any of the alternative Latin texts would be a better selection for a basis of collation than this one*, simply because each makes the collation process easier. The superiority of the Hale variants will in each case prove obvious if, say, one of the editorial principles we choose is that familiar nursery rhymes are apt to be in English. As long as we have that principle, we need not worry about the pernicious and sinister influence of the Latin readings of our basis of collation, nor need we speak of our edition 'moving' slowly toward the Hale version.

Now suppose the task is defined as producing the text of a Chaucer epitaph. Here we probably will produce a different final text, since the superiority of any of the Latin readings to the English ones should be immediately apparent. But the basis of collation? The same one that serves as the basis of collation for the nursery rhyme will probably be the most useful for this collation as well. Manly and Rickert's decision to use Skeat's *Student's Chaucer*, then, was simply one of convenience. It may have been wrong, but at least it was rational.

Records of Collations vs Editions

What I have printed above is a record of the results of collation. It appears to be an edition (and might well become one if it were so labelled), but preliminary collations (using a basis of collation) and final editions (whereby the edited text is the basis for variants) are two different things. For modern editors, they generally exist in different forms: a collation might be in a computer; it might be on draft paper; for Manly and Rickert, it exists on 5" × 8" cards. An edition, however, is in some way published, and modern editors do not normally publish their collations as editions, nor do they use their collation sheets as printer's copy for an edition. Historically, however, this has been an ordinary and convenient method of producing editions: an editor simply wrote variants into the margins of an already printed edition. For early Chaucer editions, the basis for the new edition was a copy of an old edition; thus the basis of collation and the base text (of an eclectic edition) were necessarily combined. This was the method used to produce sixteenth-century Chaucer editions, where earlier editions were used even for purposes of casting off.[9]

In modern editing, collation and editing should not be conflated unless the purpose of the editing is only to update a vulgate text (the obvious and legitimate goal of many editions). Indeed, Manly and Rickert did separate them: Skeat's *Student's Chaucer*, of no more authority than a nursery rhyme, served as basis for collation. After those collations, editorial decisions (very mysterious ones, to be sure), resulted in the critical text. The critical text then served as the basis for the printed collations: the Table of Variants in later volumes.

Here is where the unquantifiable matters of editorial psychology come into play. Did the Skeat text possess a psychological authority that Manly and Rickert's stated method clearly denied it? To believe Pearsall and Baker on this specific issue is to believe that Manly and Rickert were prejudiced in favour of the Skeat text, and that only the truth they were uncovering gradually drew them inexorably away from it. This seems very dubious to me. What drew them away from Skeat was hardly the 'true text of Chaucer,' but rather their own self-interest: they had set themselves the task of producing a new edition of the *Canterbury Tales* with a complete table of variants. Their efforts, if successful, would have completely supplanted the eclectic text of Skeat.

Now it may well be that the readings in Hengwrt are superior to those in Ellesmere or to those in Skeat's edition.[10] That is a matter of editorial opinion. It may also be the case that Manly and Rickert laboured to free themselves from the influence of Skeat. That is a matter of editorial psychology and the personal history of particular editors. Neither of these is directly concerned with editorial methodology. There is no need to be persuaded by editorial rhetoric or statistics that state no more than what is obvious: any edited text 'moves' from the basis of collation toward one of the authorities. Recent Chaucer editors may be right that Hengwrt is close to what Chaucer wrote, but Manly and Rickert's use of Skeat's *Student's Chaucer* as a basis for collation provides no evidence that they are not dead wrong.

5.2 The Electronic Chaucer and the Relation of the Two Caxton Editions

This second section turns to the CD-ROM edition by Cambridge University Press of Chaucer's *Canterbury Tales*. Two volumes are now published, the Wife of Bath's Prologue and the General Prologue, and this second volume reprints some, but not all, of the preliminary material in the first.[11] The strengths of this edition, particularly in its second volume, the General Prologue, are apparent. There is much more evidence now available to Chaucerians than any edition made available earlier, and the preliminary essays are important in dismantling some of the taxonomic findings of Manly-Rickert. What I am interested in here, however, is the way the assumptions of the edition are stated, and the way some unstated assumptions direct the questions that can be asked of the evidence it presents. I am particularly interested in the disparity between the extensive evidence the edition makes available and the built-in directives for using that evidence, and how the edition in the first of its two volumes defines the text – the object of the CD-ROM itself. In the closing pages of the chapter, I will use as a test case the relations between Caxton's first and second editions of the *Canterbury Tales*.

The Cambridge Edition and the Manly-Rickert Edition

According to the implications of the introductory essays, the CD-ROM edition is to a large extent a refinement of the 1940 edition by Manly and Rickert, although many of the particular findings of Manly-Rickert are subject to detailed criticism, particularly in the section somewhat misleadingly entitled 'Analysis Workshop' in the second volume. It is thus situated as the end point in the history of Chaucer editions, both summing up earlier editorial projects and superseding them. The Cambridge edition is the third major project in what might be called the modern history of Chaucer studies that attempts to make raw evidence available to the reader in conjunction with the production of an edition.

The first is the series of diplomatic transcripts of manuscripts produced by the Chaucer Society beginning in the 1860s – transcripts that were the basis for Skeat's multi-volume critical edition of 1894–9; the second was the Manly-Rickert edition – the first purely textual-critical Chaucer edition. These editions contain no explanatory notes, no textual commentary on individual lines; introductory essays (the Chaucer Society pamphlets containing manuscript transcriptions have no introductory essays) focus on general editorial procedures and on the textual relation of manuscripts.

The intention of Manly and Rickert was twofold: (1) to provide all manuscript readings, regardless of value (it is the first edition of the *Canterbury Tales* to do this or even attempt to do this); (2) to produce a text, O', the closest thing to what Chaucer wrote (a scribal version at least once removed), something that preceded all manuscript readings, but not a text embodied in any manuscript or best represented by any single manuscript. This text, the results of their editorial labours, was then used as the basis for recollating and publishing the various manuscript variants (as shown above, this recollation is different from the initial collation based on a previously printed text). Yet paradoxically, the Manly-Rickert edition led to the promotion of a theory that directly contradicted its aims and methods. Chaucerians came to see Manly-Rickert as promoting, not a critical text and the methodology required to produce one, but rather a new best text. Manly-Rickert's results have been interpreted (or misinterpreted) as implying the superiority of the Hengwrt manuscript to the Ellesmere (the base for the editions of Skeat and Robinson), an assumption (or conclusion) that is at the heart of many recent editions: those by the Variorum, by Blake, and now in the Cambridge edition itself.[12]

The Cambridge Chaucer challenges Manly-Rickert in several ways. To begin with, the use of 'cladistics' (presented with far greater clarity in the second volume of 2000 than in the first) rather than stemmatics produces an array of manuscript relations quite different in appearance from the genealogical stemmata used by Manly-Rickert (see the diagrams in the Analysis Workshop section of the General Prologue volume). Although what might be called the information in these new diagrams is in some cases the same or very similar to that in the Manly-Rickert stemmatic diagrams, the implications are different; they do not depend on or assume a single root origin, although the assumption of such an origin (Chaucer? his earliest scribe?) often affects discussion. In keeping with this new system, the edition at many points seems to renounce the goal of producing what might be called a 'definitive' or 'originary' text, and offers the reader a presumably disinterested array of manuscript readings; these are closer in fact to the diplomatic texts produced by the nineteenth-century Chaucer Society than to the normalized arrays of individual variants provided by Manly-Rickert (one could not, on the basis of Manly-Rickert, reconstruct the actual readings in any manuscript even if all their transcriptions were accurate). Users of the CD-ROM can view the manuscripts in facsimile, or they can read the manuscript transcriptions in various ways: as original spelling transcriptions, as normalized texts, or as editorial variants in either transcription expressed as variants of a base text (I will return to the definition of this below). How the notion of the definitive or originary text reasserts itself will be one of the points of the present chapter.[13]

The purposes of the Cambridge Chaucer, or what might be called an early statement of clearly evolving purposes, are stated in two essays: the 'Editor's Introduction' by the general editor, Peter Robinson (this is found under a special icon for 'Editorial Introduction and Acknowledgements'; the essay is included only in the first volume) and in 'Editing the Canterbury Tales: An Overview' by Norman Blake (found under the heading 'Articles' and included in both volumes). Stated goals by any editor will necessarily differ from the goals incorporated in the edition itself, and the Cambridge Chaucer provides an extreme case of these contradictions.

As characterized by Robinson, the Manly-Rickert edition faced two problems, both functions of the medium itself. The first was simply in the mass of materials. The second was in the necessary normalization required to tabulate all variants:

> This vast weight of information was simply beyond their manual methods of analysis. In addition, the printed record of their collation ... is impenetrable, to the extent that it is very difficult to reconstruct from this the actual reading of any line in any witness ... The advent of the computer, and its application to textual editing, offers a way past both these difficulties [and reconstructs] the actual reading of any line in any witness.[14]

The aims of this edition are to present much of the same information in a form that was not available in 1940:

> to present all this material in as attractive and accessible as fashion as possible ... to use the computer methods now available to us to determine

as thoroughly as we could the textual history of *The Canterbury Tales*. Here,
we face an apparent impasse: we can make no firm judgements about the
textual relations of any witnesses, for any part of the Tales, until we have
transcribed, collated, and analyzed every word in every witness of every
part of the whole text. (Robinson, 'Editor's Introduction')

Robinson draws on the rhetoric of completeness and disinterest frequent in electronic editions; such editions enable individual readers to
manipulate the text in ways not possible with printed editions. However,
the freedom readers will have is necessarily restricted. The machine may
be disinterested, but its programmers and the editors are not.

The definition of the text, the object of the edition, depends on the
difference between what is called a 'witness' to the text, and the 'history'
of the text. Robinson's introduction alludes to this problem, but only by
way of justifying what the electronic text itself does.

To discover the history of the text, even for just the earliest manuscripts,
one must therefore look at every witness. In theory, one might not wish to
stop at 1500, as we have chosen to do, but one must stop somewhere.

The problematic nature of this statement is inadvertently highlighted by
the unintentional ambiguity of '1500,' which here is a date, not a number. One stops gathering information where one defines an end to
information, not where the information itself ceases to exist. The phrase
'history of the text even for just the earliest manuscripts' is not and
probably cannot be defined. For the 'history of the text' turns out to be
something more (textually) than anything in its witnesses. E.T.
Donaldson's famous modern emendation of 'wight' for the manuscript
readings 'wright' at line 117 of the Wife of Bath's Prologue (one
recorded in his 1958 edition), is discussed at length in the general
introduction, and yet it cannot have the status as a 'witness' in any
rational sense even if Donaldson is correct in assuming that this is the
reading of Chaucer's original.[15] Furthermore, historical completeness
is something different from textual-critical relevance. In order to understand Shakespeare criticism, one does not read every article ever
written about Shakespeare, nor to understand the textual-critical history of Shakespeare does one scrupulously examine every version of
Shakespeare.

A witness, in a textual-critical sense, cannot be defined precisely; it
might be considered a contemporary, near-contemporary, or 'nearest to

being' such a near contemporary. It might be defined as 'that version of a text that repeats earlier versions no longer extant.' Or perhaps we should just despair and say that although we cannot define what a witness is, we all know a non-witness when we see one. Thus, a nineteenth-century edition of a medieval text is not in any sense a witness if the facts to which it has access are recorded earlier and those records are still available. The banal but perfectly functional textual-critical methods for dealing with late manuscripts still apply: late manuscripts or printed versions of a text are not witnesses if it can be demonstrated that the evidence to which they had access is found in earlier witnesses (thus for most Chaucer editors, Caxton's second edition is a witness, but Thynne's 1532 edition is not). If, on the other hand, the goal of the edition is to present the history of the text as opposed to witnesses of the text, then all late editions, whenever produced, are relevant as are all modern conjectures and emendations, good, bad, and indifferent. Even if one were to accept an arbitrary cut-off date, there would be no reason to limit the corpus of evidence to editions proper. Any comment, any transcription of Chaucer could be relevant and, since the object of concern is no longer an originary text but the entire history of versions of this text, any such comment could even be described as a 'witness,' not, of course, to Chaucer's own text, but rather to its history and even its distortion and misrepresentation. Thus, there would be no theoretical reason to discount the evidence assembled in, say, Spurgeon's *Five Hundred Years of Chaucer Criticism and Allusion*, or any other compendium of Chaucer commentary.[16]

These are standard criticisms that could apply to any critical edition, and for the *Canterbury Tales*, they are always present: defining and constructing the text are different from organizing the manuscripts that bear on that text. In Manly-Rickert and again in the Cambridge edition, the mass of manuscripts that can be organized (Manly-Rickert groups a, b, c, and d, and the new group 'alpha' defined in the Cambridge edition) provide far less important editorial information than do unaffiliated manuscripts or those whose relations are 'uncertain,' manuscripts that include those of greatest importance in modern editorial history: El and Hg, Harley 7334 (the basis for Wright's 1843 edition), and Gg (the first clear attempt to produce a complete works of Chaucer). The disparity between editorial relevance and textual-critical completeness is unavoidable in Chaucer editing. The Cambridge edition, however, uses the notion of textual-critical completeness (an area in which the new technology enables it to surpass all previous editions) to justify what are the very conservative principles the project both promotes and renounces – the notion of the definitive text – the desire to find what Chaucer wrote, or, more elaborately, the confusions and inconsistencies written into the text *after* Chaucer's composition of it.

Critical Assumptions

The sophistication of the technology occasionally conflicts with the announced critical assumptions. The textual-critical argument of disinterest falters when that disinterest is manifested critically. I begin with Robinson's opening statements to his general introduction:

> The Wife of Bath is one of Chaucer's most vivid creations, and one of the great characters of all literature. There are fictional personalities that appear to have a life beyond the words their creators give them.

This statement could have been made at any time in the last three centuries. Here it is in the service of a more modern notion: each manuscript is a literary text. The differences between the two 'most authoritative' manuscripts create two different Wives:

> Even without the dramatic differences of the twenty-six lines, these smaller differences are cumulatively sufficient to make reading Chaucer in Ellesmere a very different experience from reading him in Hengwrt.[17]

Note that 'experience' is something quite different from what we normally think of as experience. Experience with a physical object is touching that object, holding that object. Here experience has been textualized. There is no question of what might be called material experience – seeing or touching two manuscripts, nor is there the experience of thinking critically about them. 'Reading Chaucer in Ellesmere' means the experience of reading an editorial and textualized version of what is written in the Ellesmere manuscript.

The personification of the text as Chaucer is also significant. With multiple manuscript texts we have multiple Chaucers, the same multiplication of Chaucers that resulted from the notions of Chaucer's persona that were prevalent in mid-twentieth-century American Chaucer criticism. In this variant of that argument, however, the new transhistorical Chaucer, who once resulted from a personification of a standard text of Chaucer, becomes an unlimited number of such personifications, each the result of an individual reading of an individual manuscript.[18]

Whereas Robinson's introductory notes look back to Dryden, Norman Blake's seem to look back to the late nineteenth century. Blake begins with the notion of the *Canterbury Tales* as a series of fragments. This has been a staple of the main editorial tradition since the work of Henry Bradshaw, although Bradshaw is not cited here. For Bradshaw, the utility of such a notion of the tales had to do with the classification of manuscripts.[19] Although both Skeat and F.N. Robinson in his 1933 edition lineate the text according to these fragments, the notion of the work itself as a group of fragments was not embodied in editions until the late twentieth century: first, almost by accident, in the Variorum Chaucer, proceeding as it does tale by tale; and now in the CD-ROM.[20] The notion of multiple fragments – that cannot be organized in any definitive way implies (logically) multiple organizations, and thus multiple authorial organizational versions. Blake: 'What the early editors did not consider was that the poem could exist in multiple authorial versions.' This notion of multiple possible (and authorial) organizational versions (one that does not seem shared by Robinson in the essays in the second volume) then is extended to legitimize local textual variants as well. As Blake's essay proceeds, the notion of the difference between authorial versions or variants and just 'any old' version or variant seems to be lost. Variation is good, no matter whose:

> This outline presents in a rather sketchy manner the background to the editorial issues for the Canterbury Tales Project. One might well ask what difference the completion of this project would make to our understanding and editing of the poem. The first and perhaps most lasting benefit will be in attitudes towards the text and therefore in how the text is read. Printed editions are inflexible because they contain only what the editor wishes to present as the definitive text. This naturally breeds the assumption among readers that there is such a thing as a definitive text and so they need not bother with alternative readings. In fact, few modern editions of the poem present other readings in an apparatus criticus; a few selected variants may be discussed in the notes. Even where an apparatus criticus is provided as in the Manly-Rickert edition, it is difficult to read through it to get a feel for how an individual scribe responded to and interpreted the text.

The argument is overstated, since it is not the case that printed editions are 'inflexible,' nor were they so considered by their early readers. The handwritten marginalia in numerous copies of early printed Chaucers show that these books were read piecemeal, that variants were noted, and that readers' opinions were registered.

More important is the newly articulated purpose claimed for editions: readers need 'a feel for how an individual scribe responded to and interpreted the text.' How individual scribes responded to *what was before them* is surely a matter for editors to be concerned about: it is important to distinguish, in classical editing, the *usus scribendi* of the scribe from the *usus scribendi* of the author. However, this is not something that concerns most readers of editions, who are primarily concerned with the results of the editing process and only secondarily with the process itself. Here Blake recasts his readers in his own image: ideal users of the edition seem to be lesser versions of editors:

> The CD version will make available all the manuscripts in a readily accessible form so that a user will not only be able to consider alternative readings but also to see how those alternative readings fit into the scribes' overall presentation of the text. This response will colour our response to the text as it undermines the concept of a definitive edition and thus promotes renewed critical interest in the poem, its transmission and its reception. It will be possible to see the text as a living and developing entity, and this could also change the rather dismissive view that many modern readers and scholars have towards medieval scribes. ('Editing the *Canterbury Tales*,' penultimate paragraph)

Blake reintroduces in all these statements the very element he claims to have removed through the CD-ROM – 'the text.' What is this text? If we do not know that, how can we know how the scribe responded to it? If instead of 'text,' Blake means what some critics refer to as 'work' – the abstract entity under which all variant texts of, say, the *Canterbury Tales*, are organized – again, we can ask: 'What is it?' A scribe cannot effectively respond to that thing (the *Canterbury Tales* as we understand it), because his own work is implicated in it, and in its definition. Does Blake then mean a *Canterbury Tales* minus the work of this particular scribe? Until we know the textual affiliations, there is no way that this can have any historical existence: clearly the scribe cannot be responding to a 'work' that was to be developed later.

Base Text

The editors do not, I think, ever fully define what they mean by a base text, nor do they seem to agree on this. The editorial rhetoric often implies that there is a base text in a classical sense:

> The two major decisions which most editors have to make are what manu-
> script to use as a base text and in what order to organise the parts they
> intend to include. It is probably true to say that the only editors to have
> undertaken any comprehensive work on the manuscript tradition of the
> *Canterbury Tales* are John Manly and Edith Rickert ... The conclusions which
> Manly and Rickert reached, that there were many divergent lines of de-
> scent for the various tales or even parts of the tales, and that the manuscript
> which probably reflected the original most closely in textual matters was
> Hg, created so many problems for editors that their work has not been
> followed in any detail by subsequent editions. Consequently in their deci-
> sion as to which manuscript to follow editors have been more motivated by
> the order of the tales and what they want to include in their final version ...
> El. (Robinson, 'Editor's Introduction')

This is not quite correct: Manly and Rickert do not use and do not
construct a base text at all. To collate the variants, they used a 'basis of
collation' (Skeat's *Student's Edition*). After tabulating and organizing all
these variants, they then constructed an edited text (presumably without
reference to a base text), which itself serves as a basis for collating the
printed manuscript variants. The phrase 'base text' is only meaningful
from a textual-critical standpoint if it implies the manuscript or printed
text an editor follows generally unless better readings present themselves.[21]

The CD-ROM, however, does provide a text, one that appears to me,
and surely must appear to other users, as an edited text. Robinson,
however, defines this, in a phrase that is quite misleading in its apparent
textual-critical precision, as a 'base text for collation':

> The technique we chose was hypertext. At first, we have the reader see an
> apparently straight-forward, plain and single text. This is 'the base text for
> collation' which the reader sees on opening the electronic book: essen-
> tially, a very lightly edited representation of the Hengwrt manuscript text.
> But through hypertext, we would make this single text the starting point of
> exploration.[22]

There is no statement as to how or why this text was 'lightly edited,' or
what 'essentially' means; the phrase 'base text for collation' is put into
quotation marks, but I assume these quotation marks warn the reader

that the word or phrase does not really mean what it ordinarily means. That text is not a base text in an editorial sense (the text the edition follows unless better readings present themselves) nor is it, as far as we know, the basis for collation in the editing process (the text used to organize manuscript readings). Furthermore, the language here implies that the use of such a text does not distort the evidence the reader might find. It is just there. Anything else could be just there. Readers maintain the freedom that the electronic edition has won for them.

But clearly they do not.

Despite the technological advances and the much more accurate and complete tabulation of evidence, the Cambridge Chaucer does not advance the theoretical discussion here any more than did the Variorum project. Manly-Rickert at least attempted to produce the 'base-less' text, the purely editorial construct. Modern editorial projects are caught in a contradiction: on the one hand, they deny the definitive and authoritative text, but on the other, they claim to privilege particular evidentiary materials. The result is the translation of a manuscript into the very definitive text their rhetoric combats.

A stated goal of this and other electronic editions is that the electronic format enables the reader to construct the text, thus transforming the reader into an editorial participant, rather than reducing the reader to a passive recipient of authority.[23] That rejected authority is (or was, under classical editing) embodied in the editorial notion of a definitive version and in the physical edition itself; it is an authority more generally institutionalized by literary history and in its basic notions of authorship and the author. In volume 2 of the Cambridge Chaucer, the questioning of this authority is encouraged, particularly in the section entitled 'Analysis Workshop,' where users, at least those with a fair degree of sophistication in the use of computers, can manipulate much of the data to reproduce or challenge some of the general conclusions of the editors concerning manuscript groupings. I am arguing here that despite such readerly participation, the general claim is largely specious. There is no such thing as the presumed 'open edition' or unbiased research tool, and the presentation and organization of this particular edition serve to guide the reader into questions already formulated and to some extent answered by the editors.

The choice and construction of a base text restricts the readers in their access to evidence. The questions foreseen by the editors are two: (1) What does each manuscript witness look like in and of itself? and (2) How does each manuscript witness relate to the base text? The user cannot judge that portion of a manuscript under consideration in relation to its own manuscript context (that is, how does the manuscript present this portion of text in relation to other portions of text).[24] Rather, the manuscript section must be judged in terms of a conventional reference point (the base text), which turns out to be very much like the originary or definitive text produced by classical editions.

The only way for the researcher to get around these restrictions is through the absurd – a violation of canon. For example: 'The purpose of this essay is to determine how many times the letter *a* appears in Chaucer manuscripts whose sigla begin with C.' Such a question is not like the questions that the community of scholars employing an edition are willing to entertain. It is a question the edition and its surrounding institutions rule out-of-court. The radical question, then, is not a question that can be asked within the context of the Chaucerian community at all. The edition defines a group of questions and a procedure for answering them. The edition cannot provide the reader evidence for overturning the rules of the edition.

Practical Questions: Caxton 1 and Caxton 2

The question I will deal with below involves the specific relation (textual and material) between two of the edition's witnesses, the first and second editions of the *Canterbury Tales* by Caxton. I choose this for two reasons: (1) it is another example of the blurring of bibliographical and textual-critical language I have been examining throughout this study, and (2) it is the kind of question that the evidence provided by a database as complete and reliable as that in the Cambridge edition should be able to answer. Even though the editors provide specific conclusions about the relationship between these editions in their introductory materials,[25] the direct question itself is not one that the basic assumptions of the edition allow to be answered in any easy way or even addressed by the users.

The question of the relationship between these two editions has been asked many times in Chaucer scholarship and in printing histories, and is the only question concerning relations between various witnesses for which there is external as well as internal evidence. That external evidence is provided by Caxton's often-quoted preface to the second edition; Caxton claims he 'corrected his book' (presumably a copy of his first edition) on the basis of a book 'more correct' provided by a certain 'gentylman' – a manuscript book made 'according unto [Chaucer's] owen first book.'[26] Caxton's second edition is based on the first, but is in textual-critical terms a conflated or contaminated edition. This relationship is expressed somewhat more strongly in the two most important twentieth-century works on the editions: that of W.W. Greg in 1924 and Thomas F. Dunn, a student of Manly and Rickert, in 1940.[27] Both Greg and Dunn state that Cx2 is *set from* a marked-up copy of Cx1; that is, particular readings from the 'gentleman's copy' were inserted into a physical copy of Caxton's first edition. Conflation in the textual-critical sense, however, is more abstract than the language describing that process implies: to conflate two texts does not necessarily mean to use two material books that contain those texts. It is important to look at the way in which the question was formulated. Greg's argument in 1924 was directed specifically at the language of the Caxton preface itself, and the question of whether Caxton meant that Cx2 was copied directly from the 'gentleman's manuscript.' Greg concluded that it was not:

Indeed, I may say at once that it is clear that no print after the first was set up from manuscript; each successive printer, whatever alterations or corrections he may have introduced, set up his edition from one or other of its predecessors. ('Early Printed Editions,' 738–40)

This means only that Cx2 was not set up from the 'gentylman's book,' even though it contains readings and the tale order of that copy, and that textually it is most closely related to the text in Cx1. It is not quite the same thing as saying that Cx2 was set up in the printing shop from a copy of Cx1, the reading most scholars (and perhaps Greg himself) gave to that argument (and a reading that is of course legitimate from a textual-critical standpoint). Greg never proposed as a counter-argument a manuscript printer's copy for both editions; in textual-critical terms, to say that Cx2 was 'set from' Cx1 is the same as saying that it was 'set from' the printer's copy for Cx1, a copy that must have existed.

Dunn, like Greg, used textual collations of the two editions, in this case, the collations of Manly-Rickert, that is to say, a textualized and normalized version of the Caxton editions.[28] Although he is clearer than later scholars on the difference between 'copy-text' and actual 'printer's copy,' these occasionally become blurred as a result.[29] Nowhere in Dunn do I see an argument refuting the notion that Cx1 and Cx2 are both set from the same manuscript, with Cx1 a more accurate copy of that manuscript.

> No line appears in one edition that does not appear in the other. This in and of itself is almost certain proof that Cx1 and not its copytext was the copytext for Cx2 ... Both editions agree in the number of lines included and in the arrangement of them. (Dunn, *Manuscript Source*, 2)

> An examination of the prose of the two editions, and especially of the unique readings of Cx2, offers strong evidence that the type for Cx2 was set up from a copy of Cx1. (Ibid., 4)

The argument that Cx2 is set from a marked-up copy of Cx1 seems to be given on p. 4, n. 10, where Dunn discusses Tc2, a manuscript presumably copied 'from the exemplar of Cx1 about the date of the printing of Cx2.' For 'exemplar,' one should probably read 'textual ancestor,' since the printer's copy for Cx1 is unknown. The Tc2 scribe departs from Cx1 in specific places. 'Had Cx2 been set up from the exemplar of Cx1 at that time, it would likewise be entirely dependent upon a new manuscript in these portions, but it is not (4, n. 10).' The logic of this needs clarification. What Dunn means (and what is not finally demonstrable) is that Tc2 copies a particular manuscript that itself was printer's copy for Cx1. If Cx2 had been copied from this printer's copy, it would have been missing these pages. But this again leads to the problem of textualization and the confusion of copy-text and printer's copy, a distinction Dunn seems to make elsewhere. It is not demonstrated that the exemplar for Tc2 is the exemplar for Cx1, but only that they exist in a textual-critical schema with the same 'subarchetype.' That is a text, quite distinct from the physical object that embodies it.[30]

Dunn notes on pp. 4 and 7 that in prose sections, the two editions seem to agree: 'Caxton attempted, in the prose, to do no more than to reproduce the text of Cx1' (2); 'Indeed, long passages in these tales are passed over without an alteration of text' (7). What Dunn thus means by 'examination' of those prose sections is examination of their texts, not, say, their format and layout – elements that make prose much more useful in determining printer's copy than verse.[31] He means the regularized readings of Manly-Rickert, an excellent source for information regarding textual affiliation (substantives), but an extremely poor vehicle for making conclusions about printer's copy.[32]

The advantages of precise transcriptions are now apparent, since the textual transcriptions used by Greg and Dunn can only lead to 'textual-critical' conclusions. To determine printer's copy, we need to know exactly how Cx2 differs from Cx1, and we need to know that not only in terms of substantives (which can be introduced from external sources such as the gentleman's manuscript mentioned in Caxton's preface) but in terms of accidentals and page or line format as well. We need to distinguish between the two possibilities: Cx2 was copied from Cx1; Cx2 and Cx1 were both copied from the same manuscript.

The computerized transcriptions and facsimiles of the Cambridge Chaucer provide more information and more accurate information than is available in earlier editions. What I ask is simply: collate Caxton 2 against Caxton 1. This should prove an excellent basis for solving the problem of its printer's copy. The computer program, however, refuses to provide this information directly. I can collate either Caxton edition against the 'base text for collation' (a text that is already edited according to editorial assumptions and conclusions about Chaucer's text) but I cannot collate them against each other. It is as if I were to ask: What is the numerical relation between 9 and 10? and I were given the perfectly correct answer: 9 is 7 more than the square root of 4, and 10 is 8 more than the square root of 4.

From the Cambridge DynaText reader, one gets a list of witnesses, which can be viewed a number of ways: as regularized transcriptions, unregularized transcriptions, or images. The black-and-white facsimile images are generally only fair, far inferior to, say, the colour images available in the SEENET *Piers Plowman* edition. However, since printing is, at least in principle, a black-and-white technology, for Caxton, they are serviceable. At this point, precisely what we want here should be restated: what we want is Cx2 expressed as a variant of Cx1; what we want to see are the precise differences introduced by Cx2, so that we can determine whether each of these is compatible with a theory of the second edition being a direct copy of the first. For this, we should probably compare both the unregularized text (complete with differing accidentals) and the regularized text. We already know the direction of variation, and we already may concede that Cx1, from a textual-critical standpoint, serves as copy-text for Cx2.

It should be a simple matter to display the two texts together and record variants, but electronic technology can put an extraordinary number of obstacles in one's way. One must view them alternately, maintaining in one's head (or on a notepad) the readings of one text to compare with those of the other. It is not possible (apparently) to put them side by side on the screen (or if it is, I have not found out how to do this). To view the texts simultaneously, at least one of them must be transcribed (introducing unique errors and variants) or printed out; that hard copy could then be held against the other on the screen, a procedure that defeats simultaneously both the virtues and vices of the electronic edition.

The method for comparing two texts provided by the computer program seems to be as follows. Pressing a button, one comes up with an array of variants (seen against the ill-defined base text), and this array can be displayed in two ways: either in regularized spellings (such that, say, *onis* and *onys* are the same) or in unregularized spellings (such that these two would appear as variants). Once this appears on the screen, one can proceed through a word-by-word search in the line, carefully recording the variants. For the next line, one must leave the display of variants, return to the level of the texts and select the next line, click down through the various levels to the unregularized collations, and once again proceed word by word through the evidence.

The information should be there, but problems quickly arise in extracting it. The apparatus is not always entirely clear.[33] On line 14 of the Wife of Bath's Prologue, for example, I read the following:

sholde / wedded be but ones
The lemma for the following word variant or variants is: ne
Agreeing with the lemma: 44 witnesses ... Cx2
Reading: wedded: ... Cx1 ... 5 witnesses

Without the transcribed versions of the complete texts, I cannot understand this. I click back to the two lines of text to see the readings on which this code is based, and read:

Cx1 that / wedded' sholde be but onys
Cx2 That / ne weddid/ shold/ be but onys

What I assume the display means is that 'the variant we are discussing below is "ne"; and 44 witnesses including Cx2 have that.' I believe the meaning of the phrase 'Reading: wedded' is: 'instead of *weddid ne*, Cx1 reads *wedded*,' but only with the actual evidence in front of me can I translate the code that presents it.

This procedure is exasperating, but there are more difficulties. To get to the next line, one closes the three windows (each representing a level of the display) and returns to the transcriptions of the two Caxton editions. Before leaving one of the transcribed editions, I had set the line in question at the top of the screen, thinking that once I had both editions so set, I could at least switch rapidly back and forth between their texts. I quickly found, however, that these texts do not stay put. They are jealous texts, and when you leave them, they instantly revert to what might be construed as their first loves: their opening lines. To get to the next line, one has to scroll down on one text (Cx1), find the line, and then turn to Cx2 (which will be at its opening line), and scroll down again. When one switches back to Cx1, one finds that Cx1 has again gone back to its opening line.

Obviously, this problem is correctable and does not necessarily bear on the fundamental properties of the edition or its programs (the same answer could of course be given to complaints about many difficult or malfunctioning computer programs). Had anyone foreseen a particular question being asked of the edition, a program could have been written to provide the information in a more efficient manner, but it is not practical to write or revise a program to deal with every new question, and what cannot be eliminated in this or in any other edition project are the restrictions of initial editorial assumptions – the edition will answer only questions the editors see fit to be asked.

The CD-ROM as a Facsimile Machine

The present CD-ROM positions itself as the end point in a history of classical editions of Chaucer. The edition is, by its own claim, a 'corrected' Manly-Rickert, precisely the thing that George Kane called for in his 1984 review of Manly and Rickert.[34] It claims the raw evidence it presents allows its users to 'read' individual scribes and (by implication) compositors.[35] To 'read' the work of any compositor or scribe, however, we need to know what they had in front of them; without that information (what was the compositor of Caxton 2 working with?) the scribe or compositor becomes a parodic variant of a New-Critical poet, working in a textual vacuum free of the copy-text. In addition, by positioning itself so squarely in editorial tradition, the Cambridge Chaucer actually creates a new tradition, and promotes an editorial genre its own technology supersedes – that of the facsimile edition. When I ask a question not foreseen as legitimate by the editors, the computer edition is transformed from a powerful editorial device to a mediocre facsimile machine, one that can only be viewed through another machine costing several thousand dollars, and is only productive of information by the physical and exhausting labour of transcription.

The diplomatic transcriptions of Chaucer manuscripts produced by the Chaucer Society in the late nineteenth century were duplicitous. To print them in parallel columns, as was done in several of their volumes, required adjusting their lineation and organization, but this made them only marginally 'readable' as individual texts. They did not remain diplomatic editions but became rather variants of some material or imagined base text.[36] The Chaucer Society transcriptions thus are a hybrid, one that led to two sorts of projects. The first was embodied in Skeat's edition. The second was the evolving genre of diplomatic editions (by the late twentieth century called 'facsimiles') that were the result of both an increase in technology (presumably economic photographic processes) and a growing dissatisfaction with editorial intervention.

Growing out of this was the Variorum Chaucer of the 1980s, an editorial project that, like the first Chaucer Society project, had dual aims: first, to present the evidence itself and second, to produce an edition. The edition, which now seems stalled, was published in a series of fragments, themselves the embodiment of the critical assumptions of the scholars who produced it, but the related facsimile series became something else entirely. These facsimiles included such central manuscripts as Tanner 346, Bodley 638, Fairfax 16, Pepys 2006, Hg – an assortment of materials, in part justifying the precedence of Hg for the *Canterbury Tales* (the only *Canterbury Tales* manuscript in the series), in part following the assumptions of Eleanor Hammond and Aage Brusendorff on the relations of collections of shorter poems.[37]

Ralph Hanna has pointed out that the facsimile project of the Pilgrim Press and now other presses has a strangely belated and nostalgic quality; it harkens back, not to the evidence itself, but to a brief period just before computers began to revise the way this evidence was presented and challenge the evidence as previously published. The large, expensive, lavishly produced facsimile is, according to Hanna, a monument to a brief period in medieval studies (early 1970s), when evidence was defined differently. Scholars could now have access to a manuscript and its readings by an outlay of money roughly equivalent to what it would cost to visit the archive itself.[38]

Where, then, does the electronic Chaucer fit? To Hanna, the computer facsimiles (including those of the *Piers Plowman Archive* project in which Hanna himself is involved) were the driving force behind the production of the facsimiles in codex form – a rear-guard action against new editorial technology. However, Hanna's argument can also apply to the production of the computer facsimiles themselves. In large part, they are an extension of the older facsimiles produced, according to Hanna, by the anxiety caused by the electronic edition. There is no rift between the electronic facsimile and the material one.

In the exercise above, the best use of the computer edition was to reconstruct its evidence *as* a material facsimile. The electronic Chaucer, then, becomes a much more lavish version of the Chaucer Society transcriptions of the 1860s. Because the evidence that the editors make available for criticism is so complex and the methods for analysing it beyond the competence of most Chaucerians, the user is put less in the position of critiquing than of throwing up the hands in despair. This is precisely the reaction I had some twenty-five years ago, when trying to make sense of a pile of unbound Chaucer Society pamphlets that a local library had thrown away in my direction. Chaucer? or a nineteenth-century scholar's dream of Chaucer? Those pamphlets now sit on my shelf next to the volumes of the Variorum, once heavily annotated, now in large part ignored. There is just enough space there for the CD-ROMS, which may or may not finally come my way.

Conclusion

Advances in editorial technology provide a convincing image of scholarly advance. No doubt Chaucerians as a group were much better versed in Chaucer in the late nineteenth century than they were in the late sixteenth century. As a group, they were much better versed in Chaucer in the mid- to late twentieth century than they were in the nineteenth century. This obvious progress can be easily mapped onto various aspects of scholarly history: the work, scholarly and editorial, of the late nineteenth-century Chaucer Society; advances in editorial theory and technology. When we look at the sometimes aggravating details, however, the relation between these parallel histories becomes less clear. In the cases examined here, editors working on what will doubtless be the last edition produced under old technology do not seem to understand or, perhaps, they are simply unable to articulate even the most basic principles of editing within that tradition. Have editorial conventions become too familiar? As editorial methods advance beyond their roots, do editors become too complacent, and apply procedures and editorial rhetoric mechanically? By contrast, the edition destined to be the first produced under new technology seems in some cases to bury the very evidence it is designed to reveal. To what extent is the growing sophistication of Chaucerians dependent on or even related to the editions they claim to read? If we extend this argument to other literary fields – Shakespeare and Shakespeareans, classicists and the objects of their studies – are the results similar? Are we to treat with condescension, for example, those fifteenth-century readers of Vergil, Ovid, and Terence, who laboured under their demonstrably bad editions? In what sense is it meaningful to claim that late twentieth-century readers have a better understanding of these authors than did their fifteenth-century counterparts simply because their editors do?

When we view bibliographers in relation to editors, or editors in relation to a greater scholarly community, the relationship becomes so complex that it could be regarded, paradoxically, as a purely accidental one. That is, the more we study the relation between these branches of scholarship and scholarship in general, the less we can say with certainty about it. No doubt editors believe, perhaps correctly, that their branch of scholarship has advanced, but if the only group of scholars able to perceive this consists of other editors, it is hard to see how we can treat their evidence and conclusions as worthy of the consideration both seem to deserve.

6 Editorial Variants

The following section examines the gap between material and text as it is manifested in certain editions and in the reception of editions. I will be dealing with a number of related problems: the text vs its material embodiment, the difference between colometry and metre, and the often curious divergence of the reception of these editions from the editions themselves. These editions can be understood and even defined as existing on different levels, and these levels are often at odds: critical evaluation of editions proceeds on one level; editorial myth of succession proceeds on another (series of texts); actual editorial production proceeds on a third – the transmission of particular printed objects (printer's copy).

I will be dealing with four cases: the Erasmus edition of Terence (1532) and the transmission of Terence's text in early printing; Bentley's edition of *Paradise Lost* (1732); Malone's edition of Shakespeare (1790); and finally the late nineteenth-century edition of Chatterton by W.W. Skeat. Many of the these have been well studied, but generally from the assumption of their significance: these are considered monumental editions, and thus worthy of attention. I begin with a contrasting and sceptical assumption: until proven otherwise, there simply *is* no such thing as an Erasmus edition, a Bentley edition, or a Malone edition; there are, rather, books that go under this appellation and critical statements about such books. If what the scholarship tells us about the importance, the scandal, or the cultural significance of each is even partially true, this assumption should be easy to disprove. However, it is somewhat unnerving, when examining the pages of the editions in question, to discover how resilient that mischievous assumption is. The books often do not distinguish themselves from other books; the texts remain curiously normal.

6.1   Early Terence Editions and the Material Transmission of the Text

Terence's metre was not well understood in the fifteenth century and printed editions represented it in various ways: sometimes as straight prose; sometimes as metre that, at least for certain of the easier metres (iambic senarii), is recognizable today; and sometimes simply as arbitrarily defined colometric lines; that is, lines begin with capital letters and the right margin is ragged, but the lines have no prosodic integrity. What we now consider standard Terence colometry (the material embodiment of abstract metrical principles) came into the modern editorial tradition largely through the collation of the fifth-century 'Bembo manuscript' (MS A) by Politian in 1492. Politian's collation then served as the basis for the Giunta edition (1506), an edition that initiated a series of editions that constitutes what might be called the vulgate printed text of Terence: editions by Aldus Manutius (1517); Robert Etienne (1526, 1529); Erasmus (1532; usually singled out for his work both on the text and on Terentian metre); and presumably one by Melanchthon. These editions are not, it seems, editions in the modern sense at all. Their material embodiment is quite at odds with the notion of what we consider 'editing.'[1]

The transmission of Terence's text in the first fifty years of printing was one that involved repeated cases of contamination. Substantives could come from one tradition; colometric lines could come from another. About half of fifteenth-century editions contain no commentary, and the margins of these were particularly useful for introducing readings from other manuscripts and editions, or for full collation of other copies. Politian used a copy of the 1475 Venice edition for transcribing the variants and metre of the Bembo manuscript. In this case, the printed base text is nearly obliterated by the contaminating variants; if this book were itself copied, that copy would show little to no trace of the edition that is its documented base text.[2]

The Myth of the Erasmus Edition

Erasmus is generally listed as an editor of Terence, although the evidence itself is ambiguous. Erasmus's editorial work presumably took place twice, first in a visit to Aldus Manutius (1507–8),[3] and second prior to publication of the Froben edition in 1532. Erasmus's work on Terence during his visit to Aldus is known in part through the parodic version of it given in the colloquy 'Opulentia sordida.' Erasmus's own references suggest that his work on Terence was limited to notes on metre,[4] although most modern accounts seem to credit Erasmus with more extensive editorial work.[5]

Erasmus worked for a second time on Terence for Froben, and he is generally listed as the editor of this edition. However, he claims in his introductory essay 'De metriis' that he was able to give over only four days to the work, and this only to help 'distinguish' metres for the benefit of schoolboys:

> Here scholars have erred; while they have taken care to identify the metrical forms and scan them, they have added certain words to fill voids in the verses, or have cut out what seemed superfluous ... Thus we have undertaken this 'four-day work' that we might alleviate a small part of this difficulty for boys, not indeed in all the plays, but thoroughly in one and sporadically in others.[6]

I assume that the play Erasmus claims to have worked on the most was *Andria*, although metrical notations in the various plays seem uniform.[7]

Erasmus's work on Terence thus seems minimal, but his editing of the *New Testament* established his reputation as a major figure in editorial history, and because of this reputation, scholars seem to assume that any editing by Erasmus must be significant, whatever the evidence may be. A simple look at the Terence edition itself is sufficient here. I include two plates: one of the Froben edition of 1532 (presumably edited by Erasmus) (fig. 3); the other the folio edition of 1529 produced by Etienne (fig. 4). When we look at these pages, there is no question as to what Erasmus's editorial work involved. Erasmus had a copy of Etienne's edition, and in the four days he had to work, he annotated it. An annotated copy of this then went to Froben, who reprinted Etienne's edition with Erasmus's metrical annotations. Erasmus may well have laboured over the editing of Terence but little of that editing found its way into the so-called Erasmus edition. Despite the claims of modern scholars and some of Erasmus's contemporaries, the Erasmus edition is not an edition in the modern sense at all, but simply a contamination of the Etienne edition.

It is interesting here to consider Etienne's own stance toward what seems to us as clear piracy: editorial rhetoric and editorial products do not necessarily cohere. Etienne was proud of his own editorial work and said as much in the introduction to his own edition. In an introductory note, Etienne speaks heatedly about his editorial labours. He claims that

A N D R I A   37

quanquam illam Menander Dianam appellet,& hoc fentiat in Bucolicis Virgilius. Hui,
tam cito?)Tam cito,ut felicitatem partus oftendat incredibilem. Tam cito,ad reprehenfio∕
nem. Ridiculum.)Ad irrifionem.& infpice,ridiculum aduerbium fit,an nomen,ut fit,ui∕   *Ridiculum*
de hominem ridiculum, fed aduerbium eft magis. Non fat commode diuifa.) Confufa
funt tibi omnia,inquit: nec unumquodcp fuo tempore geritur. qua re proderis. Non fat,
rion fatis. Diuffa funt,digefta,& compofita,& diftributa temporibus,id eft per tempora.
Mihin'?)Adhuc Dauus non percipit,& bene,quafi dicat,cum ille loquatur,illæ agant.
Nũ immemor es?difcipuli.)Difcipuli Myfis, Lesbia.& Pamphilus,omnes per quos agit
fallacia. Bene ergo difcipulos imperitos oftendit, & magiftrum Dauum , quia fuprà dixit,
Tum fi quis magiftrum cepit ad eam rem improbum. Num immemor es difcipuli ? Alij   *Difcipulus*
hic Pamphilum fignificari putant difcipulum:quia Dauus magifter. Nam nomina ad ali∕   *Magifter*
quid funt,difcipulus & magifter.& tunc difcipuli,geniciuus eft fingularis cafus. Alij nomi∕
natiui pluralis putant:ut difcipulos dixerit,omnes per quos agitur fallacia, fecundũ illud,
Tum fi quis magiftrum cepit ad eam rem improbum. Ego,quid narres,nefcio.) Quafi
fabulam. Num immemor es difcipuli? Deeft,nunc. Et bene difcipuli : quia ipfum magi∕
ftrum fuprà fecit. Ego,quid narres,nefcio.Semper ita refpondet Dauus feni,tanquã non
intelligat quid loquatur. Hiccine me fi imparatum.)Redit ad illam fententiam.Simul fce
le atus Dauus,fi quid confulti habet,ut confumat nunc cum nihil obfint doli.   Adortus
effet.)Adortus dicitur qui ex infidijs repente inuadit . dictum ab eo ,quòd corpora aggre∕
dientium exurgant fubito,atcp increfcant. Adortus,aggreffus.Omnia hæc, ex translatio
ne*maris dicta funt μεταφορικός.   *alʼ. Maris*

A C T V S   T E R T I I   S C E N A   I I
LESBIA. SIMO. DAVVS.

L.   D H V C Archillis quæ adfolent.quæcp oportet   *Iambici dime*
      Signa ad falutem effe,omnia huic effe uideo.   *tri tres,qui_*
      Nunc primùm faciftæc ut lauet poft deinde   *bus acciuũtur*
      Quod iuffi ei dare bibere, & quantum imperaui.   *duo trochei*
Date,mox ego huc reuertat.   *Dimeter cataleĉticus*
Per ecaftor fcitus puer natus eft Pamphilo.   *Iambicus trimeter*
Deos quæfo,ut fit fuperftes,quandoquidem ipfe eft ingenio bono. *Iamb.te∕*
Cumcp huic ueritus eft optumæ adolefcenti facere iniuriam.   *trametri*
s. Vel hoc quis non credat,qui norit te,abs te effe ortum? D.quidnam id eft?
s. Non imperabat coràm,quid opus facto effet * puerperæ. *Puerperæ trifylla_*
Sed poftquam egreffa eft,illis,quæ funt intus,clamat de uia.   *bum eft*
O Daue,itáne contemnor abs te?aut itáne tandem idoneus
Tibi *uideor,quem tam aperte fallere incipias dolis? *Si legas uidebor conftat*
Saltem accurate,ut metui uidear?certè fi refciuerim.   *uerfus*
D. Certè hercle nunc hic fe ipfus fallit,haud ego. s.edixin tibi?
Interminatus fum,ne faceres?num ueritus?quid retulit?
Credóne tibi hoc nunc peperiffe hanc è Pamphilo?   *Iambicus trimeter*
D. Teneo quid erret quid ego agam habeo. s.quid taces?   *Item hic*
D. Quid credas? quafi non tibi renuntiata fint hæc fic fore. *Iambici tetrametri*
s. Mihi ne quifquam? D.Eho an tute intellexti hoc adfimulari? s.irrideor.
D. Renuntiarum eft.nam qui iftæc tibi incidit fufpectio?
s. Qui?quia te noram. D.quafi tu dicas factum id confilio meo.
s. Certe enim fcio. D.Non fatis me pernofti etiã qualis fim Simo. *Troch.tetr.*
                                            e   Egóne

3. Terence, *Comoediae*, ed. Erasmus (Basel, 1532), p. 37.

A N D R.   17

GRINA ʃéκλαψ·ἱς περ ἀποσιώπησιμ apta cogitanti.reliquum autem ſic pronũtiat, quaſi repetꝰ con
Ex peregrina ſilio.Et bene adeo: quia tam demens eſt quòd amat ex peregrina,id eſt ex meretrice. Mulieres enim
amare   peregrinæ,inhoneſtæ ac meretrices habebãtur.Sic ipſe alibi,Samia mihi mater fuit,ea habitabat Rho
              di.Et ſeruus,Poteſt taceri hoc quidem.hoc eſt, meretricem habuiſſe te matrem veriſimile eſt.   EX
              PEREGRINA! ἀποσιώπησις.deeſt enim,vt filium ſuſcipiat/aut aliquid tale.   VIX TANDEM
              SENSI STOLIDVS.Pulchro colore inducto,poeta oſtendit non minus falliʃʃuſpicioſum, quàm qui
              ſtultus eſt.huic enim veritas fallacia videtur,dum nimis eſt acutus ac perſpicax.& hoc eſt quod ab euē
              tu fingit poeta.non enim in Dauo eſt ſic errare nunc ſenem.   Vix tandem ſenſi ſtolidus. Q̃ uinque
Senſus   ſunt ſenſus,quorum duos,viſum & auditum,magis ſenſibiles habemus, quàm pecora. Vnde Cicero,
Auditus   Non ſolum videam,ſed etiam audiam, planèque ſentiam. quaſi ad tactum retulit, quo etiam pecora
Viſus   impelluntur ad ſenſum.duabus ergo rebus ſcimus:aut ratiocinatione, aut ſenſu:quibus maxime præ
              ſtamus cæteris animalibus.Ergo ſenex ſe non ſenſu,non ratiocinatione ſenſiſſe,ſed veluti calcaribus &
              ſtimulis punctum.   HAEC PRIMVM.Satis ſe ſagacem ſenex oſtendit,quando principia ipſa ince
              ptioneſque comprehendit.   Hæc primum.Bene primum: quaſi ex multis quas parauerat Dauus cõ
              tra Chremetē.   QVO.Qua re.   IVNO LVCINA FER OPEM:SERVA ME.Iuno Lucina, Iuno
Iuno Lucina   nis filia,græce ἀλίθυα dicitur. Latine Iuno à iuuando dicta.Lucina ab eo quòd in lucem producat.Et
              gemina vota ſunt,vt & partus,& patiens ſeruetur.nam FER OPEM,propter partum:SERVA ME,
              •propter parientem dicitur.   Iuno Lucina fer opem:ſerua me obſecro.Nota,hoc verſu totidem vert
              bis vti omnespuerperas in Comœdijs,nec alias induci loqui in proſcenio: nam hæc vox poſt ſcenam
Obſtetrix   tollitur.   Fer opem.Propter quod Lucina eſt, inde obſtetrix,quòd opem tulerit.   Serua me obſe
              cro.Hoc,extra etiam hanc poteſtatem,Iunoni attribuitur:quanquam illam Menander Dianam appel
              let,& hoc ſentiat in Bucolicis Virgilius.   HVI,TAM CITo!Tam cito, vt felicitatem partus oſten
Ridiculum   dat incredibilē.Tam cito,ad reprehēſionem.   RIDICVLVM.Ad irriſionē.& inſpice,ridiculum ad
              uerbium ſit,an nomen,vt ſit,vide hominem ridiculum.ſed aduerbium eſt magis.   NON SAT COM
              MODE DIVISA.Confuſa ſunt tibi omnia,inquit:nec vnſiquodque ſuo tempore geritur. qua re pro
Diuiſa tem   deris.   Non ſat,non ſatis.   DIVISA SVNT,digeſta,& compoſita,& diſtributa TEMPORIBVS,
poribus   id eſt per tempora.   MIHIN'Adhuc Dauus non percipit,& bene,quaſi dicat, cũ ille loquatur, illæ
              agant.   NVM IMMEMOR EST DISCIPVLI.Diſcipuli Myſis,Leſbia, & Pamphilus,omnes per
              quos agitur fallacia.Bene ergo diſcipulos imperitos oſtendit,& magiſtrum Dauum, quia ſuprà dixit,
              Tum ſi quis magiſtrum cepit ad eam rem improbum.   Num immemor es diſcipuli? Alij hic Pam
Diſcipulus   philum ſignificari putant diſcipulum:quia Dauus magiſter. Nam nomina ad aliquid ſunt, diſcipulus
Magiſter   & magiſter.& tunc diſcipuli,genitiuus eſt ſingularis caſus.Alij nominatiuiʃpluralis putant:vt diſcipu
              los dixerit,omnes per quos agitur fallacia,ſecundum illud, Tum ſi quis magiſtrum cepit ad eam rem
              improbum.   EGO,QVID NARRES, NESCIO.Quaſi fabulam.   Nũ immemor es diſcipuliʃDe
              eſt,nunc.Et bene diſcipuli:quia ipſum magiſtrum ſuprà fecit.   Ego,quid nartes,neſcio. Semper ita
              reſpondet Dauus ſeni,tanquam non intelligat quid loquatur.   HICCINE ME SI IMPARATVM.
              Redit ad illam ſententiam,Simul ſceleratus Dauus,ſi quid conſilij habet,vt conſumat nunc cum ni
              hil obſint doli.   ADORTVS ESSET.Adortus dicitur qui ex inſidijs repente inuadit.dictum ab eo,
Adortus   quòd corpora aggredientium exurgant ſubito,atque increſcant.   Adortus,aggreſſus. Omnia hæc,
              ex tranſlatione maris dicta ſunt μεταφορικῶς.

ACTVS TERTII SCENA II.

LESBIA. SIMO. DAVVS.

L.   DHVC Archillis quæ adſolent,quæque oportet
A   Signa ad ſalutem eſſe,omnia huic eſſe video.
      Nunc primùm fac iſtæc vt lauet·poſt deinde
Quod iuſſi ei dare bibere,& quantum imperaui
Date.mox ego huc reuertar.
Per ecaſtor ſcitus puer natus eſt Pamphilo.
Deos quæſo,vt ſit ſuperſtes,quandoquidem ipſe eſt ingenio bono.
Cùmque huic veritus eſt optumæ adoleſcenti facere iniuriam.
s. Vel hoc quis non credat,qui norit te,abs te eſſe ortum? D. quidnam id eſt?
s. Non imperabat coràm,quid opus facto eſſet puerperæ.
Sed poſtquam egreſſa eſt,illis,quæ ſunt intus,clamat de via.
                                                                    e.j.

4. Terence, *Comoediae*, ed. Etienne (Paris, 1529), p. 17. Photo courtesy of the
Henry E. Huntington Library, San Marino, CA.

earlier editions are chaotic: even pages are reversed. All this is corrected: 'I pass over the fact that in the case of Terence, we faithfully corrected not a few places partly from the commentaries of Donatus, and partly from the collation of the best copies.' His edition is thus as good as new ('veluti novum, nedum instauratum'). Anyone who doubts this and troubles himself to compare this edition with others will find some 6000 corrections in the exemplar.[8]

The edition in which Etienne makes these claims is the folio with commentary (1529, Lawton #199), a book that represents only one of three series of editions Etienne was printing. There is a second folio edition as well, a bare-text edition without commentary and with lines widely spaced to permit the insertion of handwritten glosses (Lawton #200). The most often reprinted series is the octavo series, which begins in 1526. The fourth edition of this third series is dated 1533 (Lawton #212), with reprints in 1534 and 1535. This 1533 edition, however, turns out to be a hybrid. In the preface, Etienne claims he once promised to expound metres – a promise he did not fulfil. But lo! Another edition 'just happened' to come his way with Erasmus's commentary and distinction of metres. This was clearly the Froben edition, which itself used Etienne's earlier edition as printer's copy and copy-text. Etienne reprints this without apology, making no reference to the fact that the text was the very one he had loosed on the world with such editorial fanfare four years earlier. Two years later, in 1536, Etienne reprints his original folio edition (Lawton #225), now with these same additions of Erasmus from the Froben edition, and, as Lawton notes, even part of its title.[9] Modern notions of editorial propriety obviously do not apply.

6.2 Richard Bentley: Milton and Terence

The second editor I will deal with is Richard Bentley. As an editor of classics, Bentley is, like Erasmus, one of the editor-heroes in histories of textual criticism. In English literature, however, Bentley has become an editor-villain, the hero of the *Dunciad* (along with another editor-villain – Theobald) and the man responsible for the 1732 *Paradise Lost.*[10]

The rhetoric of English scholarship on Bentley follows a set form. The question is framed as one of textual disfigurement: Bentley disfigured the text of *Paradise Lost.* The scholarly debate then proceeds from this premise: to his critics, Bentley's editing is simply 'bad.' In one of the more recent versions of this criticism, Hale claims Bentley disgraces both himself and the entire field of textual criticism: 'By persisting in a misguided undertaking he was making a fool of himself, and of textual scholarship to boot' (Hale, 'Paradise Purified,' 73). What he does can hardly be judged in terms of 'true editing': his *Paradise Lost* is 'neither imposture nor true editing, just a deeply-flawed ego-trip' (ibid.). For Bentley's defenders, such as Marcus Walsh, Bentley must be judged in terms of something other than classical editing:

> The notorious edition of *Paradise Lost* represents an early case of non-objective editing, and that the controversy which it immediately provoked parallels surprisingly exactly the modern polarizing of opinions I have described.[11]

Bentley perhaps is not really editing at all; he is rather producing a 'reading,' and it is the reading, not the editing, that scholars are to judge as good, bad, or historically determined. The now classic example of this argument is by Empson: Bentley is not editing in a classic sense, but responding to contradictions in Milton's text. A more recent variation on that argument is by Bourdette: Bentley is producing not an edition, but a smooth 'Augustan' version of Milton.[12] In all these arguments, Bentley either did a bad thing, and it is the business of true scholarship to explain precisely how and why this was a bad thing, or he did a historically determined or interesting thing, and it is the purpose of genuine criticism to reveal the context that makes it so.

Hale's study of Bentley's own marginalia showed that the more closely one looks at specific material, the less certain abstract arguments about 'great' editors or even 'interesting' editing seem to hold. In this section I examine a copy of Bentley's *Paradise Lost*, and a similar argument applies. The material book should be the basis for all the above arguments, but the book provides little support for any of them; it does not even support the terms of the debate.

Bentley's Collations

A number of Milton scholars have objected to Bentley's claim in his Preface that no manuscript of *Paradise Lost* exists:

> The Printer's Faults are corrigible by retrieving the Poet's own Words, not from a Manuscript, (for none exists) but by Sagacity, and happy Conjecture ... the Editor's Interpolations are detected by their own Silliness and Unfitness. (sig. a2v)

Hale, studying Bentley's marginal annotation of the Tickell text, notes that it contains many collations of the extant manuscript of Book I, but objects that this collation is not careful: 'For classical and biblical texts, he knew the need of the fullest possible collating, and practiced it ... The margins of his Terence or his new Testament in the Wren Library teem with collations' ('Paradise Purified,' 70). Thus, 'his collating is partial and slapdash in the marginalia, careless or willful in the edition.'[13] This is a standard often invoked (positively and negatively) in regard to classical editing, but the 'fullest possible collation' was not often feasible until the computer age, and not even a desideratum. The example Hale cites is a particularly unfortunate one. A book-copy of Terence 'teeming with collations' could not in any sense be a 'fullest possible collation,' nor could Bentley's particular book-copy be intended to provide such a collation. There are some 700 manuscripts of Terence. No one has collated them, nor does anyone want to collate them. There are, in addition, hundreds of early Terence printed editions, including over one hundred incunable editions. Doubtless, some of the fifteenth-century editions have, from a textual-critical standpoint, as significant a status as, say, one of the hundreds of negligible fifteenth-century manuscripts, but no one has collated these books either.[14]

Explicit and implied criticism of anything short of 'fullest possible collation' is familiar in textual-critical contexts,[15] but the criticism is invalid. Classical textual criticism engages in the process of the elimination of witnesses (Lachmann's *eliminatio codicum descriptum*), not in compiling their often useless information. From a scholarly point of view, Bentley's treatment of the Milton manuscript may be objectionable, but only if Bentley himself defined that manuscript as an important one, which (rightly or wrongly) he did not.[16]

Let us look at what Bentley did. I have taken at face value the claim of Milton scholars that Bentley grew tired and weary as he neared the end, and that the latter parts of his *Paradise Lost* have far fewer corrections than does the beginning. I have two points. First, I do not see why this is a scandal. To expend more effort at the beginning of a task than at the end is typical of editing, teaching, and work in general. Second, the differences between Bentley's emendations in the initial books and in later books are not extreme. Examples of the numbers of Bentley's proposed readings (all placed in the margins or at the foot of the text on each page) are as follows: Book 1 – 125 proposed readings in 795 lines; Book 4 – 109 proposed readings in 1015 lines; Book 5 – 82: 905; Book 8 – 62: 653; Book 9 – 83: 1185; Book 11 – 52: 900; Book 12 – 31:

645. Certainly there is a steady progression here but nothing particularly startling.

Bentley's critics have also made note of his 'silent' emendations, which Bentley himself discusses in his Preface:

> The Faults therefore in Orthography, Distinction by Points, and Capital Letters, all of which swarm in the prior Editions, are here very carefully, and it's hop'd, judiciously corrected: though no mention is made in the Notes of that little but useful Improvement. (Bentley, *Paradise Lost*, Preface, sig. a1r)

W.W. Greg expounded exactly the same distinction and principle in his 'The Theory of Copy-Text' some two centuries later. The distinction Bentley is making here is between accidentals and substantives. According to Bentley, editorial changes in accidentals need not be recorded and can be made silently; these are matters so easily marred in printing and transmission that there is no way to return to Milton's original. In his own use of accidentals, Bentley indicates certain metrical features: for example, he includes an apostrophe to indicate elision, as in the phrase 'difficulty' and ...' This is no different from the type of punctuation found in many modern Terence editions, where three of the six stresses are marked – a system of metrical indices introduced by Bentley himself.

Let us look at further figures, beginning with Book I, the example generally cited as the most egregious. I have collated this, not with the Tickell text, but rather with an everyday edition, Tonson's Tenth edition (16mo). If Bentley's assault on the text is of any particular significance, there ought to be some evidence of it here.

A collation of the first fifty lines shows thirty-seven differences in accidentals (typical of Bentley's 'silent changes'). These are among the 800 changes Bentley makes to this book, and those numbers, in and of themselves, seem high. But what do they represent?

First] first
'till] till
Aid] aid
Heart] heart
aid] Aid

Generally, capitals are reduced, but as is typical with books of this period, neither the conventions of one style nor the other are entirely articulable.[17] Other changes involve punctuation:

Illumine,] Illumine;
Creator,] Creator;

Changes of this order constitute the majority, and all changes in point-
ing follow the same pattern or direction: Bentley introduces a comma
for an unmarked pause; a comma becomes a semicolon (never the
reverse); a semicolon becomes a colon (never the reverse). Bentley's
changes, thus, are not really emendations at all, but re-representations of
what is in the text before him.

If we eliminate changes in capitalization and the changes in punctuation, then we are left with two or three spelling changes:

out-spread] outspred
Oreb] Horeb

Such changes are banal, comparable to what one finds when comparing
at random any of the early editions of *Paradise Lost*, or when comparing
those editions with the manuscript of Book 1.[18] The changes that have so
vexed Bentley's critics are probably what we would call 'substantives.' But
none of these appears in the text; all proposed readings are printed in
the margins, a procedure found in contemporary editions as well.[19]
Although these proposed emendations are highlighted by layout, that
very layout makes it almost impossible for those proposed readings to
affect any normal reading of Milton's text. To my knowledge, there is not
and never has been a printed copy of a *Paradise Lost* text constructed with
Bentley's emendations – one that removes these from the margin and
places them in the text. The only printing venture to include Bentley's
emendations was a small contemporary edition of the marginalia alone.[20]
Perhaps the purpose of this volume was to allow readers to copy these
emendations into their personal copies of *Paradise Lost*, but I have never
seen such an annotated book-copy cited by a Miltonist.

Walsh compares Bentley's work on *Paradise Lost* to Tate's *King Lear* and
to what he calls Dryden's 'dramatic transversion' of *Paradise Lost*.[21] A few
parallel passages, however, make such a comparison hard to maintain.
First, a few lines from Bentley's *Paradise Lost* (italicized readings are those
Bentley rejects or emends):

Is this the Region, this the soil, the Clime,
Said then the lost Arch-Angel, this the Seat

That we must change for Heav'n? this mournful Gloom
For that celestial Light? Be it so, since He
Who now is Sov'rain can dispose and bid
What shall be right: farthest from him is best
Whom Reason [*hath*] equal'd, Force hath made supream
Above his equals. Farwel happy Fields,
Where Joy for ever dwells! Hail Horrors, hail
Infernal World! and Thou profoundest Hell
Receive thy new Possessor: One who brings
A Mind not to be chang'd by Place or Time. (Book I, 242ff.)

Then, Dryden's 'State of Innocence,' which is supposed to provide a parallel:

Is this the Seat our Conqueror has given?
And this the Climate we must change for Heaven?
These Regions and this Realm my Wars have got;
This Mournful Empire is the Loser's Lot:
In Liquid Burnings or on Dry to dwell,
Is all the sad Variety of Hell.
But see, the Victor has recall'd, from far,
Th'Avenging Storms, his Ministers of War:
His Shafts are spent, and his tir'd thunders sleep;
Nor longer bellow through the Boundless Deep.
Best take th'occasion, and these Waves forsake,
While time is giv'n. Ho, Asmoday, awake
if thou art he: but Ah! how chang'd from him
Companion of my Arms! how wan! how dim!
How faded all thy Glories are! I see
My self too well, and my own change, in thee.   (sig. B1r–v)[22]

And finally, a passage from the last scene of Tate's 'The History of King Lear,' one that does not really have a parallel in Shakespeare:

Lear: Ingrateful as they were, my heart feels yet
A pang of nature for their wretched fall.
But, Edgar, I defer thy joys too long
Thou served'st distressed Cordelia; take her crowned,
Th'imperial grace fresh blooming on her brow.

> Nay, Gloster, thou hast here a father's right,
> Thy helping hand t'heap blessings on their heads.[23]

Now we can look at page 1 of Bentley's *Paradise Lost* (fig. 5), and compare it with page 1 of another, this the Baskerville edition of 1759 (fig. 6). It is difficult to believe that either Bentley's critics or defenders, in their more ardent moments, could have had the actual 1732 book in front of them, or a clear and distinct idea of that book in their minds. (Only Walsh, in his 1997 monograph, provides facsimile pages.) However, they have all used that particular book, or at least a facsimile of it. Despite its notoriety, it was never reprinted until the 1974 AMS reprint, and it clearly did not compete effectively with other Milton editions. No copy I have seen has been annotated, and I find no evidence that it had the slightest effect on Milton's text.

The scandal of Milton's *Paradise Lost*, then, has little to do with Milton's *Paradise Lost*. It is based on two assumptions, one of them a fallacy. The first is that Bentley was working within the strictures of a presumed ideal of textual criticism often articulated but never demonstrated (the desirability of fullest possible collation), and that Bentley practised such textual criticism in his classical works, which he did not. The second is that Bentley's *Paradise Lost* is somehow the 'idea' of Bentley's *Paradise Lost*. The book itself can hardly be the true object of the criticisms of Bentley or the scandal of his edition. Rather, the book has been absorbed into 'Bentley' – the Bentley of the *Dunciad*, the Bentley of Cambridge, and now, more amusingly, the romanticized 'Great Editor and Conjecturer' Bentley, whose towering achievements were somehow belittled by his work on Milton.

Coda on Bentley's Terence

A second edition of Bentley often cited as monumental is his edition of Terence. How does this differ from his *Paradise Lost*? In the now standard Oxford Classical Texts edition, Bentley is mentioned only seven times in the notes to *Andria*, and as far as I can tell, none of his emendations are accepted into the text itself.[24] Classical scholars thus seem less certain about the merit of his emendations here than do nonclassicists.

In the Preface, Bentley claims to follow the edition of Faernus; my reference copy below is *Publii Terentii Afri Comoediae, Phaedri ... ex recensione et cum notis Richardi Bentleii* (Cambridge, 1726). Bentley says he collated this with various manuscripts; he collated this book against his own

ɪ

PARADISE LOST.

BOOK I.

OF Man's firſt Diſobedience, and the Fruit
Of that forbidden Tree, whoſe mortal taſte
Brought Death into the world and all our woe,
With loſs of *Eden*, till one greater Man
5 Reſtore us, and regain the bliſsful Seat,
Sing Heav'nly Muſe ; that on the *ſecret* top   *ſacred*
Of *Horeb* or of *Sinai* didſt inſpire
That Shepherd, who firſt taught the choſen Seed,
In the beginning how the Heav'ns and Earth
10 Roſe out of *Chaos* : Or if *Sion* hill
Delight thee more, and *Siloa's* brook that flow'd
Faſt by the Oracle of God ; I thence
Invoke thy aid to my adventrous *Song*,   *Wing,*
       That

V. 6. *That on the* ſecret *top Of* Horeb.] *Secret Valleys, ſecret Caves,* come frequently in Poetry ; but *ſecret top of a Mountain,* viſible ſeveral Leagues off, is only met with here. Our Poet dictated it thus, *That on the* SACRED *top Of* Horeb : from *Exod.* iii. 5. *Moſes came to the mountain of God, Horeb. And God ſaid, Put off thy ſhoes from off thy feet ; for the place whereon thou ſtandeſt is* HOLY *ground.* So our Author, V. 619. VI. 25. *Sacred Hill.* And *Spenſer,* in *Fairy Queen,* I. 10. 54 ; and as frequently in the Claſſic Writers, *Mens Sacer,* ἱερὸν ὄρος. Some perhaps may prefer the preſent Reading, *Secret top* ; becauſe in moſt Countries the high Mountains have againſt rainy Weather their Heads ſurrounded with Miſts. True ; but yet it's queſtionable, whether in the wide and dry Deſert of *Arabia,* Mount *Horeb* has ſuch a cloudy Cap. I have in my Youth read ſeveral Itineraries, where the Travellers went up to the Top of *Horeb* ; and I remember not, that they take notice of its Cloudineſs. And a juſt Preſumption lies againſt it from Holy Writ, *Exod.* xvii ; where the *Iſraelites,* encamp'd at the foot of *Horeb,* could find no Water ; which was provided miraculouſly, when *Moſes* ſmote the Rock with his ſacred Rod : for all Natural Hiſtory informs us, and Reaſon vouches it, That a Mountain, whoſe Head is cloudy, has always running Springs at its Foot. But allowing all, and granting that *Horeb* was like the *European* Hills ; yet no Poet hitherto has on that account ſaid *The Secret* ; but the *Cloudy, Miſty, Hazy, Grey Top.* Nay, allow further, That *Secret Top* is a paſſable Epithet ; yet it is common to all Mountains whatever : but *Horeb,* whoſe *Ground was holy,* Horeb *the Mountain of God,* Exod. iii. 1 ; 1 Kings xix. 8, deſerved a Peculiar Epithet. If therefore (which the beſt Poets have adjudg'd) a Proper Epithet is always preferable to a General one ; and if *Secret* and *Sacred* are of a near Sound in Pronunciation ; I have ſuch an Eſteem for our Poet ; that which of the two Words is the better, That, I ſay, was dictated by *Milton.*

V. 13. *To my adventrous* Song, *&c.*] Some Acquaintance of our Poet's, entruſted with his Copy, took ſtrange Liberties with it, unknown to the blind Author, as will farther appear hereafter. 'Tis very
     B   odd,

5. Richard Bentley, *Milton's Paradise Lost: A New Edition* (London, 1732), p. 1.

PARADISE LOST.

BOOK I.

OF Man's firſt diſobedience, and the fruit
    Of that forbidden tree, whoſe mortal taſte
Brought death into the world, and all our woe,
With loſs of Eden, 'till one greater Man
Reſtore us, and regain the blifsful ſeat,   5
Sing heav'nly Muſe, that on the ſecret top
Of Oreb, or of Sinai, didſt inſpire
That ſhepherd,who firſt taught the choſen ſeed,
In the beginning how the Heav'ns and Earth
Roſe out of Chaos: Or if Sion hill   10
Delight thee more, and Siloa's brook that flow'd
Faſt by the oracle of God; I thence
Invoke thy aid to my adventrous ſong,
That with no middle flight intends to ſoar
Above th'Aonian mount, while it purſues   15
Things unattempted yet in proſe or rhime.
And chiefly Thou, O Spirit, that doſt prefer
Before all temples th'upright heart and pure,
Inſtruct me, for Thou know'ſt; Thou from the firſt
Waſt preſent, and with mighty wings outſpread 20
Dove-like ſatſt brooding on the vaſt abyſs,
                                 And

6. John Milton, *Paradise Lost: A Poem* (Birmingham: Baskerville, 1959), p. 3.

collations of manuscript readings ('cum meis ubique comparo') and has made a thousand changes ('textum autem mille ... locis immutavi'). One thousand emendations and changes is probably a slight exaggeration, but may be on the right order. The changes, however, like those in *Paradise Lost*, are more impressive collectively than when looked at individually.

The changes are of various kinds; some are based on sense, for example, the emendation *cohibebant* for *prohibebat* (the reading in Faernus).[25] Occasionally Bentley refers to manuscripts: 'Nostri codices plerique omnes, In ignem inposita est ... Recte, et ex poetae more ...' (102). But even in this case, his proposed reading is merely a rejection of Faernus and a return to the reading of the *textus receptus*, one found in the Cambridge 1701 edition. Some of his emendations are stylistic:

pedibusque] pedibus: ('Vehementior & melior oratio est, sublato isto *que*').
Si tollas interrogationem, melius procedet sententia, seu priori respicias, seu sequentia ...

The number of emendations seems to be about ten in 100 lines. The text itself is unmarked. To recover the *textus receptus*, one would have to work back from Bentley's notes, which is not always easy. Editorially Bentley does about what he does with Milton, while making his base text much more difficult of recovery. Whether one accepts Bentley's emendations or not, no one would consider this edition a scandal.

The major innovation of Bentley was in the metrical representation. Earlier editions had adopted numerous systems for representing metre, in general through marginal notes or notes at the beginning of each scene. In the modern Oxford edition, metrical identifications of all lines are listed in an appendix. For many of us, however, knowing what the metre is, and knowing how a particular line can be scanned according to that metre are two different things. The list of metres in the modern Oxford edition thus does essentially what Erasmus's or Melanchthon's verbal identifications of metre do in early sixteenth-century editions.

What is difficult for readers in many cases is applying those metres to individual lines, and numerous typographical schemes have been invented to help. One of them appears in the edition of Faernus by Franciscus Hare nearly contemporary with Bentley's edition: *Publi Terentii Comoediae Ad Exemplar Faernianum A Petro Victorio editum anno mclxv* (London, 1724). Hare provides a 'new method' for indicating scansion which he claims is easily learned, but the result as printed is often bizarre and mystifying in the extreme; for example, the following scansion is given in the introduction:

Proh Phor-mio=nem Phor-mio=nem Phor-mio=nem Phormio.

Hare's double hyphen indicates the division of the line into dipodies; the single hyphen indicates metrical feet. Under Bentley's system, the scansion of this line would be represented by marking the first accent of each dipody.

Proh Phórmionem Phórmionem Phórmionem Phórmio.

This is a system still used by many modern editions. It is unobtrusive and allows a reader to recover from any metrical wandering and return to Bentley's own idea of how the line should be scanned, an idea likely to be as good or better than what most readers would come up with on their own.

What Bentley did with Terence, then, was to produce a Terence as defined in the western educational tradition: an easily read, basic text. (It is less easy to make this case for his Horace, although even here, Bentley's work is sometimes overstated.)[26] His indications of metrics are unobtrusive, and his textual changes are marked only in the notes. Readers ignoring these notes will find an easily readable text.

When we compare this with the Milton edition, we see a striking difference. The Milton text itself is free of substantive emendation, but Bentley's changes, though kept in the margins, are the more obtrusive. Far from producing what has been called a smooth Augustan text (something that might be better said of the Terence), what Bentley produces is a questioning, self-reflexive text, with his own nagging voice in the margin and in the notes.

6.3 Malone Verbatim: The Description of Editorial Procedures

Interest in Edmond Malone's 1790 edition of Shakepeare and its place in the history of Shakespeare editing was revived with the publication of Margreta de Grazia's *Shakespeare Verbatim* in 1991.[27] In this section, I will focus on a simple problem: the gap between Malone's description of his editorial procedures and the actual procedures suggested in the work itself.[28]

The 'Old Copies'

I begin with Malone's statements about the uses of the quarto editions. Scholars and enthusiasts of eighteenth-century editing tend to construe the stated reliance on these quartos as evidence of editorial advances. Most of the eighteenth-century Shakespeare editors (with the exception of Johnson) fit this narrative. Recent scholars of Rowe have emphasized his use of such quartos;[29] for Lounsbury a century ago, Theobald becomes an editorial hero in this regard. Pope laudably uses quartos, and Malone follows Pope.[30]

When one looks at how editors use these quartos, however, one sees little evidence of modern editorial theory or practices. They are merely 'the old copies,' and their evidence is gathered and presented unsystematically, in a scholarly manner little different from what is sometimes condescendingly referred to as 'antiquarian.' As pointed out by Seary, such 'old copies' are not always quartos, but include the early folios. Pope treats the First Folio as he does the quartos; he checks his base text (the received text) against it, as one more of the 'old copies.'[31] Malone also includes both folio and quarto editions within such phrases as 'ancient copies,' 'old copies,' 'the first copies' – all to be distinguished from 'modern editions' (that is, eighteenth-century editions) (notes to *Lear*, vol. 8, pp. 503, 512, 514, 529). Each editor is judged, and to some extent judges himself, by the number of antiquarian details added (that is, number of old readings 'restored') to a preceding edition.[32]

Despite this concern with 'restored' readings, these editors show little concern about what is used as a base text or even awareness of its effect on the text. The copy-text (as well as the printer's copy) remains the same – some form of the received text based on late folio editions. Rowe's edition was based on the fourth folio (I assume he sent a marked copy of this or a copy of such a marked copy to press). Theobald used a marked-up copy of Pope's second edition, for whose text Tonson believed he held copyright. For Seary, this editing tradition is thus one determined largely by the economics of publishing firms.[33]

Malone's treatment of earlier quartos is based on the same principles stated by Theobald, vol. 8: 'A Table of the several editions of Shakespeare's Plays, collated by the Editor.' Under '1. Editions of Authority,' Theobald lists the 1623 and 1630 folios, and twenty-six quartos, all with printed dates earlier than 1623. His 'Editions of Middle Authority' include the third folio and eleven quartos, all with dates later than 1623. His 'Editions of No Authority' are modern: Rowe's edition of 1709, 1714, and Pope's first and second editions of 1725 and 1728.[34] A quarto thus is of 'authority' if it is printed prior to the First Folio. There is not a single exception in the list of authoritative editions. Also important is the meaning of the word 'collated' in Theobald's introduction. All this means, and all Theobald claims, is that copies are somehow 'brought together' in a physical way, just as the titles are brought together in the list itself. There is no systematic collation in a modern editorial sense, and Theobald refers to such things as 'the old quarto,' 'generality of the editions,' or at times to all of these books indifferently as 'all genuine copies' in his notes.[35]

Malone does not substantially change this procedure. The main difference is in his description of what the procedure is:

> The various readings found in the different impressions of the quarto copies are frequently mentioned by the late editors: it is obvious from what has been already stated, that the first edition of each play is alone of any authority, and accordingly to no other have I paid any attention. All the variations in the subsequent quartos were made by accident or caprice. Where, however, there are two editions printed in the same year, or an undated copy, it is necessary to examine each of them, because which of them was first, can not be ascertained; and being each printed from a manuscript, they carry with them a degree of authority to which a re-impression cannot be entitled. (1: xviii)

The principle enunciated here is not sound, and was known not to be sound (although Lachmann, a half century later, is generally given credit for refuting it). Furthermore, it requires an uncritical acceptance of the dates printed on the quartos (dates now known to be in many cases false, although they would not have seemed so to Malone).

Malone's claim 'to have paid no attention' to any but the first edition is obviously overstated. Malone's description of his specific procedures is on 1: xliv:

> My late friend Mr. Tyrwhitt, a man of such candour, accuracy, and profound learning, that his death must be considered as an irreparable loss to literature, was of opinion, that in printing these plays the original spelling should be adhered to, and that we never could be sure of a perfectly faithful edition, unless the first folio copy was made the standard, and actually sent to the press, with such corrections as the editor might think

proper. By others it was suggested, that the notes should not be subjoined to the text, but placed at the end of each volume, and that they should be accompanied by a complete Glossary.[36] The former scheme (that of sending the first folio to the press) appeared to me liable to many objections; and I am confident that if the notes were detached from the text, many readers would remain uninformed, rather than undergo the trouble occasioned by perpetual references from one part of a volume to another.

Malone describes here a contaminated text: the folio is the copy-text in Greg's sense (the basis for line references and for providing conventions for accidentals), but what would appear to be a base text (the presumptive authority for substantives) would be any of the most authoritative quartos.

For our purposes, the question of note placement is unimportant. In the next paragraph, Malone addresses the actual procedures of printing and editing:

In the present edition I have endeavoured to obtain all the advantages which would have resulted from Mr. Tyrwhitt's plan, without any of its inconveniences. Having often experienced the fallaciousness of collation by the eye, I determined, after I had adjusted the text in the best manner in my power, to have every proofsheet of my work read aloud to me, while I perused the first folio, for those plays which first appeared in that edition; and for all those which had been previously printed the first quarto copy, excepting only in the instances of *Merry Wives of Windsor* and *King Henry V* which, being either sketches or imperfect copies, could not be wholly relied on; and *King Richard III*, of the earliest edition of which tragedy I was not possessed. I had at the same time before me a table which I had formed of the variations between the quartos and the folio. By this laborious process not a single innovation, made either by the editor of the second folio, or one of the modern editors, could escape me. (1: xliv–xlv)

The discussion is not straightforward. The introductory theme concerns spelling. Tyrwhitt believes in maintaining early spelling. This should be a relatively easy thing to do, as long as an early edition (either Q or F) is used as both copy-text and printer's copy. The original spelling (an accidental) ought thus to be reproduced. However, Malone's proofreading procedures undermine this. Oral proofreading of the kind described here, where one copy is simply read while the other is 'perused,' will not catch such differences. Malone's procedures commit him to a modern spelling edition and the 'table' he has before him apparently lists only substantive differences.

Malone never details the 'inconveniences' of sending the First Folio to press, but they are obvious. The First Folio by the eighteenth century was an expensive book, and copies could not be wasted.[37] Therefore, what Malone sends to press is a copy of a cheaper printed edition. He does not mention this here, nor does he seem to realize what Tyrwhitt clearly sees: to send the First Folio to press is the only way to ensure that what we now call its 'accidentals' get printed. Malone's editorial theory, thus, is completely subordinate to the material procedures of getting something printed.

Malone claims that the edition of most authority is the earliest one, and according to his own theory, applied to the case of, say, *Lear*, he ought to use Q as a base text (Q here defined as the 'text of the quarto considered earliest'), and insert into that text all superior readings from F. Even a brief collation of *Lear* proves he does not do that. The central polemical opposition for Malone is not one between Q and F readings, but rather one between 'the old copies' and 'modern editions.'

If we compare the variants listed in Malone's own notes, we find the proportions between Q and F readings about equal (Q and F here mean 'that abstract text represented by one of the quartos or folios'). It is difficult to be precise, since Malone generally accepts a Q or F reading in cases where the reading is lacking in the other; for those readings where Q and F offer a real choice (that is, where Malone's notes provide the alternative reading), I count, for Act I, thirty F readings against twenty-two Q readings; and the proportion in Act II is about the same. There is no sense here that Malone prefers one (the older reading?) to the other, but when we look at the form of the text, we see that the lineation of F has, in all instances, been followed. If there were no other physical books than these, Malone's procedures would be obvious: he has taken a copy of 'F' (that is, a book that uses the folio colometry, whether an actual folio or one of the eighteenth-century editions based on a folio) and inserted into that copy some, but not all, readings of Q. Q is thus neither base text nor copy-text.

Malone's choice of readings is not systematic. The F readings do not seem to me to be obviously superior to the Q readings Malone rejects – readings presumably recorded in his table of variants. But if we compare Malone's variants with the Q readings included in Theobald's edition, we see that Malone does not always choose his Q readings because he has judged them individually against F readings; many of the readings from

Q Malone includes had already been inserted (just as unsystematically) into the 'vulgate' eighteenth-century text of Shakespeare. Malone's text is thus one more step in the slow, unsystematic, and often uncritical accrual of Q readings and other alternate readings into the base-text F.[38]

The 'inconveniences' Malone mentions are economic in several senses. He cannot afford to send a copy of the folio or a quarto to press, nor does he copy either by hand. Instead, he sends to press the received text, obviously in modern spelling, with the accumulated variants from Rowe, Pope, and Theobald. The much vaunted oral collation was designed to improve on 'Mr. Tyrwhitt's plan,' and to remove the variants introduced through the second folio and by these later editors. Instead, it makes Tyrwhitt's goal (the production of an original spelling edition) impossible, and furthers the very editorial innovations to which Malone objects by making indifferent the distinction between folio and quarto.

6.4 W.W. Skeat, Chatterton's Rowley, and the Definition of the True Poem

W.W. Skeat is generally considered one of the 'great' late nineteenth-century editors of early English literature.[39] Skeat defined for medievalists the three 'forms' of *Piers Plowman* (presumably the three authorial versions), and his parallel-text edition was basic to Langland studies for over a century.[40] Even more influential was his Chaucer edition, an edition that not only embodied the views of canon, but also materialized the notion of apocrypha in a supplemental volume. Here, Skeat placed himself squarely in line with Thomas Tyrwhitt (1774–8) on matters of canon; his decision to use the Ellesmere manuscript as base for the *Canterbury Tales* was continued in the most widely used American edition of this century, that of F.N. Robinson.[41] Skeat's editorial procedures have been criticized. He is 'eclectic,' or, in the case of the *Canterbury Tales*, relies overly heavily on a manuscript that is no longer in favour. His repeated claims to have judiciously examined certain manuscript evidence cannot always be supported. He relied too heavily on the transcriptions provided by the Chaucer Society. His editions, however, with their easily accessible texts, glossaries, and voluminous notes, were the points of departure for nearly all twentieth-century editions of these texts and for most serious readers.

Skeat did not hesitate to engage in editorial polemic, and yet when it comes to a clear description of what his editorial procedures actually were, Skeat is surprisingly reticent. The seven-volume Chaucer edition has headings that promise at least introductory editorial discussion for certain poems (for example, 'The Plan of the Present Edition,' 4: xvii, on the *Canterbury Tales*), and there are several statements concerning general editorial procedures and assumptions:

> The text of the *Canterbury Tales*, as printed in the present volume, is an entirely new one, owing nothing to the numerous printed editions which have preceded it. (*Complete Works of Chaucer*, 4: vii)

Skeat's 'absolutely new text' (4: vii) will rely solely on manuscript evidence and owes nothing presumably to previous printed editions. However, there is little in Skeat describing what his actual procedures and assumptions were – what text he used as a basis of collation, how he recorded alternative readings, what principle of selection went into the recording of those readings. In addition, as far as I can determine, there is no statement in Skeat clearly defining what it was he was presenting to his readers. In the case of the *Canterbury Tales*, for example, the Ellesmere manuscript is good because it 'not only gives good lines and good sense, but is also (usually) grammatically accurate and thoroughly well spelt' (4: xvii). What grammar or spelling, or whose grammar and spelling is being accurately presented – these things are not made clear,[42] nor is there a clear definition of whose 'good sense' is being presented in the manuscript, or presented in Skeat's edition itself.

The present section considers Skeat's editing from a different standpoint. Here, I will examine one of Skeat's lesser known productions: his edition of Chatterton's Rowley poems, first published in 1871 and reprinted in the Aldine British Poets series in 1890 (roughly contemporary with Skeat's work on Chaucer).[43] As in the Chaucer edition itself, Skeat was here following Thomas Tyrwhitt as a predecessor, whose views on Rowley and procedures for analysing the language of the poems Skeat by and large followed. Skeat's apparent modernizing of the poems and his justification for doing so, however, reveal certain assumptions about how he conceived the poetic process and what he believed a poem actually to be, and it is likely that he used these same assumptions when he produced some of his major works as well.

The Rowley poems of Thomas Chatterton were first published in 1777; the third edition adds an essay on the Rowley controversy by Tyrwhitt.[44] Tyrwhitt argued that the poems were forgeries and exposed one of the methods Chatterton had used. According to Tyrwhitt, Chatterton used as a basis for his vocabulary Skinner's etymological Dictionary, and simply substituted for the ordinary word in the definition, the medieval word in the entry itself.[45] If we take Tyrwhitt's statements in their most literal sense as implying a set of poetic procedures (Tyrwhitt himself did not do so), then Chatterton actually composed the poems in modern English, and substituted 'hard words' for ordinary ones (this is a procedure that Skeat makes even more explicit). Obviously, such a method of composition will lead to mistakes, and these mistakes Tyrwhitt duly recorded.

Skeat's two-volume edition and its reprints in the Aldine series were not the first of Chatterton editions to appear in small format. Almost identical in appearance is *The Poetical Works of Thomas Chatterton*, 2 vols (Boston, 1857),[46] but the texts, even in this apparently 'user-friendly' format, remained what they were in 1777. The Aldine edition, by contrast, gave the poems themselves in what Skeat claimed was an accessible form with most of the text in modernized spelling and much of the vocabulary changed. Skeat's editorial procedures did not simply produce a readable set of poems; they radically changed what such poems really were, that is, they changed the thing editing reconstructs.

Skeat's changes are seen on a number of levels. For some of the poems, what Skeat did amounts to little more than respelling. The first text cited here is the text as it appeared in the 1857 Boston edition:

The feathered songster chaunticleer
    Han wounde hys bugle horne,
And tolde the earlie villager
    The commynge of the morne:
            ('Bristowe Tragedie,' st. 1)

Skeat:

The featured songster Chanticleer
    has wound his bugle horn,
And told the early villager
    The coming of the morn:

For others, however, wholesale changes are made; see, for example, in 'Aella':

Syr Johne, a knyghte, who hate a barne of lore,
Kenns Latyn att fyrst syghte from Frenche or Greke,
Pyghte the hys knowlachynge ten yeres or more,
To rynge upon the Latynne worde to speke.
            ('Aella, Epistle to Mastre Canynge,' st. 3)

Skeat:

> Sir John, a knight, who hat a barn of lore,
> Knows Latin at first sight from French or Greek;
> Setteth his studying ten years or more,
> Poring upon the Latin word to speak.

It is no criticism of Skeat to point out such changes, and almost any procedure could be justified with these poems. Everyone knew the poems were bizarre, and without such changes as Skeat introduced, few readers could actually read them. What I am concerned about here is only what assumptions Skeat had to bring to the poems in order to make them accessible in the way he did.

Let us look first at Skeat's introductory essay. As elsewhere, Skeat presents himself as a spokesperson for truth and facts: he is the scholar, rather than the mere critic:

> The following Essay is designed to put the reader in possession of the true facts of the case as regards the Rowley poems.[47] Many writers have employed themselves to small purpose in ridiculing each other's notions, and in wasting time in the investigation of a few isolated words, instead of setting steadily to work to analyze the whole of them ... Anything like accurate information about the forms of words occurring in our old authors seems, with one exception, to have been possessed by none of them ... and it is not too much to say that Tyrwhitt is the only writer among those that have hitherto handled the subject who had a real critical knowledge of the language of the 14th and 15th centuries (1: viii–ix)[48]

Skeat's refutation of the idea that Chatterton's poetry is genuine is no real advance on Tyrwhitt's essay included in the editions of the Rowley poems over a century earlier. Skeat follows Tyrwhitt here the same way he follows Tyrwhitt in his *Canterbury Tales* edition, sometimes with effusive acknowledgment, sometimes with no acknowledgment at all.

> According to Skeat, Chatterton speaks in a particular language: 'Yet for all this, Chatterton coined a language which he so far mastered as to be able to employ it with considerable ease and skill' (1: xi).

That is, he does not simply plug in words, but writes in a definable language or dialect.[49] Still, there is an implied difference between the language Rowley composed these poems in, and the language in which they appeared (or at least, there must be such a difference in order for Skeat's essay to maintain any consistence).

Skeat describes four different methods for editing the Rowley poems.

1 'To reprint the old text, with old notes, merely compiling them from former editions.' (The old notes in the former editions are, Skeat says, those of Tyrwhitt.)
2 'To reprint the old text, with sound critical notes, fully explaining every error.'
3 'To do away with the needless disguises in spelling and, on the supposition of the genuineness of the poems, to reduce them to the usual *sufficiently* uniform spelling of some good MS. of the fifteenth century.'
4 'To do away with the needless disguises, and, on the supposition of their *not* being genuine, to give them as far as possible in modern English.' (1: xxxviii–xxxix)

Skeat opts for the fourth:

> The last of these methods has been adopted. The process of thus re-writing the greater part of the poems has been rendered easier by frequently substituting Chatterton's words in his *footnotes* for the words in the *text.* (1: xxxix)

The question, however, is what does this modern English represent? It is not intended as a translation, for Skeat believes it is in fact the real poem:

> The actual language of these poems may be conveniently called the Rowleian dialect. It is a thing *per se*; but it is quite an error to suppose that it must have cost him much time to learn that it is difficult to compose in. It can be learnt, by a careful study of Kersey, in a few weeks; whilst the spelling is of that debased kind which prevails in *Chevy Chace* and *The Battle of Otterbourn* in Percy's *Reliques*, only a little more disguised. (1: xl–xli)

But what is the Rowleian dialect and what does it have to do with what might be called the 'actual' poem rather than the hypothetical real one?

> The reader has now a chance, *for the first time*, of judging what the poems are really like, without being continually pulled up, sometimes three times in a line, by hard words (1: xli)

According to this, 'what the poems are really like' does not involve the 'hard words' (for most readers, the most distinctive feature of the Rowley poems); such extraneous hard words are eliminated by 'the process of thus re-writing the greater part of the poems.'

What does this imply?

Skeat does not say he is simply translating the poems; he is rather allowing the reader to see what the poems are 'really' like. What they are 'really' like has apparently nothing to do with the Rowleian dialect in which the poems are written and in which Skeat himself (as well as Chatterton's most recent editor, Taylor) says that Chatterton has some fluency.

There seem to be multiple levels on which these poems exist:

1 what the poems are really like = Skeat's revision
2 Chatterton's 'first thoughts' = what is obscured by hard words
3 'the actual language' = the Rowleian dialect

According to this, the order of composition must be this: Chatterton's 'first thoughts,' the writing of those thoughts in 'ordinary expression,' the composition in the 'actual language' of the poems (that is, 'Rowleian dialect'), and finally the addition of 'hard words.' What Skeat is doing, then, is not translating (providing a fifth level, or a text four times removed from whatever the poem itself is). He is, rather, reconstructing an original poem. He is providing in 'ordinary expression,' access to Chatterton's 'first thoughts,' and the poem is a structure of ordinary language expressing such thoughts.

The Rowley poems, paradoxically, seem not to be written in Rowleian dialect. There is only one significant exception to this preposterous rule; hard words that rhyme are different from hard words that do not:

> But many words, especially at the end of the lines, had to be left. These are spelt as in the old editions, though occasionally made to look a little less bizarre. (1: xxxix–xl)

This principle can be seen in Skeat's version of 'Aella,' stanza 5. First, the version of the 1857 edition:

> To maydens, huswyfes, and unlored dames,
> Hee redes hys tales of merryment and woe.
> Loughe loudlie dynneth from the dolte adrames.

Skeat:

> To maidens, housewives, and unlearned dames,
> He reads his tales of merriment and woe.
> Laugh loudly dinneth from the dolt adrames.

Skeat's note on line 3 reads: 'Foolish churls. But dolt is a substantive, and the only authority for "adrames" is "adraming, churlist" in Bailey.' Because he needs a rhyme, Skeat cannot translate 'adrames' even though his note claims it is a solecism. However, these rhymes also contradict Skeat's notions of what the poem 'really' is. Chatterton could not write the poems in standard English and 'translate' them into Rowleian dialect. If there is such a thing as the Rowleian dialect, Chatterton's rhymes show that he composed his poems in that dialect, or at least in the words associated with it.

The case of Chatterton and Skeat is interesting not only for what it tells us of Skeat's attitude toward Chatterton. It also reveals editorial assumptions and techniques used in his once standard editions of Chaucer and Langland. What was the thing the editor was producing through what is now known as 'eclectic' editing? Was it something he was attempting to reconstruct out of the past? Or was it an ersatz past, imagined in the mind of the editor himself?

If we translate the sets of assumptions Skeat used for Chatterton to the situation for his medieval poems, we find the same problems arising: there are the poet's historical thoughts, and there is a coherent language (a correct grammar, one analysed by late nineteenth-century grammarians), a coherent set of rules regarding metre and rhymes, and there are potential poems composed in each of these forms.[50] Skeat's eclecticism, then, is not simply an eclecticism over manuscript readings, choice of base text, and selection of interesting variants. The eclecticism under which Skeat edits is much more radical, one in which the poem itself – the thing edited – moves freely between three, and sometimes four, specific and opposing historical and linguistic contexts.

7 Bibliographical Myths and Methods

This final chapter is in two sections. The first discusses a popular and amusing myth of book history: that in late nineteenth-century America, paper was manufactured with Egyptian mummy wrappings. It is an extreme example of the resistance of scholarly and bibliographical mythology to the very evidence that scholarly and bibliographical inquiry uncovers – a good case of the operation of 'urban mythology' in bibliographical studies. The particulars of this case may be more accessible than those discussed earlier, but the problem is the same. The myth of the mummy paper persists (as does much of the mythology I have discussed earlier of print culture) in part because that uncritical myth is interesting, coherent, and easily expressed – something that cannot be said about the masses of conflicting evidence that never quite cohere enough to support it. The second section, which is both the origin and conclusion to this study, states the problem I have discussed throughout in both its most general and its most personal terms.

7.1 The Curse of the Mummy Paper

One of the most popular books on papermaking is Dard Hunter's *Papermaking: The History and Technique of an Ancient Craft* (1943), a work that both sums up and adds to material Hunter gathered and compiled in earlier works. Hunter was primarily interested in papermaking as a craft, and the history Hunter presents as background has been characterized by John Bidwell as nostalgic.[1] An implied moral runs through Hunter's work, with the history of technological progress competing with the history of a decline in the paper making art. Thus an exotic history competes with a history of technological progress; early paper making in China, Egypt, Japan, and even America provides the initial steps in one history (a history of technology), and the allegorical goal of the other (a history of craft). Such a scheme provided a frame for the organization and presentation of a wealth of material, but little incentive to question specific historical details in which Hunter had only a passing interest.[2]

This chapter examines one such detail in that history. On pp. 382–7, Hunter somewhat casually provides evidence that in mid-nineteenth-century America, linen wrappings from mummies were used in commercial paper manufacture, and that serious proposals were set forth by those who believed that such wrappings could provide a cheap source of material for paper manufacture on a large scale. We hear of unlimited supplies of this material, cholera epidemics among rag workers, and the much-retailed notion that Egyptian railways used mummies for fuel – an anecdote that finds its way into a 1996 *New Yorker* article.[3] No such mummy paper has ever been discovered, and some of Hunter's sources are untraceable. Nonetheless, this appealing legend persists, and versions are found in standard paper histories both preceding and following Hunter; for example, Munsell (from which Hunter drew much of his material), Weeks, and even the 1987 monograph on New England paper making by McGaw.[4] Part 1 below surveys the background for this myth, both in paper history and in western Egyptology; part 2 examines the specific evidence brought by Hunter – an editorial in the Syracuse *Daily Standard* and a grand projection by one Isaiah Deck.

Material Shortages

The myth itself is consistent with a number of historical facts in paper history, most notably, the chronic shortages in materials. Until the late nineteenth century, paper shortages and the shortage of material for its manufacture seem to have been chronic in England (or at least were felt to be so) and, of course, in America. These shortages and the sense of crisis were especially acute in the 1850s, just prior to the introduction of wood pulp and the very moment when the myth of mummy paper developed.[5]

The history of the search for alternative fibres has been told many times, with one of the best surveys in Hunter's own book.[6] There are several major figures in this history: René Antoine Ferchault de Réaumur, who speculated in 1719 that paper could be made from wood, as wasps make their paper (Hunter, *Papermaking*, 314–16); Jacob Christian Schäffer,

whose series of pamphlets from 1765 to 1771 contained actual specimens of paper made from various materials (Hunter, *Papermaking*, 320–
3); and finally, Matthias Koop (1800), whose historical survey of alternate
materials is itself printed in part on paper made from straw.[7] There are
numerous minor figures as well, who hypothesized, like Swiftian Projectors, that paper could be made of everything from caterpillar cocoons to
cow dung.[8]

In the mid-nineteenth century, the search became more serious. The
paper historian Richard Herring claimed in 1856 that in England, the
annual consumption of rags was 120,000 tons, three-quarters of which
was imported.[9] Herring describes the 'agitation of late ... that there was a
great scarcity of fibrous materials fit to be used in paper making' (54),
and notes further that these shortages may have been more imagined
than real, since the price in paper actually declined: 'During the most
exciting period of last year, the scarcity so much talked of, was, in fact,
comparatively trifling' (59). The central motif in these histories of shortages is the offer by the London *Times* in 1855 of £1000 for the discovery
of a new paper-making material – an offer Herring saw as being partly
responsible for the crisis.[10] Interestingly, it is precisely at this date, according to Munsell, that 'Egyptian rags' made an appearance in America,
at a cost of between 3 and 4 cents per pound (*Chronology*, 144).

From a purely technological standpoint, most of the materials proposed during the nineteenth century as a base for making paper could
be so used. Seaweed, straw, corn husks, asbestos, wood pulp and, of
course, mummy wrappings – all will do. Mummy wrappings, however,
have a different cultural value from most of these; in the late twentieth
century we all understand quite clearly (and quite perversely) that making paper out of wood and even rocks is somehow more reasonable.

The Egyptian Connection

The earliest reference to the making of paper from mummy wrappings
is from Abd al-Latif (the transliteration of this name varies wildly), a
Baghdad physician of the late twelfth century. The anecdote, found in
many standard paper histories, concerns the Bedouins' theft of these
wrappings:

> There are, however, circumstances which really contribute to strengthen
> their covetousness ... They occasionally discover, under ground, vast cav-
> erns of very solid construction, containing an immense number of corpses,

deposited there at some very distant period. The corpses are enveloped in winding-sheets of hempen cloth; for some of them, more than a thousand yards have been employed ... The Bedouins, the Arabs established on the cultivated lands, and all those who employ themselves in search of these sepulchral caves, carry away the winding-sheets and every thing which continues to possess a sufficient consistency; these they employ in making dresses, or sell to the manufacturers of paper, who use them in the fabric of paper for the grocers.[11]

Like most scholars who have referred to this, paraphrased it, or quoted it in one of its various translations, I have no competence to judge its date or authenticity. The anecdote appears in numerous important studies: Hunter's *Papermaking*, Karabacek's *Das arabische Papier*, and most important for English scholars, Thomas Pettigrew's *History of Egyptian Mummies* of 1834.[12] No further contemporary evidence is cited in support, and much of this description is second-hand ('I have been told that ...' etc.). In addition, even what little context I have for this text shows that the statement is part of a general satire against greed. The author is criticizing those who turn everything, even mummies, into money: 'Among those covetous men of whom I speak, some ... have lost all they possessed in these fruitless researches ...' etc.[13]

Mummies had been part of the 'prodigies' of Egypt to Western travellers for some time, but the interest seemed confined to the drug presumably extracted from them.[14] Among the descriptions of visits to the mummy pits prior to the nineteenth century, there seems no support for the anecdote of the Baghdad doctor or even mention of it.[15] The bandages appear to have no value and the Arab guides, much complained about, are never credited with suggesting a use for them to gullible Western visitors.[16] The most that is said about the bandages in early descriptions is that they are prodigiously long. John Greaves in 1646 speaks from experience and authority, combining the usual authorities (Herodotus) with his own observations. Greaves speaks of the 'fillets' in which Herodotus says the bodies were wrapped: 'Of these Ribbands I have seen some so strong, and perfect, as if they had been made but yesterday. With these they bound, and swathed the dead body, beginning with the head, and ending with the feet: over these again they wound others, so often one upon another, that there could not be lesse then a thousand els upon one body.'[17] The heavily subscribed and much more lavish account of Thomas Greenhille, *Nekrokedeia* (1705), repeats the figure from Greaves: 'There could not be less than a 1000 ells upon one body.'[18] A more scholarly and accurate work, even more lavish than Greenhill's, is Pococke, *A Description of the East and Some other Countries*, vol. 1, *Observations on Egypt* (1743). Pococke speaks in great detail of the bandages, distinguishing, as others do not, between the bandages that can be removed and those inner layers which are essentially destroyed (232). Pettigrew in 1834 is generally credited with being more scientific, and on p. 56 notes with apparent precision and exactitude that Davidson's mummy had nine yards of cloth, three inches wide, stuffed in the head. However, in his chapter 7, 'On the Bandages,' the same figure found in Greaves appears: 'In some there are 1000 elles; other sources say over 1000 yards' (89).[19]

As for the value of the bandages, Pettigrew's section, 'On Deceptive Specimens of Mummies' (227–30) is suggestive. Pettigrew says he has bought three mummies; two were fake. The method used in their manufacture, a common one according to Pettigrew, was to cover fake mummies with real bandages (228). Since the price of these 'well-wrapped mummies' could run into the thousands, a shrewd businessman might be reluctant to part with such materials for the mere 3 cents per pound that rags for paper making would fetch.[20]

Dard Hunter and Mummy Paper

Hunter cites a series of anecdotes in support of mummy paper. The most important is an editorial from the Syracuse *Daily Standard* of 19 August 1856, quoted in extenso:

> An Onondaga county man, worshipful of the golden Eagle and not of the Egyptian Ibis, has put upon the market 'paper made from the wrappings of mummies.' Could anything better illustrate the practical character of this age, and the intense materialism of America? With an intense materialism that shears right through sentiment, and world's ideas and usages, this American sees fibre in all the mummied dead of Egypt ...

Hunter's note refers to Munsell:

> Munsell ... states that the Syracuse *Standard* 'boasted' that one of its issues was printed on paper made from the wrappings of Egyptian mummies. A diligent search through the files of this publication did not reveal a copy of this newspaper printed on paper manufactured from this unusual material. The only reference to mummy paper found in the files of the *Standard* was

the article of 1856 (herewith given), and this was reprinted from the Albany *Journal.*

The full Munsell quotation, not given by Hunter, is as follows:

> The Syracuse *Standard* boasted that its issue was printed on paper made of rags imported directly from the land of the Pharaohs, on the banks of the Nile. These were said to have been stripped from the mummies. (*Chronology*, 149)

Munsell must be mistaken, as Hunter realized. The *Standard* was not printed on mummy paper, nor did it ever claim it was. Nonetheless, the clearly false statement led only to further collaboration. Hunter's note on p. 383 continues:

> These two references led to an investigation of the making of mummy paper in New York State, and through the interest of Miss Ida Benderson of the Syracuse University Library the Syracuse *Post-Standard* reprinted the original 1856 story in its issue of December 22, 1940. This article brought forth a communication from Mrs. John Ramsey of Syracuse, the interesting contents of which are here set down: 'Upon reading the article in the *Post-Standard* recently about paper made of wrapping from mummies, I am reminded of a story told me about forty years ago by an old friend of my father. His name was Dr. Myron K. Waite ... Dr. Waite said that when he was a young man (about 1855–1860) he worked in a paper mill in Broadalbin where they received great bundles of old linen wrappings from Egyptian mummies, which they made into paper. He said that the rolled-up vestments retained the shape of the mummy, so that when the workmen tried to straighten or unroll the "cocoon," as it might be called, it sprang back at once into the shape of the mummy it had encased so long. He described the material as cream-coloured linen and fragments of the embroidery still retained on some of the edges, somewhat like modern cross-stitch borders.'

The evidence Hunter cites on the preceding page is also a product of oral history. The following concerns I. Augustus Stanwood, who opened a mill in Maine in 1869, and some of the information here is supported by the New York obituaries Hunter refers to:

> The information here set down regarding the mummy paper was given to me by Stanwood's son, Daniel, a retired professor of international law ...

During the Civil War, according to Professor Stanwood, his father was
pressed for raw material ... [He responded] by importing mummies from
Egypt for the sole purpose of stripping the dried bodies of their cloth
wrappings and using the material for making paper. Professor Stanwood
informed me that his father brought several shiploads of mummies to his
mill in Gardiner, Maine, and threw the woven wrappings as well as the
papyrus filling into beaters and manufactured from these substances a
coarse brown wrapping paper, which eventually found its way into the
shops of grocers, butchers, and other merchants who used paper of this
kind.

So far, the testimony of Prof. Stanwood seems a dubious narrative built
on two facts: the shortage of paper, and the importation of Egyptian rags
during the mid-century. Although a classicist might cringe, the professor
of international law was unruffled by the thought of papyrus fragments
being ground up in a Maine hollander. Hunter continues:

It was further stated that the rags stripped from the long-dead Egyptians
caused an epidemic of cholera among the rag-pickers and cutters in the
Maine mill, for at that period there was no regulation regarding the
disinfection of rags. Professor Stanwood also related that the only competi-
tion his father encountered in purchasing the mummies was the Egyptian
railroad, for during a ten-year period the locomotives of Egypt made use of
no other fuel than that furnished by the well-wrapped, compact mummies,
the supply of which was thought at the time to be almost unlimited.

In a pamphlet serving as a guide to a paper exhibit in 1950, Hunter
much embellishes this anecdote. The actual sample that instigates the
telling of this anecdote is of papyrus (no. 2, cabinet 1). Again, no specific
source is given; I assume some details are from Stanwood *fils*:

About 1860, in Gardiner, Maine, an enterprising papermaker named I.
Augustus Stanwood found it increasingly difficult to obtain rags for operating his mill which manufactured a coarse brown wrapping paper. Stanwood
had his agent in Cairo buy for him a vast quantity of Egyptian mummies
which in turn were thrown into the hulls of American ships and brought to
the nearest Maine port where they were unloaded and transported to the
Gardiner mill by oxcart. It is stated that the mummy cloth and the wrappings of papyrus were stripped by women workers from the dried bodies
and cast into the beaters where the fibrous material was reduced to a pulp

suitable for the making of brown wrapping paper. In removing the rags and cutting them into small usable pieces the women of the village developed a dread sickness that no local doctor could diagnose and eventually a frightful epidemic broke out in the community. It was this pestilence that was thought to have originally supplied the impetus for the U.S. government to demand that thereafter all imported rags be sterilized ... The brown wrapping paper, made from the wrappings of the Egyptian mummies, had a ready sale among the grocers and butchers of the vicinity. During the years from 1850 until 1860 the Egyptian government used no other fuel for their locomotives than the well dried mummies and in the purchase of this unusual paper making material Stanwood was forced to bid against the manager of the railroad. At that period it was thought that the supply of mummies was inexhaustible, but at the present time a well preserved mummy is worth from twenty-five to a hundred dollars, F. O. B. Cairo, a price much too high for the modern papermaker.[21]

The Egyptian railroad story is one still alive, as the joke retold in *The New Yorker* article proves. Obviously, the joke will have a different force with each telling (and it is not at all clear that *The New Yorker* writer understands the precise irony involved). It may be, as is the editorial from the *Standard* and as is the first story from Abd al-Latif, a Tacitean satire about materialism. Or it may be a simpler joke. The great period of Egyptian railroad building was in the 1850s and 1860s.[22] The joke may be that in an earlier decade, Egyptian locomotives are themselves mythical and could have been fueled by ambrosia. A more likely source for Prof. Stanwood is Mark Twain, in *Innocents Abroad* (1869):

I certainly shall not tell the hackneyed story of the massacre of the Mamelukes, because I am glad the lawless rascals were massacred ... I shall not tell any thing about the strange, strange city of Cairo, because it is only a repetition, a good deal intensified and exaggerated, of the Oriental cities I have already spoken of ... I shall not speak of the railway, for it is like any other railway – I shall only say that the fuel they use for the locomotive is composed of mummies three thousand years old, purchased by the ton or by the graveyard for that purpose, and that sometimes one hears the profane engineer call out pettishly, 'D—n these plebeians, they don't burn worth a cent – pass out a King!'

Twain adds in a note: 'Stated to me for a fact. I only tell it as I got it. I am willing to believe it. I can believe any thing.'[23]

Hunter's most bizarre source is given on pages 384–5: 'In 1855 ... a New York scientist, Dr. Isaiah Deck, compiled a manuscript in which he advanced the idea that the wrappings of Egyptian mummies could be used in making paper' (*Papermaking*, 384). I have not been able to locate this 'manuscript,' nor is there anything in Hunter's published writings to offer any guidance.[24] I am quite willing to concede that this manuscript exists exactly dated and exactly written as Hunter claims, but if so, he has been snookered. The quotations from Hunter begin with references to Pettigrew about the weight of linen from individual mummies (over 3 pounds).

> The supply of linen rags would not be limited to the mummies of the human species alone; independent of that obtainable from this source, a more than equal amount of cloth could be depended on from the mummies of the sacred bulls, crocodiles, ibides, and cats, as all of these animals were embalmed and swatched in a superior quality of linen ... some bandages, from 5 inches to 5 feet wide and 9 yards long, have been stripped from mummies their entire length without tearing.

Hunter continues, still quoting Deck:

> The question, Will it pay? may be readily answered by assuming the value of rags to be from 4 to 6 cents per pound; in the United States this is considered under the market estimate of fine linen rags; the cost of purchasing, collecting, and transportation of the Egyptian material would be under 3 cents per pound.

According to repeated entries in Munsell's *Chronology*, this is not an unreasonable price for rags. In 1850, the average price of imported rags is given as 3.61 cents per pound, although in 1854, the price of paper is 2½ cents per pound. In 1855, the year of the *Times* offer, there is a half-cent price rise. Also in 1855, Munsell lists the arrival of Egyptian rags (a cargo of 1215 bales), at a price of 4 and 3⅜ cents per pound (were these headed for Gardiner, Maine?).

Deck is quite specific, stating that 405 million pounds of rags are required in the U.S. (the figure is a bit extravagant; Munsell lists under 10 million pounds imported in 1846 and 1847, and 10 and 26 million pounds imported in 1850 and 1851). Apparent precision, in such arguments, is more important than a precise relation to fact. The final sentence Hunter cites from Deck's compilation concerns the ancillary benefits of this importation scheme:

The substances used in the process of embalming would be far more valuable than the swathing cloths – aromatic gums of the rarest and most expensive qualities, and such as are now used in preparing incenses for the Catholic Church: olibanum, labdanum, issoponax, ambergris, etc.

The suggestion that the Catholic Church might substitute mummy for their current incense should have warned Hunter that something was amiss. The inspiration for such proposals is obvious; it is Swift's 'Modest Proposal':

Infant's flesh will be in season throughout the year, but more plentiful in March, and a little before and after. For we are told by a grave author, an eminent French physician, that fish being a prolific diet, there are more children born in Roman Catholic countries about nine months after Lent than at any other season.

Those portions of Deck's 'compilation' quoted by Hunter all have precedent in Swift. References to thrift: 'a fair, cheap, and easy method.' Concern with alleviating shortages: 'Those who are more thrifty (as I must confess the times require) may flay the carcass ...' Precision: 'Of the hundred and twenty thousand children, already computed, twenty thousand may be reserved for breed, whereof only one fourth part to be males ...' And anti-Catholic satire: 'It will have one other collateral advantage, by lessening the number of Papists among us.' Deck has written this manuscript in the spirit of the Projectors of Book 3 of *Gulliver's Travels*, who propose extracting sunbeams from cucumbers, or reducing excrement to its original components.

It is probably this treatise of Dr Deck that serves as the source for another reference listed in Hunter's 'Chronology,' under the date 1855: 'About this time Egyptian mummies were imported to America, the wrappings and other fibres to be used in making of wrapping paper for grocers, butchers, etc.' (*Papermaking*, 557). This reference is cross-referenced by his earlier entry under 1140: 'A physician of Baghdad writes of the source of the wrapping paper used by the grocers ...' the much-cited anecdote from Abd al-Latif. Hunter has conflated his sources here. The 1855 date is one from Deck's 'manuscript' and also the date given by Munsell for the importation of Egyptian *rags*, 'said to be' from mummies. The 1856 date is from the Syracuse *Standard*; the most emphatic reference to actual importation of mummy cloth is by Stanwood, whose father's mill was not begun until 1863.[25]

The references to mummy paper have much in common: first, they are vaguely documented or pure products of oral history. The copy of the *Standard* printed on mummy paper cannot be found; Deck's manuscript compilation can be quoted, but no published source I know of specifies its origin or whereabouts; the importing of Egyptian mummies by a Maine paper mill is known only in a second-hand account, as is the 1940s statement of other mills using mummy paper. Second, they have the aura of a Swiftian projection, based on real needs – the chronic shortages of material. Third, nearly all of the supposed original writers have clear satiric intentions: Abd al-Latif is criticizing the Bedouins, who are willing to convert anything to money. The exact same stance is assumed by the *Standard* editorial – the commercialization of mummy wrappings is an example of crass American materialism. Deck's projection has the same target: exaggerated thrift and the extravagance of Catholic ceremonies. Many arise during the mid-nineteenth century, when Barnum is making a living from the American quest for the exotic; if there was ever a time, prior to Tut-mania, that Americans were susceptible to a myth of mummy paper, this would be it.[26]

The myths are persistent. I have discussed this with a number of paper historians, and all claim to have heard it. Most deny that their source is Munsell or Hunter (one, the most eminent, concedes that the source is 'probably Munsell' but allows that he would 'like to believe it is true').[27]

It may well be that paper was made of mummy wrappings, and that people in Gardiner, Maine, during the 1850s, just like the Egyptians of the twelfth century, carried their groceries about in mummy-unguented grocery bags. It may also be that there were serious efforts to inquire into the economics of importing this material. In the hopes of eliciting some of the thus far elusive evidence, I will here state the sceptical case in its strongest sense: an occasional supporting fact for a myth or legend cannot entirely repair the flimsy foundation for that myth. An alligator may one day be found in the New York sewers, but those who believe that these critters are there should not feel vindicated if one is wrestled to the surface. Those who believe in alien abductions should not feel they are less than crazed should a visitor from Mars, much to the relief of us all, finally spirit a handful of them off. In the case here, 'all the instruments agree' that in nineteenth-century America, mummies provided the materials for paper making, and it is quite possible, I suppose, that a reasonable explanation for such a consensus is that it is true. I am personally inclined to conclude the opposite: when all the authorities agree, they are far more apt to be suffering under the same delusion.

Addendum: Note on Cholera and the Wiscasset Mummy

One of the recurrent motifs in this history is a cholera epidemic in Gardiner, Maine, caused by the use of mummy rags in paper mills. I have spent some time in search of the evidence that such an event occurred. I admit that I am not entirely certain what 'cholera' might mean in these contexts, particularly a cholera that 'no local doctor could diagnose,' but if the disease referred to is the disease now known as cholera, both the cause and the possible association with paper making are fairly clear: the disease is carried by feces, and until the invention of paper pulp, the standard material for making paper was rags, that is, underwear. The connection is obvious. No doubt mummy wrappings also can contain diseases, and perhaps one should stay clear of them. But they would not cause cholera in the strict sense. Therefore, if there had been a cholera epidemic in Gardiner that originated with paper workers, it is likely that ordinary rags and not mummy wrappings were the cause.

Was there such an epidemic?

In the City of Gardiner 'Mayor's Address and Annual Reports' for Gardiner from 1851 to 1859, there is no mention of any epidemic until 1859, when we hear of a 'confluent form of small pox': 'In April small pox broke out in the thick settled part of Water Street near the New Mills.' The Physician's reports included in these pamphlets for 1861 and 1867 are specific on the absence of disease:

[1861] There has been no epidemic or contageous disease among the inmates of the Almshouse ...

[1867] The inmates of the Alms-house, and the poor of the city, have been very free from disease during the past year; no case of cholera, small-pox, or other contagious diease has required treatment by me.

Unless the 1859 'confluent form of small pox' was that special mummy-related variety no local physical could diagnose, cholera was not a major problem in Gardiner. In the 1880s and 1890s, there are better statistics on health available, due to the surge in government publications, itself a function of the availability of pulp paper. The First Annual State Board of Health report, dated 1886, includes a section on cholera, a disease which apparently did make an appearance in Maine:

> In 1849, this disease appeared in Bangor and there resulted 320 cases of decided cholera. Dr. S.B. Morrison, who was at the time City Physician, sends a very interesting account of the epidemic. In 1854 this disease appears in Richmond ... Bath, Biddeford, Castine, Damariscotta, and Lewiston.

I am reasonably familiar with these towns, those said to have been afflicted with cholera in 1854, and, with the exception of Lewiston, they are not major mill towns. If there had been an epidemic associated with paper mills in the Richmond / Bath area, it would have occurred in Brunswick. But paper making was not responsible for the epidemics in these towns, nor was it so considered. There is little doubt as to the origin of the disease, as proved by the section 'Practical Facts about Cholera' (24ff.), which speaks of 'discharges of bowels and vomitted matter' (25), and 'articles of clothing' imported from Holland, Sweden, and Russia, clothing responsible for the epidemic of 1873. There is no mention of the dreaded medium of mummies.[28]

In these annual reports, there are two reports concerning Gardiner, the first by W.P. Giddings, MD (161–3). Giddings reports on the last six years, and speaks only of smallpox: 'The last time in 1880. It has been brought in the rag used in our paper mills more frequently than any other way.' The following report is by A.F. Plimpton, MD, also of Gardiner, who speaks specifically of cholera:

> Cholera morbus, cholera infantum and diarrhoea are usually more or less prevalent during every summer and fall. In the past 27 years ... that I have been practising medicine here I think we have had Small-Pox and varioloid in this town about 10 times, the cases numbering from one to twenty-five each time. The origin of this infection has almost always been exposure to some persons affected with the disease or from handling old rags in the paper mills. (163)

Plimpton claims not to recall any epidemic of cholera since 1860. Again, any such infections related to paper mills would have been caused by the handling of ordinary rags, not mummies. It is hard to believe that wagonloads of infectious mummy wrappings would have escaped these witnesses; the source richest in detail remains the anecdotal account of Daniel Stanwood as told by Dard Hunter.

Shortly after the original version of this paper trying to debunk the mummy paper myth, further events promoting that myth were taking place in Maine, that hotbed of urban mythology. In the fall of 1996, CBS Sunday Morning with Bill Geist reported on Mr Terry Lewis, owner of an antiques store in Wiscasset. For as long as I remember visiting this establishment, there has been a mummy in a glass case just inside the main door. The mummy is interesting, but less interesting than its owner. The rest of the story depends on who one happens to hear tell it, and on the mood that person is in. In one version of the story, the Egyptian authorities in 1996 demanded that Mr Lewis return the mummy as a national artifact. Mr Lewis refused and threatened then to throw it off the Wiscasset bridge in protest (the Egyptian authorities, of course, would have had no way of knowing what an idle threat that was, summer traffic in Wiscasset at the time making all access to the bridge impossible).

The *Lincoln County Weekly*, 22 August 1996, 'Mummy Roils Media Madness,' recounts this story, and quotes Mr Lewis as saying: 'Around the turn of the century rags were hard to come by. Sailors used to buy mummies just for the wrappings, rags that were used to make paper.' I cannot remember who referred me to the *Lincoln County Weekly* report, but I believe the reference came to me along with several communications by people claiming to have found the evidence of mummy paper that I could not find (in each case, the ultimate source was Dard Hunter). In any event, in the summer of 1998, I drove to Wiscasset and asked Mr Lewis where he had heard that particular story. He denied ever having heard it or having referred to it.

In July of 2000, I again drove to the Wiscasset / Damariscotta area, thinking to recheck back issues of the *Lincoln County Weekly*. There turned out to be no need, since the perfect bibliography on the matter exists in Wiscasset, where I stopped, waiting for the traffic on the bridge to quiet down. Mr Lewis has all of the newspaper clippings related to the incident taped in perfect chronological order on the walls surrounding the mummy case in the entryway to his antiques store. His quotation is featured prominently on A4 of the 22 August 1996 issue of the *Lincoln County Weekly*, as I have given it above. There is little mention of mummy paper in further clippings, those from the *Portland Press Herald* or the *New York Times*, for example. However, *USA Today*, 11 September 1996, has an interesting embellishment:

Legend has it that Maine paper companies imported mummies by the ton in the 1800s. The bodies were unceremoniously discarded, legend says. Folklorists have tried to debunk the tale, but archaeologists insist there's truth to it.

My article 'The Curse of the Mummy Paper' appeared in 1995, and I believe in my e-mail files there is at least one message from someone connected with a news agency, a message sent before the *USA Today* article appeared. *USA Today* researchers are aggressive and well paid, but evidently so are their editors. The reference to 'folklorists' and 'archaeologists' is curious. Wouldn't it be the archaeologist who would debunk such a myth? the folklorist who would seek some level of truth in it? In all my research, I never found one archaeologist or folklorist who had the slightest thing to say about mummy paper. Just who are these archaeologists and folklorists? Only the copy-editors know for sure, but I assume these copy-editors felt that *USA Today* readers would not be much moved by references to 'paper historians' and chose as a euphemism these more reputable professions.

It is time to turn to Mr Lewis again. Mr Lewis is an extraordinary and brilliant man, with a very interesting and exotic career in the merchant marines; he was a raconteur of no small notoriety even before his mummy made national news. A more sober report from the *Lincoln County Weekly*, now of 5 September 1996, states of the CBS Sunday Morning show: 'At times it seemed that Lewis and Geist were engaged in a comedy act ...' In my second trip to Wiscasset, in July 2000, Mr Lewis not only claimed to remember our earlier conversation, but gave me a complete history of the mummy paper myth, a myth two years earlier he had denied knowing at all. In *Down East Magazine* of, oh, twenty years ago, there was a story of a ship sailing from the 'east Med' (i.e., the eastern Mediterranean); like many ships of that period on that route, it was full of mummies. In fact, ships sailing from the east Med 'always topped off with mummies,' although this fact 'is not generally known in Maine.' On one ship, 1500 mummies were used in the boilers. In England, 'hundreds of thousands were shipped as fertilizer' (think of *that* when munching on your next Brussels sprout). Taped to the wall behind Mr Lewis is a yellowing slip of paper – mummy paper? – no, just a scrap torn from a newspaper margin – this a reference to a phone call ... from someone near Boston, 'Old Mansion Company' – whose father's friends 'always had a pile of mummies out back' for paper making. And we thought (we?) that that practice had ended forty years earlier, with the invention of pulp. Maybe the area code for that number has changed ...

More details; more evidence. Mr Lewis is only the second person I have encountered who can quote the passage from Mark Twain's *Innocents Abroad* dealing with Egyptian locomotive fuel. The cholera epidemic in Gardiner was in 1855, during a period when there were 'wagon trains of mummies miles long' heading from Portland to Gardiner. Again, a fact 'not generally known in Maine.' A woman enters, half our age. I am close to forgotten. He laughs. 'I'd like to see a manifest on those things!' he says; 'You know, all merchant ships had to carry manifests of their cargoes.' (Does his tone mean that he thinks that manifests and mummies are equally difficult to document?) He laughs again. 'Hell, I'd like to see the manifest even on the one in the hallway!' The origin of that mummy, one the Egyptian government has now left in peace, is also obscure. I leave, now fully forgotten.

7.2 The History of Irony as a Problem in Descriptive Bibliography

The history of irony, and of many literary-critical concepts, can be seen in two ways.[29] The traditional way involves what I will call the academic method: here, the first step is to define one's terms – 'What is irony?'; the second step is to find examples of this new definition. This method can support histories of particular concepts (for example, 'romantic irony'); it can also support what I will call the 'culture of readings' of modern literary study, about which I will say more later. In *The Critical Mythology of Irony*, I tried to develop a different approach, one that I described as 'critical.' Under this method, the subject of discussion (in this case 'irony') is defined as a word, not a phenomenon. What is at issue is the history of the word and the implications such a word has in our reading of literature. How, for example, does the labelling of a work as 'ironic' change the nature of the work itself?

Most serious discussions of irony have of course critical elements and I do not wish to imply otherwise. Many begin with histories of the word, citations of early uses, and most acknowledge that the history of the word is problematic. But the difficulties encountered here are rarely seen as essential to the discussion of the presumed reality of irony; they are rather seen as mere linguistic infelicities, the predictable products of our post-lapsarian critical language. And radical though many histories of irony claim to be, the operative assumption in all that I have read is the same: that there is in the real world (the world of literature) a genre or technique that has rightfully been identified as 'irony,' and it is job of the literary critic to clarify the relation between the critical language and these works. Why assume this? My own work begins with an opposing assumption: that there is nothing in the real world or the literary world properly called 'ironic,' nor any phenomenon properly called 'irony.' To discover anything interesting about irony, one needs to assume it does not exist. To write a history of irony then is to limit oneself to real evidence rather than imaginary evidence, that is to say, specific invocations of the word itself. This is the only way I see to avoid the circularity of literary critical discussion – the analysis of increasingly subtle varieties of increasingly subtle critical concepts.

In literary-critical terms, the problem is purely textual – the mapping of critical terminology onto textual artifacts. While some scholars may revel in that, others, including myself, have attempted to escape, by turning to problems of physical books and what seems to be their comforting materiality. In the final pages here, I will consider the biblio-graphical analogue to the literary-critical history of such terms and concepts, that is, the rules of descriptive bibliography bearing specifi-cally on the cataloguing of books printed during the hand-press period, or, perhaps more appropriately, 'books printed prior to the rise of romantic irony.'

The entry in a book or library catalogue, whether in the form of an index card or computer screen, is an extremely problematic piece of evidence, and it is one that literary scholars confront daily. In a catalogue for a particular library, the primary meaning of the card is clear. Mislead-ing though the library card may be, it is an index, a finding aid. It refers to a physical object housed in the library, let us say, a copy of the 1952 edition of Beckett's *En attendant Godot.* What is disturbing about the library card is not its function, but its method – the curious convention-ality of the description, a description that is clearly intended to make that card similar to other cards in other libraries, cards that refer to different physical objects; *other* copies of the 1952 edition of *En attendant Godot*; later editions of the same play; the 1954 Grove Press edition of *Waiting for Godot.* We interpret the conventionality of these cards as a reference to a real phenomenon, or intention, in the real world. There was a writer named Beckett who wrote a play (varied, as we know, in every performance) that we call *Godot*; various printing firms undertook to produce editions at different times. Each of these editions produces a series of interchangeable objects to be distributed among owners and libraries. The conventionality of that library card is thus a reflection of a set of conventional assumptions: that every object that comes from the Grove Press during the press run of 1954 is somehow 'the same'; that all the editions produced over time are variants of the same text; that the biological entity Samuel Beckett whose name appears on the first edition is the same biological entity whose name appears on the title page of the most recent imprint, and that somehow his literary or authorial sameness transcends the biological facts of his growth and death.

With earlier books, we have a variant of the same problem. As anyone knows who has used books from the pre-romantic-irony period, the uniqueness of each book-copy asserts itself at every turn. Books were changed during the press run. Books were bound differently. Mistakes were made. Unless the book cataloguer falls into despair and defines his catalogue as a mere index of singular objects, that cataloguer must construct a conventional description. How does one describe, for example, the sameness of a book in the British Library and one in the Bibliothèque Nationale, in the face of obvious differences in materiality? And what would a book dealer tell a client who claimed: 'I don't need *that* Shakespeare folio dated 1623; I have the *same* book dated 1664.' The result of these negotiations are the rules of descriptive bibliography. In Anglo-American bibliography particularly, these descriptions are focused on the notion of 'ideal copy' or 'an ideal copy' – a phrase whose horrific ambiguities in English are most easily seen when it requires translation.

Each early book has its own singularities: missing quires, sophisticated title pages, printing errors, etc. The ideal copy description is intended to filter out these singularities: the description is based on printers' hypothetical intentions, or more precisely a highly idealized version of these intentions. Suppose the evidence suggests that the printer intended, say, a press run of 1000 copies and that a year later, many of these were unsold. If the printer produced a second title page to sell off these remaining copies, we have two 'issues.' If the printer decided to add two or three chapters, and revise and reprint significant portions of the unsold books, we have two separate 'editions.' When the changes we find are merely the correction of routine printer's errors, however, then we have mere variant 'states.' Among its many virtues, descriptive bibliography provides a norm against which certain objects can be measured. Is this book that I hold, one lacking a title page, a copy of the 1623 Shakespeare folio? or the 1664 folio? The page numbers are entirely disturbed. Is this disturbance a fact of printing processes? or a product of later history (provenance)?

One of the most intriguing aspects of these books and their place in what I will call contemporary bibliographical culture concerns the irreducible singularities of each book-copy; its binding, its marks of provenance, its structure, its paper – all challenge at every turn the ideal copy description. Yet that book cannot be discussed without some form of ideal copy description. Without the description, preposterous as it may be, there is no variation.

I would like to return now to the question of irony and what I called the 'culture of readings' of contemporary literary scholarship. On the one hand, if I accept and support the obvious absurdities of descriptive bibliography (and I do), I seem to lend support to the traditional reception of irony and other critical concepts. 'The definition of irony,' one might argue, 'is of course provisional and arbitrary: it promotes the real work of the literary scholar, which is study of the individual work. It is the same as your bibliographical "ideal copy."' That may well be true, but if any form of that argument could convince me, I would now be well into volume 2 of my work on irony, and would never have allowed myself to be distracted by the insecurities of book history.

Bibliographers are necessarily taxonomists, and they are taxonomists of objects (extremely valuable ones) that exist in the real world. The descriptive bibliographer who decided that descriptive bibliography could proceed without reference to the real world of books and book dealers would soon have nothing to discuss. Book owners or scholars of early books who decided to ignore the intricacies of descriptive bibliography and deal only with the singularities of particular collections would quickly find themselves absorbed into other taxonomic communities, communities interested in the history of particular libraries, the history of bindings, the history of paper manufacture. Without such communities, the singular object not only has no value, it has no meaning and thus is of no interest.

The ideal copy description serves different functions for the different communities: book owners, of course, are enmeshed in the peculiar system of value associated with the institution of collecting – a system involving such indefinable concepts as 'association,' 'marketability,' and 'rarity' – that is, the singularity that increases value also threatens value. Something that cannot be 'exchanged' cannot be sold. These are of course interesting problems, but they are not those of primary concern to the bibliographer: to the bibliographer, descriptions are valid to the degree to which they reflect the present array of extant copies and the more banal history of printing house records and implied historical intentions of moderately intelligent, and (as external evidence proves) often inebriated workmen. Without some notion of these historical ba- nalities, a bibliographical taxonomy has no more intellectual value than, say, the shelf on the book collector's wall (one of far greater monetary value) containing 'books bound in red covers.'

These problems interest me greatly, and I am particularly struck by the gap between the sophistication and intricacy of modern bibliography and the irritatingly complex 'banality' of its objects. Any printer can decide to increase a press run, or change paper stocks, without even considering the end product, but to the modern bibliographer, this has to be interpreted in terms of rational intentions, and it must be demon- strated in actual physical objects in libraries. Is this not the same, one might argue, as the situation confronting the modern literary critic? Any ironist can substitute one word for another, but it is the task of the academic critic of irony to describe this in terms of rationalities.

It would be an overly romantic view, but an easy one, to describe this apparent analogue between the bibliographer and the literary critic in terms of the materiality of objects. There are literary taxonomies (of, say, irony), and literary objects of those taxonomies (literary works, or rather, literary works interpreted in terms of the taxonomy). The difference is simply that the bibliographer acts under the constraints of physical objects, rather than textual ones, and these physical objects have an irreducible immobility that the textual objects of literary criticism do not. Thus, my own method in *Critical Mythology of Irony* was simply to assume that the critical taxonomy might as well be considered in its own terms: its presumed objects were textual and abstract, not material. Literary works may indeed exist, for all I know, but 'ironic' works are purely a mirage – a product of the taxonomy.

However, the literary critic and scholar of irony is in my opinion facing a much deeper crisis, and this has to do with the participation in what in America has become (or perhaps always has been) the 'culture of read- ings' characteristic of contemporary literary scholarship. As has been often pointed out, any method based on 'readings' or in the service of readings is inevitably self-validating. The fact that particular readings of Rabelais, Goethe, Marx, Sterne, or Flaubert are interesting (and how could they not be?) has nothing whatsoever to do with the validity of the method used to produce those readings. Most of these readings and the academic methods that produce them doubtless promote the Common Good, whether it be political, ideological, intellectual, or aesthetic. It is certainly a comfort to know, for example, that Elizabethan theatre was produced under the auspices of a powerful queen named Elizabeth, or that Rabelais often used obscenity. It is also, doubtless, of great social import to be reminded that there are gay themes in the plays of Oscar Wilde. But the literary scholar who deals with these subjects in the public sphere is in grave danger of becoming merely a highly paid, socially respectable circus performer. And as most literary scholars have more than once discovered, there is no use arguing with a clown over whether he should wear polka-dots, stripes, or perhaps nothing at all.

Conclusion

When I look at the books on my shelf, I see that I have organized them much as a late nineteenth-century auction catalogue might have organized them. I know that I am supposed to be interested in their contents, or at least in the material aspects of their production and construction, of their imprint and date, and yet what I see, materialized on my shelves, are the same categories that appear so quaint in the auction catalogues: folios, large quartos, small quartos, octavos. In that folio section, a few books lie on their sides, too large for the shelf. A few are upright, indistinguishable from the large eighteenth-century quartos. In smaller format, there are a few sets, valuable insofar as they are complete; it takes a few moments for me to remember what their contents might be, who their printers might be, of what consequence they might be for either the early or a modern reader.

In what way does my own glance at these books reflect any of the realities of the economics and literary culture that produced them? A 1719 Matthew Prior folio stands next to a four-volume edition of Addison produced by Tonson in 1721. These editions were much praised by Daniel Updike in *Printing Types*, and since they once stood next to each other on a local dealer's shelf, is not their existence here more a product of a belletristic remark by Updike than a reflection of facts of eighteenth-century book history? There are no marks of ownership in these books. Why has neither been read? Next to those is a series of Chaucer folios, incomplete and now no longer nearing completion. The best and worst is perhaps the 'hospital' copy of Stow's Chaucer (1561), whose many missing leaves I imagine to be tipped in to other once-defective copies of the same book. Again, what does this series reflect? the reception of Chaucer in the sixteenth and seventeenth centuries? the propensity of late nineteenth-century collectors to seek out folio copies of the 'great English poets'? or rather my own earlier scholarly interest, and the accidental indifference of the book trade of twenty years ago to English books of this period that made them cheap and readily available.

There are numerous other items here: a few Aldines, whose cramped and nearly unreadable italics I always must look at directly to remind myself how preposterous are statements and claims about their presumed legibility. There is an Elzevier or two – that these editions were once valued is almost unimaginable; any modern book seller has shelves of better things. There are, by contrast, eminently readable Tonson editions from the early eighteenth century, books whose physical qualities cast severe doubt on often repeated statements about the depraved state of English printing at the turn of the century. There are sets of *Spectators* and *Ramblers*, their essays extracted, as usual, from their original sources. No English reader's bookcase should be without them, but I believe I am the first to have even glanced at pages in these particular copies. The 20-volume British Theatre series sits there – did late eighteenth-century readers actually want these texts? or did they, like modern dealers still urge, buy them 'for the plates'? My copy is still unread.

One could imagine a book history based on these book-copies – a book history dealing with the physical evidence here, physical evidence that in many cases was saved from being pulped only because of statements made in *earlier* book histories. These books, then, would support a book history that to some extent projects as historical evidence the assumptions and goals of early book histories. That history could have a narrative, perhaps dealing with changes in English printing practices, typefaces, or paper. It could involve a more self-reflective and far less interesting narrative, cataloguing the accidents of acquisition, with its oblique bearing on the far lower end of the late twentieth-century book trade. But the coherence of those narratives would be misleading, for of these books, there simply is no account to be given that could be at the same time intelligible, coherent, and even minimally correct. It is perhaps only a somewhat grander illusion to imagine that the histories embodied in the material objects organized and preserved by others should possess a greater coherence than what is so elusive here.

The singularity of the individual book and the singularity of the problems any book or group of books pose will always challenge such narratives, although even to express that challenge involves the construction of another narrative, one that itself is subject to other labels: 'sceptical,' or perhaps simply 'querulous' and 'obstructionist.' The present group of essays has attempted to confront these problems both directly in their contents and indirectly in their organization, with as many of the necessary illusions noted as possible.

Notes

Introduction

1 See the interesting notes by Philip Connell, 'Bibliomania: Book Collecting, Cultural Politics, and the Rise of Literary Heritage in Romantic Britain,' *Representations* 71 (2000): 24–47, on D'Israeli's use of the anecdote as a response to a similar situation in late nineteenth-century bibliographical scholarship.

2 By *ISTC* I refer to *The Illustrated ISTC on CD-ROM*, gen. ed. Martin Davies, 2nd ed. (London, 1998). The contents may differ from the actual British Library database. Pollard and Redgrave, *A Short-Title Catalogue*.

3 See my 'The Lure of Oral Theory in Medieval Criticism: From Edited "Text" to Critical "Work,"' *TEXT* 7 (1994): 145–60, and references. For the fluidity of this term in bibliographical studies, see G. Thomas Tanselle, 'Textual Criticism and Deconstruction,' esp. 23–8.

4 See Grafton, *Commerce with the Classics*, esp. 19–43, on the differences between the ideal books and libraries imagined by humanists and the real ones they had to deal with.

5 Darnton, 'What Is the History of Books?'

6 See the roundtable comments by David Vander Meulen in *The Status of Evidence, PMLA* 111, no. 1 (special issue, 1997): 22, and the introductory essay in the same volume by Heather Dubrow, 'Introduction,' 7–20.

7 Needham, *The Bradshaw Method*, letter to Furnivall, 7 Aug. 1868, quoted also in Prothero, *A Memoir of Henry Bradshaw*, 349.

8 Dane, 'The Importance of Importance,' *Huntington Library Quarterly* 56 (1993): 307–17.

1 The Myth of Print Culture

1 These figures include books in series collections such as the University of Massachusetts Press series, Studies in Print Culture and the History of the Book. Books with the term 'print culture' in the actual title or subtitle, however, do not generally discuss the implications of the term itself. See, for example, the essays in Peter Isaac and Barry McKaw, eds., *The Human Face of the Book Trade: Print Culture and Its Creators* (Winchester, Hampshire, 1999), on the provincial book trade.

2 For an exercise in this methodology applied to a critical term, see my *The Critical Mythology of Irony* (Athens, GA, 1991).

3 Eisenstein has now put McLuhan back in ordinary scholarly discussion of print culture; see, for example, the casual, but uncritical reference in Lisa Gilelman, 'The First Phonographs: Reading and Writing with Sound,' *Biblion* 8 (1999): 3–16. Although McLuhan speaks of 'typographic logic' (212), 'manuscript culture' (84, 149), and 'scribal culture' (105), I cannot find the term 'print culture,' despite my certainty that it is there; McLuhan, *The Gutenberg Galaxy*.

4 See also similar statements by Darnton, 'What Is the History of Books?' For an example of the more abstract levels of evidence Eisenstein's study inspires, see the excellent introductory essay by Michael D. Bristol and Arthur F. Marotti, in *Print, Manuscript, Performance: The Changing Relations of the Media in Early Modern England* (Columbus, 2000), 1–29.

5 These works are discussed in more detail below, chap. 3. An excellent contemporary work in English in this tradition is Hessels, 'Prototypography.'

6 Proctor, *An Index to the Early Printed Books in the British Museum*; *Catalogue of Books Printed in the Fifteenth Century Now in the British Museum*; Ph. E. Gold-schmidt, *Gothic and Renaissance Bookbindings: Exemplified and Illustrated from the Author's Collection*, 2 vols (London, 1928); N.R. Ker, *Pastedowns in Oxford Bindings* (Oxford, 1954).

7 Examples are the essays in Sandra L. Hindman, *Printing the Written Word: The Social History of Books, circa 1450–1520* (Ithaca, 1991).

8 Johns, *The Nature of the Book*, 12; some of the points here are made in my review in *TEXT* 12 (1999): 244–9.

9 A critique of such arguments is David Aers, 'A Whisper in the Ear of Early Modernists: Or, Reflections on Literary Critics Writing the "History of the Subject,"' *Culture and History (1350–1600): Essays on English Communities, Identities and Writing*, ed. David Aers (Detroit, 1992), 177–202. Paul de Man, in *Blindness and Insight: Essays in the Rhetoric of Contemporary Criticism*, 2nd ed. rev. (Minneapolis, 1983).

10 This was also reprinted as *The Culture and Commerce of Texts* ... (Amherst, 1998). See also Beal, *In Praise of Scribes*, opposing 'manuscript culture' to 'print culture' (vi).

11 Among numerous studies arguing this is H.R. Woudhuysen, *Sir Philip Sidney and the Circulation of Manuscripts, 1558–1640* (Oxford, 1996); see further the review by Ian Frederick Moulton in *Huntington Library Quarterly* 60 (1998): 459–69.

12 See esp. chap. 4, 'Some Metaphors for Reading' 141ff., on how original readers saw these texts as different from print.

13 See chap. 5, 'The Social Uses of the Scribally Published Text,' 177. Reference is to Ong, *Orality and Literacy*.

14 Kernan, *Printing Technology;* Kernan's terms 'print-culture' (49) or 'print logic' (again with reference to McLuhan) are subject to the same criticisms stated earlier in this chapter.

15 Febvre and Martin, *L'Apparition du Livre*, trans. Gerard, ed. Nowell-Smith and Wootton, *The Coming of the Book*, 9.

16 'Then, at the other end of the period, we deal with the second great epoch, another age of confusion ...' (11).

17 That Febvre and Martin are cavalier in their use of bibliographical sources is a point made by Needham, 'Fragments in Books: Dutch Prototypography in the Van Ess Library.'

18 *L'apparition du livre*, 112–13: 'gothique' and 'l'écriture romaine.'

19 See also p. 81 and the reference to 'a semi-roman letter' used by Sweynheym and Pannartz.

20 The same three categories of gothic are recognized by Updike, *Printing Types*, 1:57–9, 92, and by McKerrow, who describes 'lettre de somme' as one of the 'three great classes' of gothic (*An Introduction to Bibliography for Literary Students*, 289). The illustration below is from Isaac, *English and Scottish Printing Types*. Updike's classification is adopted and his discussion paraphrased by Greetham, *Textual Scholarship*, 224–40. On the conceptual differences of manuscript scripts and the use compositors made of these, see Paul Needham, 'Palaeography and the Earliest Printing Types,' in *Johannes Gutenberg: Regionale Aspekte des frühen Buchdrucks* (Berlin, 1993), 19–27.

21 Other scholars, such as A.F. Johnson, substitute the large rounded gothic typeface of Ratdolt (Italian rotunda) – typefaces with no particular relation to professors or theologians – for the smaller varieties of rounded gothic that are the basis of this classification ('The Classification of Gothic Type,' with ref. to Stanley Morrison).

22 Examples include Caxton's type 1. Among many studies, see, for example,

Paul Saenger, 'Colard Mansion and the Evolution of the Printed Book,'
Library Quarterly 45 (1975): 405–18.

23 *STC* 21599. In the earlier sections of the book Berthelet replaces similar
text in bastard type with roman.

24 This is suggested in fig. 1 and can be seen clearly simply by skimming
through the Isaac's facsimiles in *English and Scottish Printing Types*; see in
particular the use of bastard type by Rastell and Godfrey. The use of such
type by Berthelet is also noted by Johnson, *Type Designs*, 23.

25 See the introductory chapter to Haebler, *Handbuch der Inkunabelkunde*,
1–33.

26 See Amelung, *Der Frühdruck im deutschen Südwesten, 1473–1500*, Bd. 1, *Ulm*,
59, Abb. 99, 100; and discussion in Dane and Lange, 'An Unrecorded
South German Incunable.

27 See Febvre's own *Le Problème de l'incroyance au XVIe siècle: La Religion de Rabelais*
(Paris, 1947); see also M.A. Screech, *Rabelais* (Ithaca, 1979), 24, 129; Stephen
Rawles, 'La Typographie de Rabelais: Réflexions bibliographiques sur les
Éditions faussement attribuées,' *EtudesRabelaisiennes* 21 (1988): 37–48.

28 See my 'Bibliographical History versus Bibliographical Evidence: The
Plowman's Tale and Early Chaucer Editions,' *Bulletin of the John Rylands
University Library of Manchester* 78 (1996): 47–61, on folio editions of
Chaucer and Gower in the early sixteenth century.

29 'Le livre imprimé a été tout autre chose qu'un réalisation technique' (xxv).

30 Robert Darnton, *The Business of Enlightenment: A Publishing History of the
Encyclopedia (1775–1800)* (Cambridge, MA, 1979): 'for *l'histoire du livre*, as
it is known in France, opens onto the broadest questions of historical
research' (1).

2 Twenty Million Incunables Can't Be Wrong

1 Anderson, *Imagined Communities*, 18.

2 The empirical statement is immediately followed by a statement of the
highest abstraction: 'If manuscript knowledge was scarce and arcane lore,
print knowledge lived by reproducibility and dissemination.' The illogical
'if ... [then]' construction common in late twentieth-century academic
criticism is worth note.

3 For 'before 1500' (Anderson's 'by 1500'), one should probably read 'by the
end of 1500.' The arithmetic seems easy, but see Frederick R. Goff, 'Char-
acteristics of the Book of the Fifteenth Century, in *Buch und Text im 15.
Jahrhundert, ed. Lotte Hellenga and Helmar Härtel* (Hamburg, 1981), 33–4,
whose estimate of '35 or 36000' editions produced in edition sizes of '100

to 2000 copies' yields a figure of 'approximately 185,000,000' (corrected in the German summary to 'ca. 18 Millionen').

4 The review by B.C. Loublinsky, 'The Book in Social History,' is on pp. 162–7, quotation at 164. I thank Barbara Dash of the Library of Congress and Prof. Paulina Kewes of the University of Wales for deciphering the relevant passages for me.

5 For the gap between various narratives and the books printed and distributed that presumably support these narratives, see the comments by Kurt Flasch, 'Ideen und Medien oder: Gehört Gutenberg in die Geschichte der Philosophie?' *Gutenberg-Jahrbuch* 2000, esp. 28–35.

6 Now *Gesamtkatalog der Wiegendrucke*, vols 1–7 (Leipzig, 1926–38); vols 8 – (Stuttgart, 1978–); The first *GW* volume, *Nachträge zu Hain* (1910), contained a catalogue of additions to Hain; the second concerned broadsheets: *Einblattdrucke des XV. Jahrhunderts, ein bibliographisches Verzeichnis herausgegeben von der Kommission für den Gesamtkatalog der Wiegendrucke* (Halle a. S., 1914). An excellent history now exists in English: Paul Needham, 'Counting Incunables,' esp. 470–5.

7 Kurt Ohly, 'Der gegenwärtige Stand der internationalen Inkunabelinventarisierung,' 29. See Dachs and Schmidt, 'Wieviele Inkunabelausgaben gab es wirklich?' on which much of the following discussion is based.

8 Bowers, *Principles of Descriptive Bibliography*, 39–42, 113–17.

9 Needham, 'Counting Incunables,' 514. Dachs and Schmidt also quote Erich von Rath, 'Vorläufer des Gesamtkatalogs der Wiegendrucke,' in *Werden und Wirken: Ein Festgruss Karl W. Hiersemann* (Leipzig, 1924), 288–305 – the catalogue as designed could never be considered absolutely complete. Needham notes that this figure of 27,500 is some 850 short of the number now listed in *ISTC*.

10 Dachs and Schmidt, 'Wievele Inkunabelausgaben gab es wirklich,' 89; Hain, *Repertorium bibligraphicum*.

11 Haebler, *Handbuch der Inkunabelkunde*, 169. See Dachs and Schmidt, 'Wievele Inkunabelausgaben gab es wirklich,' 87–8 and n. 22, with reference to Carl Wehmer, 'Zur Beurteilung des Methodenstreits,' *Gutenberg-Jahrbuch* 1933, 267, n. 2

12 Haebler, 'Der Gesamtkatalog der Wiegendrucke.' Needham, 'Counting Incunables,' 472, notes that the 'arbitrarily assigned numbers' of *GW* show that very early the total number of incunables must have been estimated at 35,000. This estimate, whatever it might have been based on, must be the basis of the assertions by Ohly and Wehmer against Haebler.

13 Haebler noted in 1921 the difference between the number of incunable editions and the number of *GW* descriptions, and dealt with it directly

(Dachs and Schmidt, 'Wieviele Inkunabelausgaben gab es wirklich?' 93–4).

14 Dachs and Schmidt, ibid., 87, and n. 21, comment on the quick acceptance of the figure 40,000 by German scholars Barge and Juchhoff. See further, Needham, 'Counting Incunables,' 463.

15 See, for example, Hellinga, 'Further Fragments of Dutch Prototypography.' The number of Donatus fragments catalogued in *GW* does not differ appreciably from the number catalogued in the 1998 *ISTC.*

16 See my 'An Example of Netherlands Prototypography in the Huntington.' There is no complete survey of Huntington Library bindings, but in their nearly 6000 incunables, I have found only one set of Ohly's hypothesized fragments.

17 A number of these entries involving fragments occur under 'Donatus,' itself contained in one of the early volumes of *GW*.

18 'Jede Bibliothek hat ein Recht zu erfahren, welchen Anteil ihr Inkunabel-besitz an der Buchproduktion des 15. Jahrhunderts darstellt' (94).

19 Arnold Schoenberg, *Theory of Harmony*, trans. Roy E. Carter (Berkeley, 1978), 19.

20 Needham, 'Counting Incunables,' 489.

21 U. Neddermeyer, 'Möglichkeiten und Grenzen einer quantitativen Bestim-mung der Buchproduktion im Spätmittelalter.'

22 Most of the books and editions listed in extant book inventories (for ex-ample, the often cited list by Pannartz and Sweynheym) can be matched with extant book-copies. I am not certain whether Neddermeyer's figures include broadsheets, although the evidence here does not suggest high print runs: Falk Eisermann, 'Auflagenhöhen von Einblattdrucken im 15. und frühen 16. Jahrhundert,' in *Einblattdrucke des 15. und frühen Jahrhunderts: Probleme, Perspektiven, Fallstudien*, ed. Volker Honemann, et al. (Tübingen, 2000), 142–77.

23 For a critique of statistical analysis applied to book history, see Joseph A. Dane and Rosemary Roberts, 'The Calculus of Calculus: W.W. Greg and the Mathematics of *Everyman* Editions,' *Studies in Bibliography* 53 (2000): 117–28.

24 See, for example, Alfred Hartmann, ed., *Die Amerbachkorrespondenz*, esp. Band I, *Die Briefe aus der Zeit Johann Amerbachs, 1481–1513* (Basel, 1942); some of these contain information bearing on edition size, see, for ex-ample, #11 (p. 15); the correspondence is now partially available in a translation from University of Michigan Press.

25 That the grammars were printed on vellum may have a bearing on the size of print runs. For cheap books such as this, would large supplies of vellum be available and immediately ready at hand for use in printing?

26 Boghardt, 'Partial Duplicate Setting'; Curt F. Bühler, 'The Two Issues of the

First Edition of the *Manipulus Florum*,' *Gutenberg-Jahrbuch* 1953, 69–72; repr. *Early Books and Manuscripts*, 198–204. The procedure is described earlier in McKerrow, *Introduction to Bibliography*, 216.

27 Joseph A. Dane, 'A Ghostly Twin Terence (Venice, 21 July 1475; IGI 9422, 9423),' *The Library*, ser. 6, 21 (1999): 99–107; 'Note on Two Presumed Editions of Bartholomaeus Metlinger, *Regiment der Kindheit* (Augsburg: Johann Schaur, 1497 and 1500),' *Gutenberg-Jahrbuch* 2001, 165–7.

28 See further, Giovanni Andrea Bussi, *Prefazioni alle edizioni di Sweynheym e Pannarz, prototipografi romani*, ed. Massimo Miglio (Milan, 1978), 5. Voullième notes that this notice is not a *Buchhändleranzeigen* in a strict sense at all in 'Nachträge zu den Buchhändleranzeigen des 15. Jahrhunderts in getreuen Nachbildungen herausg. von K. Burger.' See further, Martin Davies, 'Two Book-lists of Sweynheym and Pannartz,' in *Libri tipografi bibliotheche: Ricerche storiche dedicate a Luigi Balsame* (Florence, 1997), 1: 25–53; Konrad Haebler, *Die deutschen Buchdrucker des XV. Jahrhunderts im Auslande* (Munich, 1924), 13–14; Leonhard Hoffmann, 'Buchmarkt und Bücherpreise im Frühdruckzeitalter: Der Antoniter Petrus Mitte de Caprariis als Käufer der ersten Frühdrucke in Rom (1468/69),' *Gutenberg-Jahrbuch* 2000, 73–81; Sylvia Kohushölter, 'Lateinisch-deutsche Bücheranzeigen der Inkunabelzeit,' in *Einblattdruck*, ed. Honemann, 445–67, and references.

29 Hirsch, *Printing, Selling and Reading*, 66; also 64, n. 15. See also Hirsch, 'The Size of Editions of Books Produced by Sweynheim and Pannartz between 1465 and 1471.

30 Hirsch, *Printing, Selling, and Reading*, chap. 5: 'The Selling of Books,' 61ff.

31 Pollard and Ehrman, *The Distribution of Books*, 'The Fifteenth Century' (by A. Ehrman), 1–46. See also Pollard, *An Essay on Colophons*.

32 Horatio Brown, *The Venetian Printing Press*, 10, 'second edition of the Epistulae consisted of six hundred copies, published in two issues of three hundred each; ... the whole six hundred took four months to print'; quoted in Pollard, *Essay on Colophons*, 34: 'The fourth month must be reckoned from the date of the first edition, and we have to choose, as to the number of copies in the second, between supposing that the three hundred, the "tercentenum opus," refers to this alone ... or else that the second edition consisted of two hundred copies, and that these, with the hundred of the first, made up a total of three hundred.' See Michael Pollak, 'The Performance of the Wooden Printing Press,' *Library Quartely* 42 (1972): 218–64, esp. 235–59 on the statement by the printer Lignamine in Riccobaldus Ferrariensis, *Chronica summorum pontificum imperatorumque* (Rome: Johannes Schurener, de Bopardia, 1476; Goff R-188), and the meaning of the phrase 'trecentas cartas.'

33 Quoted, with translation, by Pollard, *Essay on Colophons*, 37.

34 Pollard, *Essay on Colophons*, 39: 'Faithfully to reecho the discords of the original is above the present translator's skill: Wendelin of Speier to Venice now once more / Of printed Sallusts hath given hundreds four. / But here all's better, all may trusted be: / This text, good reader, is from errors free.'

35 H.R. Plomer, 'Two Lawsuits of Richard Pynson,' *The Library*, n.s., 10 (1909): 115–33. See also, H.S. Bennett, *English Books and Readers, 1475 to 1557* (Cambridge, 1952), 232–3.

36 W.J.B. Crotch, ed., *The Prologues and Epilogues of William Caxton* (London, 1928), 7–8.

37 Again from Da Spira: Cicero *Epistolae* (1469) (*BMC* 5: 152): 'Quom Labor hic primus calami superauerit artem'; Pliny (1469) (*BMC* 5: 153): 'Fessa manus quondam moneo: Calamusque quiescat.'

38 Lenhart, *Pre-Reformation Printed Books*, 9–10. Lenhart's evidence is again from Haebler, *Handbuch*, 142–5, citing editions of Plato (1494) of 1025 copies; a Breviary (1491), Aristotle's *Politics* (both of 1500 copies); Caraccioli (1489) of 2000 copies. The largest print runs are editions of the *Decretals* (1491 and 1494), of 2300 copies. See also Haebler, *Deutsche Buchdrucker des XV. Jahrhunderts im Auslande*, 95–6, 112, 140–1, 262.

39 Curiously, these entries do not show up when one searches under Author for 'Persius.' They show up only when one searches 'Any Field: Persius.'

40 The proper search techniques for this database often must be learned by trial and error, and vary with each individual search. A number of extraneous books appear in casual searches here: see, for example, those printed by the 'Printer of Persius,' or Badius, *Silvae Morales*, which includes excerpts of Juvenal and Persius.

41 1469 (Juvenal) (Goff Suppl J-625a), 1470 (Persius) (Goff P-334), 1471 (Juvenal) (Goff J-627), and 1478 (Juvenal and Persius) (*ISTC* ij00638500). See, on these editions, Curt F. Bühler, 'The Earliest Editions of Juvenal' (1955), in *Early Books and Manuscripts*, 223–7.

42 Anser Tarpei custos Iouis: unde quod alis
   Constreperes: Gallus decidit: Vltor adest
Vdalricus Gallus: ne quem poscantur in usum
   Edocuit pennis nil opus esse tuis.
Imprimit ille die: quantum non scribitur anno
   Ingenio haud noceas: omnia uincit homo.
[An avenger, another Gaul, Udalricus, comes, O goose, and your quills will be valueless; he prints more in a day than could be written in a year ...] (see further *BMC* 4: 19–21).

43 There are between six and nine copies of each, the same numbers of copies that survive of the Juvenal and Persius editions.

44 For an overview, see Dickinson, *Henry E. Huntington's Library of Libraries.* On the recovery of such composite volumes, see esp. Needham, *The Printer and the Pardoner.*

3 What Is a Book? Classification and Representation of Early Books

1 A popular example is *Printing and the Mind of Man: A Descriptive Catalogue Illustrating the Impact of Print on the Evolution of Western Civilization during Five Centuries*, ed. John Carter and Percy H. Muir (London, 1967).

2 See, for example, Grendler, *Schooling in Renaissance Italy*, 176–81.

3 Steele, 'What Are Fifteenth-Century Books About? IV.' Steele's fourth class, 'Literature,' includes classics, medieval literature, and 'contemporary,' within which are included grammars and schoolbooks.

4 Dickinson, *Huntington's Library of Libraries*, 207–10.

5 The best of the English studies participating in and summarizing such discussion is Hessels, 'Prototypography.'

6 Needham, 'Fragments in Books: Dutch Prototypography in the Van Ess Library,' esp. 93–110. See, for example, Richard Rouse, 'Copy-specific Features of the Printed Book: What to Record and Why,' in *Bibliography and the Study of 15th-century Civilisation*, ed. Lotte Hellinga and John Goldfinch, British Library Occasional Papers 5 (London, 1987), 206–7, 213.

7 Dane, 'Herman R. Mead's *Incunabula in the Huntington Library* and the Notion of "Typographical Value,"' *Bulletin of the Bibliographical Society of Australia and New Zealand* (forthcoming).

8 Henry Bradshaw, 'List of the Founts of Type and Woodcut Devices Used by Printers in Holland in the Fifteenth Century,' (1871), in *Collected Papers*, 258–79, quotation at 262–3; Goldschmidt, *Gothic and Renaissance Bookbindings*, 1: 120. See further, Needham, 'Fragments in Books.'

9 See further, Bradshaw's remark (260): 'the very mode of working the plates so as to form a book, even though no type be used'; such book-forming does not constitute a book.

10 The first of a series of letters between Politian and Jacobus Antiquarius (13 November 1489; *Ep.* 3:18); *Angelus Politianus: Opera Omnia* (Basel, 1553; repr. Torino, 1971). Grafton, 'Quattrocento Humanism and Classical Scholarship'; earlier versions in *Journal of the Warburg and Courtauld Institutes* 40 (1977), and in chap. 1 of *Joseph Scaliger: A Study in the History of Classical Scholarship* (Oxford, 1983), 9–44. See also Silvia Rizzo, *Il Lessico filologico*

degli umanisti (Rome, 1973), 78–9, citing the same letter, specifically identifying the book as one unbound.

11 See my '"Si vis archetypas habere nugas": Authorial Subscriptions in the Houghton Library and Huntington Library Copies of Politian, *Miscellanea* (Florence: Misconomi, 1489),' *Harvard Library Bulletin* 10 (1999): 12–22.

12 See my 'Prototypography,' and 'Note on the Huntington Library and Pierpont Morgan Library Fragments of Donatus, *Ars minor (Rudimenta grammatices)* (GW 8995, GW 8996).'

13 Bowers, *Principles of Bibliographical Description*, 40–2.

14 *ISTC* lists 48 editions in the 36-line Bible or 42-line Bible type and 112 for Netherlands prototypography.

15 Paul Schwenke, *Die Donat- und Kalender-Type: Nachtrag und Übersicht* (Mainz, 1903), 37–49.

16 For a description and facsimile reproduction, see Zedler, *Gutenbergs älteste Type*, Tafellen 31–4. The four plates show leaf 10 conjugate with 1 (Tafel 31 has leaves 10b/1a), and leaf 9 conjugate with leaf 2 (Tafel 34 has leaves 2b/9a).

17 See the introductory note to the Donatus *Ars minor* in the *Gesamtkatalog*: 'Bruchstücke sind nur dann zu einer bibliographischen Einheit zusammengezogen, wenn ihre Zusammengehörigkeit aus gemeinsamer Bibliotheksheimat oder sonstigen Gründen erschlossen werden kann' (583).

18 Reichling, *Alexandri de Villa-Dei Doctrinalis*, iv: 'Recensui enim viginti sex editionibus postea intersertis libros 296, inter quos 166 artis typographicae incunabula sunt. Qui numerus multo maior appareret, si nostrae aetatis bibliographos secutus singulas multarum editionum partes separatim impressas separatim posuissem numerique ordine notassem, id quod proposito meo minus convenire putavi.'

19 The presumed 'humanist' animosity toward this text is I think overstated by Padley, *Grammatical Theory in Western Europe*, 5–15. The printing histories of this and the Donatus are too similar to support Padley's attempt to oppose them.

20 *ISTC* now lists 393 editions. The *GW* entry for Alexander occurs in the earliest volume, and some, but not all, the differences between cataloguing this and the Donatus *Ars minor* may be due to the evolving conventions for description in the *GW* project itself. Although considerable work had been done on the Donatus fragments prior to *GW*, vol. 5, the *GW* entry here is clearly organized (as the earlier entry for Alexander is not) as the starting point for further research.

21 Leaf 28 (Reichling, lines 1550 and 1607), as represented in GW 934/XIV and GW 934/XV, leaf 1:

XIV:

[ ]Ande[re] p[ro]posui p[er] v[er]sus sill[ab]a q[uae]q[ue] *eingedrückt* :
tris [i.e., the last syllable of the following line is printed on this one]
Q[ua]n[do] vocalem duo co[n]sona iuncta sequu[n]tur

XV:

[ ]Andere p[ro]posui p[er] v[er]sus sillaba q[uae]q[ue]
[Qua]n[do] vocalem duo co[n]sena iu[n]cta sequu[n]t[ur]

22 For specific examples, see my 'The Bibliographical Discontents of dei
   Libri's 1492 *Historie fiorentine*,' *La Bibliofilia* 104 (2002), 113–21, and references above, chap. 2, n. 26.

23 Woolley Photographs: *Photographs of Fifteenth-Century Types, of the Exact Size of
   the Originals, designed to supplement published examples, with references to Robert
   Proctor's Index of Books in the British Museum and Bodleian Library* (London
   1899–1905); Type Facsimile Society, *Publications* ... (Oxford, 1900–).

24 Bradshaw, 'List of the Founts of Type and Woodcut Devices Used by Printers in Holland'; Bradshaw's classification follows that of Campbell, *Annales
   de la typographie néerlandaise au xve siècle.*

25 Holtrop regarded types 4 and 5 as the same, except that 23a measured in
   his facsimiles 144mm, and 23b measures 123mm!

26 See I.A. Sheppard, 'Introduction to the Presses,' in *BMC*, vol. 11, and 'The
   Speculum Printer's Editions of Donatus.'

27 See memoir by Alfred W. Pollard, 'Robert Proctor,' in *Robert Proctor: Bibliographical Essays* (London, 1905), xxx.

28 Proctor's description reads 'Type 2, almost = 3, but h, I, *us* differ. M not
   as 1, the other caps. the same, h tailed and broad; 20 ll. = 94 mm.' (*Index*,
   84).

29 For what was available to Bradshaw, see Oates, *A Catalogue of the Fifteenth
   Century Printed Books in the University Library, Cambridge*, nos 3294, 3298 and
   3299. CUL has the Pontanus, but the Donatus fragments are not in type 4.

30 Alfred W. Pollard, Introduction, *BMC*, 1: xx; Haebler, *Typenrepertorium*, 1:
   x–xi.

31 Dane, 'Prototypography.'

32 It is not possible to photograph these fragments as they lie physically on the
   Hellinga plates; thus, the only reliable way to compare them cannot itself
   be illustrated.

33 Holtrop, *Monuments typographiques*, 28 and 29 associates Planches 24 [37]
   et 13 [49] abc and identifies them as printed with the same types used by
   Pontanus 23 [9].

34 I thank Barbara Ravelhover of St John's College, Cambridge, for informa-
    tion on this book. The appearance of size in the Hellinga plates is further
    enhanced by the harshly black and white reproduction.

35 'Sie hat dabei ihren Namenerhalten von einem der spätesten Drucke,
    zu denen sie verwendet worden ist'; the type should be identified as the
    'Donat-Type des Frühdruckers' (40). See Zedler's Abb. 3 on p. 39, a com-
    pendium of both types. How Zedler combined them photographically is
    not stated. Differences are detailed in the Hellinga catalogue.

36 Zedler, of course, could not have seen the images as they would be pub-
    lished when he composed his text.

37 Practical and theoretical difficulties posed by the use of facsimiles in
    bibliographical discussion have worried bibliographers for over a century:
    George Watson Cole, 'The Photostat in Bibliographical and Research Work
    – a Symposium,' *Papers of the Bibliographical Society of America* 15 (1921): 1–21
    (the entire issue is concerned with these questions), and Frank Weiten-
    kampf, 'What Is a Facsimile?' *Papers of the Bibliographical Society of America* 37
    (1943): 114–30; Franklin B. Williams, Jr, 'Photo-Facsimiles of *STC* Books: A
    Cautionary Check List,' *Studies in Bibliography* 21 (1968): 109–19. See the
    early discussion of photographic reproduction of individual letters by
    Wilhelm Molsdorf, 'Die Photographie im Dienste der Bibliographie, mit
    besonderer Berücksichtigung alterer Drucke,' *Beiträge zur Kenntnis des
    Schrift-, Buch- und Bibliothekswesens* 4 (1898): 83–9. See also, Adrian Weiss,
    'Reproductions of Early Dramatic Texts as a Source of Bibliographical
    Evidence,' *TEXT* 4 (1988): 237–68.

38 Blades, *The Life and Typography of William Caxton*. A condensed and revised
    one-volume version was produced for the Caxton celebration of 1877 and is
    often reprinted; see Blades, *The Biography and Typography of William Caxton*.

39 The following paragraphs are expansions of points I raise in my review of
    Johns, *TEXT* 12 (1999): 244–9.

40 'These Notes were made by Mr. G.I.F. Tupper while engaged in tracing the
    plates for Blades, LIFE AND TYPOGRAPHY OF W. CAXTON, 2 vols. 4to.'
    See Myers, 'George Isaac Frederick Tupper, Facsimilist,' and 'William
    Blades's Debt to Henry Bradshaw and G.I.F. Tupper.'

41 For a history and description of the various processes, see Twyman, *Early
    Lithographed Books*.

42 Twyman, *Early Lithographed Books*, 209–12; Senefelder, *A Complete Course of
    Lithography*, 80, 87, alludes to the process but does not describe it in detail.
    Tupper identifies the particular book-copies used for his facsimiles and
    none shows signs of having been so used. Cf. de Grazia, *Shakespeare Verbatim*,

222–6, who claims that facsimile reproduction was available by the late eighteenth century 'providing a seemingly exact duplicate of the original.'

43 John L. Flood, '"Caveat Lector!" Edward Schröder's "Facsimile" of the 1515 Strasbourg edition of "Till Eulenspiegel" and the Consequences for Scholarship,' in *The German Book: 1450–1750: Studies Presented to David L. Paisey in His Retirement*, ed. John L. Flood and William A. Kelly (London, 1995), 45–59, implying (not convincingly) that such early techniques were too 'crude' to have been used by later facsimilist (specifically, Emery G. Walker).

44 Twyman, *Early Lithographed Books*, 212.

45 Letter of Blades to Henry Bradshaw, 30 November 1857, quoted by Myers, 'George Isaac Frederick Tupper, Facsimilist,' 113.

46 In the Burt Franklin reprint, the 'Imitations' of course show no block impression; Mansion's red and black type is reproduced in plain black and white. Even in plate III (the *Boece*), the red ink is printed as black and the entire point of the plate is lost.

47 Quoted by Myers, 'William Blades's Debt to Bradshaw and Tupper,' 278; also in 'George Isaac Frederick Tupper, Facsimilist,' 114; I transcribe the word *the* according to modern conventions.

48 Myers, from L. Hellinga, cites J. Mathiels, *Meester Arend de Keysere (1480–1490)* (Ghent, 1973), as first embodying the twin goals implied by Tupper. Earlier projects, however, certainly deal with these problems: the facsimiles of the Gesellschaft für Typenkunde, with its full-page images opposed to its clean isolated alphabets, embody at least a *version* of these conflicting goals.

49 Blades recognized that each book-copy was unique (see quotation above from *Life and Typography*, 1: x: 'as no two copies of the same work are in all respects exactly alike ...'), but he seems less concerned than Tupper about the differences between particular type sorts. These differences are of two classes: that between recastings (Caxton 2 vs Caxton 2*) and differences between individual type sorts produced by the same matrix.

50 For early discussion of how such alphabets might be produced photographically, see Molsdorf, 'Die Photographie im Dienste der Bibliographie' (1898).

51 Such pen facsimiles seemed far more accurate to their contemporaries than they do to us. There are numerous examples; that the facsimile title page to the Hungtington Library Hoe copy of the 1542 Chaucer (RB 99596) is hand-drawn is obvious to any modern viewer, but it is described in a marginal note, apparently by a Hoe bibliographer, as 'so good as to defy detection.'

4 The Notion of Variant and the Zen of Collation

1 Lindstrand, 'Mechanized Textual Collation,' 24 (1971): 212; Randall McLeod, *McLeod Portable Collator* (Toronto, 1990).

2 Charlton Hinman, 'Mechanized Collation: A Preliminary Report,' *Papers of the Bibliographical Society of America* 41 (1947): 99–106. 'According to the story it was one of our common wartime practices to send a plane out to photograph a given target area soon after an attack on that area; and then, shortly before a new attack, to send out another plane to photograph the same area' (102). For a detailed history of Hinman's work on the collator and its construction, see Steven Escar Smith, 'The Eternal Verities Verified: Charlton Hinman and the Roots of Mechanical Collation,' *Studies in Bibliography* 53 (2000): 129–61.

3 For present locations of Hinman machines, see Smith's survey in 'Eternal Verities.' Cheaper versions employing the same principle of alternating images are discussed by Dearing, 'The Poor Man's Mark IV, or Ersatz Hinman Collator' and Smith, 'Collating Machine, Poor Man's, Mark VII.' See further, Smith, 'Eternal Verities,' 129–30, n. 2. Stereoscopic versions include Lindstrand's Mark I and the mirrored collators by Randall McLeod and Carter Hailey discussed in detail below.

4 Charlton Hinman, 'Mechanized Collation at the Houghton Library,' *Harvard Library Bulletin* 9 (1955): 132.

5 Lindstrand, 'Mechanized Textual Collation,' 211, discusses his own tests.

6 The figure appears in both studies cited above; for example, the collator 'has made possible the collation of First Folios, not only with far greater accuracy than heretofore possible, but at about 40 times the speed' ('Mechanized Collation at the Houghton,' 133).

7 See Greg, *The Variants in the First Quarto of 'King Lear.'* I cannot find where Greg describes his method, which I assume involved simple comparison but not optical superimposition of any kind. See in particular the detailed variants identified in 'Doubtful Readings,' 85ff.

8 Hinman, *The Printing and Proof-Reading of the First Folio of Shakespeare*, 1: 245, n. 1. Cf. the comments by Love, *Scribal Publication*, 90: Hinman's *Printing and Proof-Reading* 'presents us with a production-history of an edition so meticulous that it is hard to imagine what might have been added.'

9 The estimates by Smith, 'Collating Machine,' 113, for a hypothetical collating task are 2–4 hours for a mechanical collator vs 11–15 minutes for 'sight' collation.

10 Although a fairly minor flaw made my machine only marginally usable, I have seen a much more severely damaged version of the Comet in apparent

use by a reputable scholar, who seemed to be recording results from what was clearly an inoperable and unusable machine.

11 See the description in Lindstrand, 'Mechanized Textual Collation,' 209–10, describing these same effects.

12 Dearing, 'Poor Man's Mark IV,' 159, estimates that one can do 'five lines or so' without readjustment 'if all goes well.'

13 Lindstrand, 'Mechanized Textual Collation,' 210, claims that one might detect the difference between a printed (embossed) and planographic line (lithograph facsimile, for example).

14 Newer versions of these collators have solved one of these problems, and produce a hard image that can then be manipulated by computer. Paul R. Sternberg and John M. Brayer, 'Composite Imaging: A New Technique in Bibliographic Research,' *Papers of the Bibliographical Society of America* 77 (1983): 432–45: 'Rather than creating only ephemeral images, its product is a fixed image which can be recorded.' In this version, pages are collated as computer images, with differences programmed to appear in blue and red on a single image. However, even the examples published in their article reveal problems one finds with other collators: although there are areas of colour difference in the composite image that unambiguously show variations in the two original images, there is also a considerable amount of clutter that needs to be disregarded, even after the programming designed to eliminate or minimize it. Decisions as to what is or is not variation are still made by the investigator.

15 G. Thomas Tanselle, 'The Treatment of Typesetting and Presswork in Bibliographical Description,' *Studies in Bibliography* 52 (1999): 40: 'whether one uses a single control copy for all collations or different pairs of copies in order to multiply more rapidly the number of collated copies ...'

16 *English Letters of the Eighteenth Century*, ed. James Aitken (London, 1946), 120ff.

17 McKerrow, *Introduction to Bibliography*, 204–13; Greg, *Variants in King Lear*.

18 Blayney, *The Texts of King Lear and Their Origins*, 1: 1–4.

19 Greetham, *Textual Scholarship*, 7–8.

20 So also Bowers's statement in 'Purposes of Descriptive Bibliography, with Some Remarks on Methods' (1952) in *Readings in Descriptive Bibliography*, ed. John Bush Jones (Kent, 1974), 13–14: 'Let me illustrate. I hold that bibliography is properly an advanced form of independent scholarship, which is not necessarily subsidiary to other forms, and as such that it has as much right to express itself in its own technical terms as any other independent form of advanced scholarship.'

21 See Fredson Bowers, 'Old-Spelling Editions of Dramatic Texts,' in *Studies in*

Honor of T.W. Baldwin, ed. Don Cameron Allen (Urbana, 1958), 9, and discussion in G. Thomas Tanselle, 'The Editorial Problem of Final Authorial Intentions,' *Studies in Bibliography* 29 (1976): 167–211.

22 Gaskell, *A New Introduction to Bibliography*, 1.

23 For a discussion of these principles, see my 'Perfect Order and Perfected Order.'

24 'Having printed the sheets of the heap on one side, the pressmen turned it over ... and changed the first forme for the second. The register was tested, and any necessary adjustment was made by shifting the second forme slightly on the bed of the press. The reiteration was then printed off in much the same way as the white paper, the sheets going through the press in the same order as before' (Gaskell, *New Introduction to Bibliography*, 131).

25 McKerrow's discussion seemed to influence Bowers, who describes a similar disordering that occurs during gathering of printed sheets: 'Depending upon various circumstances, a corrected forme may be backed by an uncorrected or by a corrected forme so that a corrected state of both formes of a sheet can exist only fortuitously. Furthermore, since the sheets of corrected and uncorrected formes were indiscriminately bound under ordinary conditions, the corrected *state* of a book cannot exist except by accident or by a special effort on the part of the printer' (Bowers, *Principles of Bibliographical Description*, 46).

26 'Perfect Order and Perfected Order.' The last point was made in one of the earliest studies of press variation: Francis R. Johnson, 'Press Correction and Presswork in the Elizabethan Printing Shop,' *Papers of the Bibliographical Society of America* 40 (1946): 286: 'All the varieties of accidental variation which characterize every activity carried on by human beings.'

27 McKenzie, 'Printers of the Mind: Some Notes on Bibliographical Theories and Printing-House Practices.'

28 I am not concerned here with how perfected sheets are gathered together in a book. Binding does not show the same degree of regularity as perfecting (there are no 'Binders of the Mind'), but Bowers's description of these procedures as 'indiscriminate' is overstated (see above, n. 25). See my comments on 'binding integrity' in 'Perfect Order and Perfected Order.'

29 Bowers, gen. ed., *The Dramatic Works in the Beaumont and Fletcher Canon*, 3: 460. I earlier claimed some 'irreducible anomalies' in this book by misreading the sometimes baffling textual-critical language: the phrase 'first corrected state' means state 2. Sheet B, despite my claims to the contrary ('Perfect Order and Perfected Order,' Appendix) is banally regular.

30 See my critique of the bibliographical application of such textual-critical

language in 'On "Correctness": A Note on Some Press Variants in Thynne's 1532 Edition of Chaucer,' *The Library*, ser. 6, 17 (1995): 156–67.

31 Quotations from *Dramatic Works in the Beaumont and Fletcher Canon*, 4: 525–7.

32 The distinction as stated is misleading. 'Machine collation' is no better or different from any other type of collation, and the methodological distinction is one between collation pure and simple and 'checked for press variants.' Gabler's basis for collation is not identified.

33 Of the three Folger copies, Folger copy 2 has a period; copy 1 has a comma so badly printed it does not seem the same sort as copy 3.

34 The outer forme variant is on the opening page. The inner forme variant is on B2r.

35 It is possible, of course, that a printer for some peculiar reason perfected the sheets according to perfect regular procedures in the *reverse* order of initial printing. So far, no bibliographer or print historian has ever had what it takes to argue that.

5   Two Studies in Chaucer Editing

1 One of the first Variorum volumes and a model for those that follow is Pearsall, ed., *The Nun's Priest's Tale*; also cited below is Baker, ed., *The Manciple's Tale*. See my review of the first six volumes in the *Canterbury Tales* series in *Envoi: A Review Journal of Medieval Literature* 2 (1990): 292–9. Robinson, ed., *Geoffrey Chaucer: The Wife of Bath's Prologue on CD-ROM*; Elisabeth Solopova, ed., *Chaucer: The General Prologue on CD-ROM*.

2 Skeat, ed. *The Complete Works of Geoffrey Chaucer*; Robinson, ed., *The Complete Works of Geoffrey Chaucer*, and rev. ed. Larry D. Benson, ed., *The Riverside Chaucer* (Boston, 1987). The same historical situation applies to recent editorial history of *Piers Plowman*, where the last of the monumental Athlone edition, an 'old-technology' edition, appeared nearly contemporarily with the first of the SEENET editions. George Russell and George Kane, eds., *Piers Plowman: The C Version* (London, 1997); Hoyt N. Duggan, et al., ed., *The Piers Plowman Electronic Archive*, vol. 1: *Corpus Christi College, Oxford MS 201 (F)* (Ann Arbor, 2000). See the review by Anne Middleton, 'Editing Terminable and Interminable,' *Huntington Library Quarterly* 64 (2001): 161–86.

3 Manly and Rickert, *The Text of the Canterbury Tales*; and Kane, 'John M. Manly (1865–1940) and Edith Rickert (1871–1938).' For the reliance of the Variorum edition on Manly and Rickert, see Ralph Hanna III, review of Pearsall, *Nun's Priest's Tale, Analytical and Enumerative Bibliography* 8 (1984): 187–94.

4 Greg, 'The Rationale of Copy-Text.' For discussion of these distinctions, with particular reference to Greg's definition, see my 'Copy-Text and Its Variants in Some Recent Chaucer Editions,' *Studies in Bibliography* 44 (1991): 163–83. On best-text editing in Chaucer, Ralph Hanna distinguishes 'hard and soft Hengwrtism' in 'The Hengwrt Manuscript and the Canon of *The Canterbury Tales*.' For a retaliatory comment, see Blake, 'Geoffrey Chaucer: Textual Transmission and Editing,' where he seems to defend his reliance on Hg not because its readings are right, but because they are wrong (34). One of the editors of the Cambridge CD-ROM Chaucer has recently denied that Blake ever was guilty of such 'hard' Hengwrtism: Robinson, 'Can We Trust the Hengwrt Manuscript?'

5 Skeat, *The Student's Chaucer.* I believe the text is identical to Skeat's contemporary multi-volume edition.

6 Both the abbreviation SK and the term 'copy-text' are misleading, since the Variorum sigil SK refers to the multi-volume Skeat (not the smaller edition), and the term 'copy-text' is not explained. Pearsall and Baker's statements thus appear stronger than they might be: they seem to be claiming that Manly and Rickert's multi-volume edition relies on Skeat's earlier multi-volume edition. Pearsall and Baker would probably not argue that. If by 'copy-text' they mean only the authority for accidentals (see Baker's odd word 'incidentals'), then they concede that it has no authority on substantive matters.

7 'What we are attempting is the difficult task of proving at one time the text which is as near as it is possible to get to what Chaucer must have written (and we believe that for most of the *Canterbury Tales* it is that of the Hengwrt manuscript – as slightly emended – to a greater extent even than that of the Manly-Rickert text).' Donald C. Baker, Introduction to *Geoffrey Chaucer, The Canterbury Tales: A Facsimile and Transcription of the Hengwrt Manuscript, with Variants from the Ellesmere Manuscript*, ed. Paul G. Ruggiers (Norman, 1979), xviii.

8 See my 'Who is Buried in Chaucer's Tomb? Prolegomena,' *Huntington Library Quarterly* 57 (1994): 98–123. The texts collated here are by John Foxe, *Actes and Monuments* (London, 1576); Thomas Speght, 'Life of Chaucer,' *The Workes of Geoffrey Chaucer* (London, 1602); William Camden, *Reges, Reginae, Nobiles ...* (London: Bollisantus, 1600); John Pits, *Relationum Historicum de Rebus Anglicis ...* (Paris, 1619); Elias Ashmole, *Theatrum Chemicum Britannicum* (London, 1652); and John Dart, *Westmonasterium* (London, [1742]).

9 The briefest and most reliable guides to sixteenth-century editions are John Rowland Hetherington, *Chaucer (1532, 1602): Notes and Facsimile Texts*

(Edgbaston, Birmingham, 1964), and still Hammond's 1908 *Chaucer: A Bibliographical Manual.* Tyrwhitt's 1774 edition could in this context be considered transitional. Tyrwhitt's collation papers are taken from the 1687 reissue of Speght, his printer's copy from the 1602 edition. See Hench, 'Printer's Copy for Tyrwhitt's Chaucer,' and the facsimile plate in Charles Muscatine, *The Book of Geoffrey Chaucer* (San Francisco, 1963). See further B.A. Windeatt, 'Thomas Tyrwhitt (1730–1786), in *The Great Tradition,* ed. Ruggiers, 123–4, and my 'Fists and Filiations in Early Chaucer Folios, 1532–1598,' *Studies in Bibliography* 51 (1998): 48–62.

10 Baker quite correctly notes that Skeat himself in 1909 was willing to grant greater authority to Hg. See Baker, *Manciple's Tale,* 53, with reference to Walter W. Skeat, *The Eight-Text Edition of the Canterbury Tales,* Chaucer Society Publications, 2nd ser., 43 (London, 1909), 55.

11 See, in addition to the introductory essays in the CD-ROM, the series of occasional papers, beginning with Blake and Robinson, eds., *The Canterbury Tales Project.* Due to the somewhat startling price, that these editions are 'published' does not mean that they are widely used, nor that they are readily accessible or available even in well-funded libraries; this is a point made in reference to the first volume by Hanna, 'The Application of Thought to Textual Criticism in all Modes – With Apologies to A.E. Housman,' 163, and one that applies equally to the second.

12 See most recently the general editor of the Cambridge Chaucer, Robinson, 'Can We Trust the Hengwrt Manuscript?' 214: 'The excellence of the text and the even more problematic spelling and metre of other manuscripts confirm that Hengwrt is the best choice for a base text for an edition, as Manly and Rickert, the Variorum editors and Norman himself have all insisted.' Manly himself was certainly in a good position to state this directly, but did not.

13 Despite the editorial rhetoric, the final goal of the Cambridge edition seems to be more ambitious than the reconstruction of Manly-Rickert's O'; what is at issue is *O* itself. At least, this is the implication of the statements by the general editor Robinson in 'Can We Trust the Hengwrt Manuscript?' 199, and the reference to 'O' and 'O-group witnesses.' Presumably, this *O* would be the 'origin of origins' for all subsequent manuscript witnesses.

14 The statement should not be taken as implying that the impenetrability of their results (the printed record of collation) entails the impenetrability of their collation methods, which they describe in great detail.

15 Reference is to E.T. Donaldson, 'Chaucer, *Canterbury Tales,* D117: A Critical Edition,' *Speculum* 40 (1965): 626–33. The editors' treatment of manuscript relations based on variants of this line is the focal point for the highly

critical review by Hanna, 'The Application of Thought to Textual Criticism in all Modes.'

16 Caroline F.E. Spurgeon, *Five Hundred Years of Chaucer Criticism and Allusion (1357–1900)* (1908–17; repr. 3 vols., Cambridge, 1925).

17 See also, Peter M.W. Robinson, 'Is There a Text in These Variants?' 112: 'The text is Chaucer; the text is the scribes; the text is the Wife of Bath; the text is us. It is a continual delight to make an edition such as this: there is the beauty of the manuscripts, the serendipity of recovering what the scribes did from the variants, and of seeing unseen patterns of manuscript relations emerge; and then there is through all this the Wife of Bath herself speaking.'

18 See my discussion in *Who is Buried in Chaucer's Tomb?*, chap. 8: 'Unbooking Chaucer: The Drama of Chaucer the Persona,' 159–73.

19 Henry Bradshaw, 'The Skeleton of Chaucer's Canterbury Tales: An Attempt to Distinguish the Several Fragments of the Work as Left by the Author' (1871), repr. in *Collected Papers* (Cambridge, 1889). See my 'The Chaucerian Reception of Henry Bradshaw,' *Archiv für das Studium der neueren Sprachen und Literaturen* 235 (1998): 68–84.

20 'A poem which consists of fragments will appear to its readers as unfinished ... More recently, the concept that the poem is complete in its incompleteness has been argued, though this has not had any impact on the way editions are presented' (Blake, 'Editing the *Canterbury Tales*: An Overview'). I believe Blake ignores here the precedent of the Variorum Chaucer and its single-tale volumes.

21 Skeat and F.N. Robinson are the obvious practitioners of such a method in Chaucer editing.

22 Such statements are examples of what Hanna describes as the editors' uncritical and 'outspoken veneration of the Hengwrt manuscript' ('Application of Thought,' 164).

23 See the review by Susan Arvay of Murray McGillivray, ed., *Geoffrey Chaucer's Book of the Duchess: A Hypertext Edition* (Calgary, 1997), *Studies in the Age of Chaucer* 22 (2000): 513–17.

24 In the SEENET edition of *Piers Plowman*, edited by Duggan, by contrast, the unit of organization is the individual manuscript, not the section of text.

25 'The Analysis Workshop' in vol. 2 uses the early printed editions of Caxton, de Worde, and Pynson as an exercise in the use and manipulation of their database. Their cladistic diagrams show de Worde, Pynson as a 'block' next to Cx1, surely a view that would be maintained by all students of these books.

26 Text is most readily available in W.J.B. Crotch, ed., *The Prologues and Epilogues of William Caxton*, EETS 176 (London, 1928), 90–1.

27 Greg, 'The Early Printed Editions of the *Canterbury Tales*'; and Dunn, *The Manuscript Source of Caxton's Second Edition of the Canterbury Tales.*

28 'For this study I have used the collations of all the known extant manuscripts and Caxton's two editions made by Professors Manly and Rickert at the University of Chicago' (Dunn, *Manuscript Source*, 2, n. 6).

29 Blake, in his various essays on this question, seems to follow Dunn, and repeats the specific textual examples given earlier by Dunn; 'Caxton and Chaucer,' 1967, repr. Blake, *William Caxton and English Literary Culture*, esp. 149–55; *Caxton and His World*, 101ff.; and 'Aftermath: Manuscript to Print,' in *Book Production and Publishing in Britain*, ed. Derek Pearsall and Jeremy Griffiths (Cambridge, 1989), 403–32.

30 Robinson's cladistic diagram in 'Analysis Workshop' shows rather Tc2 in a group with Cx1. Tc2 is from the node that produces both Cx editions.

31 If one printed version is copied from another printed version, one can expect some sort of correspondence in line breaks, or at the end of a material unit such as the page or forme, but there seems to be no significant correspondence in the sections of the Caxton editions I have checked (Tale of Melibee and the Parson's Tale). Although a recent article claims otherwise, Cx2 was set up and printed by the page, something that reduces its relationship to printer's copy: see Donaghey, 'Caxton's Printing of Chaucer's *Boece*,' esp. 85; see also, George D. Painter, *William Caxton: A Biography* (New York, 1997), 97. In Cx2, running heads exist generally in recognizable pairs, and they alternate according to the unit of the page, not the printed forme (that is, 4v/5r are occasionally the same).

32 Dunn's procedure for finding the relation between Cx1 and Cx2 was to refer to Manly-Rickert's collation cards, which had been created by comparing each witness to an arbitrary text – Skeat's *Student's Edition* (Dunn, *Manuscript Source*, 2–3). In Melibee, Dunn states that Cx1/2 depart from this text 1475 times, but vary from each other forty-five times. Of these 1475 readings, only twenty-four are peculiar to Cx1 and Cx2. The conclusion is both that Cx1 copied 'faithfully' from a manuscript, and Cx2 copied 'faithfully' from Cx1. The problems with this method are obvious, since Skeat's *Student's Edition* is not anything from which the Caxton editions were ever copied.

33 Standard critical apparatus may not be suitable for computers, nor is it practical to incorporate a previously printed apparatus directly; see comments by Peter S. Baker, 'The Reader, the Editor, and the Electronic Criti-

cal Edition,' in *A Guide to Editing Middle English*, ed. Vincent P. McCarren and Douglas Moffat (Ann Arbor, 1998), 263ff.: 'We must abandon the notion that the critical apparatus in any form now familiar to us can be processed by the computer' (275).

34 Kane, 'Manly and Rickert,' 229: 'All the work will have to be done again.'

35 The first and now classic study of this sort is Windeatt, 'The Scribes as Chaucer's Early Critics.' George Kane has derided such interpretation of scribal habits as 'sentimental' ('The Text,' in *A Companion to Piers Plowman*, ed. John A. Alford [Berkeley, 1988], 194); see my *Who Is Buried in Chaucer's Tomb*, chap. 10: 'Scribes as Critics,' 195–213.

36 There are many examples, and I discuss one in 'The Notions of Text and Variant in the Prologue to Chaucer's *Legend of Good Women*,' *Papers of the Bibliographical Society of America* 84 (1993): 65–80.

37 The editors of these short poems paradoxically treated them as individual poems, and by and large ignored their manuscript context – a manuscript context basic to the arguments of Hammond and Brusendorff and thus the justification for the manuscripts produced in facsimile; see my discussion in *Who is Buried in Chaucer's Tomb*, 137–58. See Hammond, *Chaucer: A Bibliographical Manual*, 333–9, and Aage Brusendorff, *The Chaucer Tradition* (Oxford, 1925), 182–207.

38 Hanna, review of *Facsimile of Oxford, Bodleian Library, MS Digby 86*, and *The Works of Geoffrey Chaucer and The Kingis Quair*.

6. Editorial Variants

1 See my 'On Metrical Confusion and Consensus in Early Editions of Terence,' *Humanistica Lovaniensia* 48 (1999): 103–31. All surveys of Terence editions must begin with the catalogue of editions and their relations by Lawton, *Térence en France*, 1: 63–251 (henceforth referred to as Lawton). For Politian's use of the Bembo manuscript see esp. Riccardo Ribuoli, *La collazione polizianea del codice bembino di Terenzio* (Rome, 1981), with several facsimile pages, and 'Per la storia del codice bembino di Terenzio,' *Rivista di Filologia e di Istruzione Classica* 109 (1981): 163–77. On the role of Bembo, see Anthony Grafton, 'Pietro Bembo and the "Scholia Bembina,"' *Italia Medioevale e Umanistica* 24 (1981): 405–7, and John N. Grant, 'Pietro Bembo and Vat. Lat. 3226,' *Humanistica Lovaniensia* 37 (1988): 211–43.

2 This process of thorough contamination, where one text is transformed into another, can also be seen in cases of everyday annotation; in the Huntington Library copy of the edition of Da Spira, 1471 (Goff T-65), an alternate version of the *Eunuchus* prologue is introduced as a set of variants.

3 Aldus was given credit for editing the *Andria*, although the text of the Aldine edition of other Terence plays in the 1517 edition follows that of the Giunta edition. See the 1517 letter of And. Torresanus to Erasmus: 'Nosti enim (nam tum aderas) quantum temporis consumpsit in emendando Therentio Aldus, gener meus suavissimus et charissimus ... tum in Plauto quanta usus est industria ...' (Allen, ed., *Opus Epistolarum Des. Erasmi Roterodami*, 2:590–1).

4 Allen, *Opus Epistolarum*, 1:63, and the letter of Beatus Rhenanus on Erasmus's first visit to Aldus. Here he edited two tragedies of Euripides 'and worked on the meter of Terence and Plautus.' See also, Erasmus's own letter to Botzheim, (ibid., 1:13): 'Moliti sumus simile quiddam apud Aldum post aedita Proverbia in Comoedia Terentii et Plauti omnes, sed hic nihil aliud professi quam versuum confusorum digestionem, ubi licuisset, tum in tragoedias Senecae ... exemplaria reliquimus Aldo permittentes illius arbitrio quid de his statuere velle.'

5 R.A. Mynors, trans., *The Correspondence of Erasmus*, 11 vols (Toronto, 1974–), 9: 310, n. 96: 'During his stay in Venice in 1507–8, Erasmus assisted Aldus in the preparation of the texts that became the basis for the Aldine edition of Terence (Nov. 1517) and Plautus (July 1522)'; see also Allen, *Opus Epistolarum* 4: 388 and note. The same statement is made by Martin Lowry, *The World of Aldus Manutius* (Ithaca, 1979), 242: 'Erasmus worked in 1508 on an edition of Terence which was finally printed by Andrea Torresani in 1517.' The references cited do not support these statements. See also Allen, *Opus epistolarum*, 1: 437 (Erasmus to Aldus), and Allen's note at 1: 444, with reference to Erasmus's statement in the letter to Botzheim (above, n. 4).

6 'Nonnihil etiam hic peccarunt eruditi qui dum carminum genera distingunt ac dimetiuntur parum attenti, interiecerunt uerba quaedam, ut explerent uersus hiatum, aut resecuerunt quod uidebatur superesse ... Proinde nos quatriduanam opellam sumpsimus, ut adolescentulis aliquam huius difficultatis partem adimeremus, non quidem in omnes fabulas, sed in unam perpetuo, & in ceteris carptim: quo ceu filo adiuti, sese facilius e caeteris explicent labyrinthis' (Froben edition, sig. [alpha]3r).

7 The 'four days' Erasmus worked on this edition are mentioned again by Glareanus in his *In Pub. Terentii Carmina ... Heinrichi Glareani Helvetij Iudicium* (Lyons, 1540), quoted by Lawton, *Térence en France*, 307. Glareanus cannot reconcile the textual corruption evident in the text with the claims of Erasmus's editorial endeavours and invents a fiction of textual degeneration to account for the text in 1540.

8 The very phrase '6000 emendations' or faults is a cliché that appears also in Erasmus, *Adagia*, on Aldus's 'Festine Lente,' LC 1:403D (complaining of

printers who would prefer that a book suffer '6000 errors' to paying a corrector). Six thousand emendations is about one per line, and there is nothing like this in Etienne's Terence, which is textually close to the Giunta editions.

9 For supplements to the Lawton series, see Elizabeth Armstrong, *Robert Estienne, Royal Printer: An Historical Study of the Elder Stephanus* (Cambridge, 1954); and Fred Schreiber, *The Estiennes: An Annotated Catalogue of 300 Highlights of their Various Presses* (New York, 1982).

10 On early attacks on Bentley, see Jarvis, *Scholars and Gentlemen*, 17–42, and discussion in Walsh, *Shakespeare, Milton, and Literary Editing*, 62–75. See Theobald's own letters to Warburton, in Richard Foster Jones, *Lewis Theobald: His Contribution to English Scholarship with Some Unpublished Letters* (New York, 1919), Appendix C, 30 Oct. 1731: 'I am sory he has now dabbled in a Province, where even the Ladies are prepar'd to laugh at, & confute him' (278). See also, Theobald's introduction in *The Works of Shakespeare* ([1733], 8 vols [London, 1773]), sig. a12r. The tradition seems continued in Anthony Grafton, *The Footnote: A Curious History* (Cambridge, 1997), 111. The distinction between Bentley's classical and English editing is implied in Kenney, *The Classical Text*, and in the dismissal of Bentley's vernacular editing by Rudolf Pfeiffer, *The History of Classical Scholarship from 1300–1850* (Oxford, 1986), 146–7. See also Hale, 'Paradise Purified: Dr Bentley's Marginalia for his 1732 edition of Paradise Lost,' esp. 62.

11 Walsh, 'Bentley our Contemporary,' quotation at 162. See Levine, 'Bentley's Milton.'

12 Empson, *Some Versions of Pastoral*, 149–91; Bourdette, Jr, 'A Sense of the Sacred'; and comment by Walsh, *Shakespeare, Milton, and Literary Editing*, 74–5.

13 The manuscript is available in facsimile in Helen Darbishire, *The Manuscript of Milton's Paradise Lost, Book I* (Oxford, 1931).

14 For a discussion of these manuscripts, see Claudia Villa, *La 'Lectura Terentii,'* vol. 1, *Da Ildemaro a Francesco Petrarca* (Padua, 1984).

15 See, for example, Charlotte Brewer, *Editing Piers Plowman: The Evolution of the Text* (Cambridge, 1996), 273, 306, 308, and my review in *Envoi* 8 (1999): 30–5.

16 See Hale, 'Paradise Purified,' 73, criticizing Bentley for not systematically collating the 1667 with the 1674 edition.

17 David Foxon, *Pope and the Early Eighteenth-Century Book Trade* (Oxford, 1991), 153–236.

18 In the passage quoted below (1: 242–54), the number of such 'silent' changes between the 1690 edition and the 1674 manuscript is sixteen;

there are fourteen such changes between the manuscript and the third edition of Newton (1754); all are 'silent,' with the exception of the word 'Rea'son'; the note states the spelling indicates a scansion of one syllable. *Paradise Lost: A Poem in Twelve Books*, ed. Thomas Newton, 3rd ed. (London, 1754), 43; *Paradise Lost: A Poem in Twelve Books*, 6th ed. (London, 1690).

19 The procedure is the same stated by Pope in his edition of Shakespeare: 'The method taken in this Edition will show it self. The various Readings are fairly put in the margin, so that every one may compare 'em; and those I have prefer'd into the Text are constantly ex fide Codicum, upon authority. The Alterations or Additions which Shakespear himself made, are taken notice of as they occur' (*The Works of Shakespeare in Six Volumes, Collated and Corrected by Mr. Pope* [London, 1725], 1: xxii).

20 *Dr. Bentley's Emendations of the 12 Book's of Milton's Paradise Lost* (London, 1732).

21 'Bentley's impulse to re-create is analogous to that which led Dryden to write a "dramatic transversion" of *Paradise Lost* (*The State of Innocence and the Fall of Man*) 1677' (Walsh, 'Bentley our Contemporary,' 167).

22 To determine how the 'silent' changes Bentley introduced into *Paradise Lost* might compare with similar silent changes in two editions of Dryden's 'State of Innocence,' I took the time and endured the tedium of collating the first edition with the 1731 Dublin edition. The quality and number of changes here (punctuation, spelling, capitalization) is almost identical to those between Bentley's *Paradise Lost* and other contemporary editions.

23 James Black, ed., *Nahum Tate: The History of King Lear* (Lincoln, NE, 1975), V, 133–9.

24. Robert Kauer and Wallace M. Lindsay, eds, *P. Terenti Afri Comoediae* (Oxford, 1926 and 1958).

25 'Dum aetas, metus, magister prohibebat, ita est scitum sane manistrum seu paedagogen! qui prohibebat patrem noscere fili ingenium ... Hancine lectionem tam diu ferri? Repono: Dum eum aetas, metus, magister cohibebant, ita est cohibebent, retinebent' (p. 5).

26 M.B. Parkes, *Pause and Effect: An Introduction to the History of Punctuation in the West* (Berkeley, 1993), 115, n. 10, claims that Bentley completely repunctuates Horace to indicate parsing. My survey of other eighteenth-century Horace editions suggests, however, that his punctuation was uninteresting and traditional.

27 Malone, *The Plays and Poems of William Shakespeare*; Margreta de Grazia, *Shakespeare Verbatim: The Reproduction of Authenticity and the 1790 Apparatus* (Oxford, 1991).

28 The scholarly assumption that prefaces reflect practice is criticized by

Jarvis, *Scholars and Gentlemen*, 11, through Anthony Grafton, 'The Origins of Scholarship,' *American Scholar* 48 (1979): 260.

29 N. Rowe, *The Works of William Shakespeare in Six Volumes* (London, 1709); *The Works of Shakespeare in Six Volumes, collated and corrected by Mr. Pope* (London, 1725). The interest in Rowe's editing seems based in part on the recent availability of this edition in facsimile, at least, that is the opinion of some scholars attending the Rowe conference in Montreal, April 2000.

30 Lounsbury, *The First Editors of Shakespeare*; Seary, *Lewis Theobald*; see also, Colin Franklin, *Shakespeare Domesticated: The Eighteenth-century Editions* (Aldershot, 1991).

31 John A. Hart, 'Pope as Scholar Editor,' *Studies in Bibliography* 23 (1970): 54–8, on Pope's collations. When Theobald wrote his *Shakespeare Restored* the following year, he had not seen a copy of the First Folio (noted by Lounsbury, *First Editors of Shakespeare*, 499).

32 See the figures in Seary, *Lewis Theobald*, 62, and in Lounsbury, *First Editors of Shakespeare*, 102. Rowe presumably 'restored' 131 lines to *Hamlet*; Pope another 36. In *Lear*, Rowe restored none; Pope 142.

33 Seary, *Lewis Theobald*, 133–5. Cf. Richard Corballis, 'Copy-Text for Theobald's Shakespeare,' *The Library*, ser. 6, 8 (1986): 156–9, and Jarvis, *Scholars and Gentlemen*, 88–100. 'The numerous corrections, which I made of the Poet's text in my *Shakespeare Restor'd*, and which the public have been so kind to think well of, are, in the appendix of Mr. Pope's last edition, slightingly call'd Various Readings, Guesses, etc.' (Theobald, *Works of Shakespeare*, sig. b4v).

34 Cf. Pope, whose privileged quartos are those eleven 'printed in Shakespeare's lifetime' (Pope, *Shakespeare*, 1: xv–xix).

35 See the note on *Lear*; only 'the old quarto' is specifically identified: 'The generality of the editions, ancient and modern, stupidly place this verse to Cordelia. But I have, upon the authority of the old 4to, restor'd it to the right owner, Glo'ster; who was, but a little before, sent by the King to conduct France and Burgundy to him' (sig. a5v).

36 It is odd that this suggestion to place notes and glossary separately from the text should be attributed to 'others,' since Tyrwhitt's five-volume *The Canterbury Tales of Chaucer* (London, 1775–8), is printed in this fashion.

37 To use the First Folio as a basis of collation does not entail using it as a base text under eighteenth-century editorial theory. Tyrwhitt used a late folio edition of Chaucer (1687) as a basis of collation into which he inserted manuscript readings; the printer's copy is a 1602 folio (*also* of no authority) (Hench, 'Printer's Copy for Tyrwhitt's Chaucer').

38 Even F2 'mysteries,' for which Malone makes great noise in his note on 493,

appears in Theobald. See also Paul Werstine, 'Shakespeare,' in *Scholarly Editing: A Guide to Research*, ed. D.C. Greetham (New York, 1995), 261, whose Malone appropriates also the much-criticized edition of Capell.

39 See A.S.G. Edwards, 'Walter W. Skeat,' in Ruggiers, *Editing Chaucer: The Great Tradition*, 171–89.

40 Skeat's *Piers* edition began with *The Vision of William Concerning Piers Plowman ... Text A* (London, 1867), and culminated in *The Vision of William Concerning Piers Plowman in Three Parallel Texts*, 2 vols (Oxford, 1886).

41 Skeat, ed., *The Complete Works of Geoffrey Chaucer*; Skeat, *The Chaucer Canon*; Robinson, *The Complete Works of Geoffrey Chaucer* (1933; 1957); reedited Larry D. Benson, *The Riverside Chaucer* (Boston, 1987). On Skeat's influence on the canon, see Kathleen R. Forni, *The Chaucerian Apocrypha: A Counterfeit Canon* (Gainesville, 2001), 26–32.

42 Skeat's editing procedures (although less extreme) are similar to those used by the *Société des Anciens Textes Français*, whose texts were rewritten in a presumably 'standard' grammar, and thus comparable to classical texts. See the excellent discussion by Mary B. Speer, 'Old French Literature,' in *Scholarly Editing*, ed. Greetham, 382–416.

43 Skeat, ed., *The Poetical Works of Thomas Chatterton*.

44 *Poems, Supposed to have been written at Bristol, by Thomas Rowley, and Others, in the Fifteenth Century* [ed. Thomas Tyrwhitt], (London, 1777). The third edition adds 'An Appendix, Containing some Observations upon the Language of these Poems, Tending to Prove, that They were Written, Not by any Ancient Author, but Entirely by Thomas Chatterton.' See Taylor, ed., *The Complete Works of Thomas Chatterton*, 1: xxix–xxxi. On Chatterton, see the series of recent essays in *Thomas Chatterton and Romantic Culture*, ed. Nick Groom (New York, 1999), and on some of the topics here Margaret Russett and Joseph A. Dane, '"Everlastinge to Posterytie": Chatterton's Spirited Youth,' *Modern Language Quarterly* 63 (2002): 141–65.

45 See the list of Chatterton's source materials in Taylor, 'Glossary to the Rowleyan Writings,' *Complete Works*, 1: 1176–82.

46 The poems had also appeared in the series of British Poets by Anderson (1795) and in Chalmers 1810 (reprinting the edition of Southey and Cottle); see Taylor, *Complete Works*, 'Principal Editions and Collections,' 1: xxx. Adaptations include a 1837 Edinburgh edition by James Glassford (1: xxxi).

47 For similar statements by Skeat, see his *Complete Works of Chaucer*, 6: xxiii, distinguishing his own work from what he refers to as mere 'aesthetic criticism.' See also, my discussion of his polemic against the Moxon edition of 1843, *Who Is Buried in Chaucer's Tomb?*, 'Skeat's Moxon and the Authority of the Book,' 175–83.

48 Among those specifically criticized here is Thomas Warton, *An Enquiry into the Authenticity of the Poems Attributed to Thomas Rowley* (London, 1782; repr. 1993). Warton follows Tyrwhitt, but condemns Chatterton as a forger through praising him as a poet. 'This hyperbole of panegyric perhaps proves too much ... It is Chatterton's misfortune to be convicted of forgery, not only by himself, but by his friends ... His pretensions to [antiquity] are alike endangered by the excellence of his own poetry, and the praises of his commentators' (Warton, *Enquiry*, 16–17). Baines, *The House of Forgery*, 159ff., on the legalistic language used in this debate.

49 So Chatterton's most recent editor, Taylor, *Complete Works*, 'Glossary,' 1178 ('his proficiency with this language grew steadily and rapidly ...').

50 The notion of such coherent rules applying to metrics is central to Skeat's work on the Chaucer canon; see Skeat, *The Chaucer Canon*, 106–8.

7. Bibliographical Myths and Methods

1 Dard Hunter, *Papermaking: The History and Technique of an Ancient Craft*, 2nd ed. (1947; repr. New York, 1978); John Bidwell, 'The Study of Paper as Evidence, Artefact, and Commodity,' in *The Book Encompassed: Studies in Twentieth-Century Bibliography*, ed. Peter Davison (Cambridge, 1992), 77. Pages 170–81 reprint my 'The Curse of the Mummy Paper,' originally published in *Printing History* 34 (1995): 18–25.

2 On some controversies, Hunter was reluctant to change his initial views, even when he was clearly in error. See his dismissive introductory statement in *Old Papermaking* (Chillicothe, OH, 1923): 'Nor is it a desire to enter into the controversy as to the priority of cotton or linen as a papermaking material.' In fact, there was no controversy, since Hunter's views had been decisively refuted decades earlier. See Karabacek, *Das arabische Papier*; and Charles M. Briquet, 'La legende paléographicque du papier de coton,' (1884) and in a review of Karabacek, 'Le Papier Arabe au moyen Age et sa fabrication' (1888), in *Briquet's Opuscula*, Monumenta Chartae Papyraceae Historiam Illustrantia, gen. ed. E.J. Labarre (Hilversum, 1950), 112–15, 162–70; see also introduction by Allan H. Stevenson, 'Briquet and the Future of Paper Studies,' xxff.

3 Preston, 'Annals of Archeology,' 56: the conversation is between archaeologist Kent R. Weeks, paleontologist Elwyn Simons, and the author. Simons suggests grinding up a skull and putting it in soup. 'When the laughter has died down, I venture that I didn't get the joke. "In the Middle Ages, people filled bottles with powdered mummies and sold it as medicine," Simons explains. "Or mummies were burned to power the railroad," Weeks adds. "I don't know how many miles you get per mummy, do you, Elwyn?"'

4 Munsell, *Chronology of the Origin and Progress of Paper and Paper-making*, 149 (entry for 1855); Weeks, *A History of Paper-Manufacturing in the United States, 1690–1916*, 212 (from Munsell); McGaw, *Most Wonderful Machine*, 219 (from Weeks and Munsell). The version found in a later exhibit pamphlet by Hunter is much expanded; see Hunter, *Story of Early Printing*, 8–9.

5 Richard L. Hills, *Papermaking in Britain, 1488–1988: A Short History* (London, 1988), 119–36; D.C. Coleman, *The British Paper Industry, 1495–1860: A Study in Industrial Growth* (Oxford, 1958), 209. For America, see McGaw, *Most Wonderful Machine*, 190–206. For the earlier period, see J.N. Balston, *The Elder James Whatman: England's Greatest Paper Maker (1702–1759)*, vol. 2 (West Farleigh, Kent, 1992), Appendix V, Part 1: 'The Nature of the Rags Used for Making White Paper in the 17th and 18th c. Paper Mills of the British Isles,' 183ff.

6 Hunter, *Papermaking*, 314–23; Henk Voorn 'In Search of New Raw Materials,' *Papermaker* 21, 2 (1952): 1–14; and A.H. Shorter, *Paper Making in the British Isles: An Historical and Geographical Study* (New York, 1972), 113–16. See also B.G. Watson, 'The Search for Papermaking Fibers: Thomas Routledge and the Use of Esparto Grass as Papermaking Fiber in Great Britain,' *Papermaker* 26, 1 (1957): 1–6.

7 Koops, *Historical Account of the Substances Which Have Been Used to Describe Events and to Convey Ideas*; see Hunter, *Papermaking*, 332–3. For Schäffer, Hunter cites in *Old Papermaking*, 'Sämmtliche Papierversuche' (Regensburg, 1756–72); in *Papermaking*, Hunter cites 'Versuche und Muster ohne alle Lumpen oder doch mit enem geringen Zusatze derselben zu machen,' 6 vols (Regensburg, 1765–71), with an issue of 1772.

8 See Voorn, 'In Search of Raw Materials,' with reference to Jean Etienne Guettard 1715–1786. Munsell's *Chronology* provides a convenient survey of these materials: licorice wood, hemp, corn husks, dwarf palm, esparto grass, straw, hops, asbestos, and, indeed, mummy wrappings. See also Weeks, *History*, 'The Search for Raw Material,' 211–38, with reference to Munsell and Charles T. Davis, *The Manufacture of Paper* (1886), 64, who lists some 500 materials. The search, at least in the sphere of craft, continues; see, for example, C.F. Hill, 'Making Paper with Foliage and Flowers,' *Hand Papermaking* 3 (1988): 15–17; and Marilyn Wold, 'Oregon Seaweed Paper,' *Hand Papermaking* 8 (1993): 23. See also Clarence J. West, *Bibliography of Pulp and Paper Making 1900–1928* (New York, 1929), 555ff., indexing the various trade and technical journals of the early twentieth century, where hundreds of articles and notes on substitute fibers can be found.

9 Herring, *Paper and Paper Making*, 54. Herring is probably the source for Munsell, *Chronology*, who notes that in 1854, paper was selling for 2½c per pound, amid 'universal' complaints of price and shortages. On Munsell's

Chronology, see Paul A. Cyr, 'Joel Munsell, Aldus's Disciple in Albany,' *Printing History* 30 (1993): 13–22.

10 Herring, *Paper and Paper Making*, 54; Munsell, *Chronology*, 140–1. Similar prizes were offered in America: in 1804, the American Company of Booksellers offered a $50 gold medal for the greatest quantity of paper of material other than rags, and a $20 medal for wrapping paper (*Chronology*, 60).

11 John Pinkerton, *A General Collection of the Best and Most Interesting Voyages and Travels in All Parts of the World*, 17 vols (London, 1814), vol. 15, p. 802ff.: 'Extract from the Relation respecting Egypt of Abd Allatif, an Arabian Physician of Bagdad, translated into French by Mr. Sylvestre de Sacy' (quotation at 815).

12 Hunter, *Papermaking*, 472–3; Karabacek, *Das arabische Papier*, 37–8; Pettigrew, *A History of Egyptian Mummies*, 89. The source for the latter two is S. de Sacy, ed., *Abd el-Latîf, Relation de l'Egypte*, 198. Karabacek is, of course, well versed in Arab sources but, as far as I can determine, cites this exclusively with reference to the French translation.

13 By this time, the robbing of tombs had been going on for over two millennia: see John Romer, *Ancient Lives: Daily Life in Egypt of the Pharoahs* (New York, 1984), 145–55.

14 See the summary in Pettrigrew, *History of Egyptian Mummies*, chap. 2 'On Mummy as a Drug,' 7–12. It was already on the wane in popularity in the eighteenth century; see Richard Pococke, *A Description of the East and Some other Countries*, vol. 1, *Observations on Egypt* (London, 1743), 54.

15 See William Foster, *The Travels of John Sanderson in the Levant, 1584–1602*, Hakluyt Society, II, 67 (1931; repr. Nendeln, 1967), (44–5) along with a description of an examination of the mummy pits in 1586. See also, *Voyages en Egypt de Jean Coppin (Lyon, 1720)*, ed. Serge Sauneron (Cairo, 1971), 191–2, who speaks both of visiting the mummy pits and of seeing whole mummies, wrapped in bandages, in Cairo. For a survey of these works, see Karl H. Dannenfeldt, 'Egypt and Egyptian Antiquities in the Renaissance,' *Studies in the Renaissance* 6 (1959): 7–27, and John David Wortham, *The Genesis of British Egyptology, 1549–1906* (Norman, 1971).

16 Vansleb, visiting Egypt in 1672 and 1673, complains specifically about the mercenary nature of these guides; see *The Present State of Egypt; or, a new relation of a late voyage into that Kingdom, performed in the years 1672. and 1673. by F. Vansleb, R.D.* (London, 1678), 89–93.

17 John Greaves, *Pyramidographia: Or a Description of the Pyramids in Aegypt* (London, 1646), 50, note d.

18 Thomas Greenhille, *NEKROKEDEIA: Or the Art of Embalming* (London, 1705), 290.

19 For a modern account, see Renato Grilleto, 'Mummification and Embalming,' in *Egyptian Civilization: Religious Beliefs*, ed. Anna Maria Donadoni Roversi (Turin, 1988), 183, claiming one mummy produced 845 square metres of material.

20 For an earlier statement on prices, see Vansleb, *The Present State of Egypt* (1678), 127. The price of a mummy is given as 2 abukelb, slightly more than 2 piaster. The same weight in spices costs over 20 piasters; an equal weight in flax or hemp is 5–10 piasters. Rollin's popular history, translated into English in 1730, notes: 'These embalm'd Bodies are now what we call Mummies, which are daily brought from Egypt, and adorn the Cabinets of the Curious' (*The Ancient History of the Egyptians* [London, 1730], 49).

21 Hunter, *Story of Early Paper*, 8–9. In *Papermaking*, 363, Hunter claims that in the 'various obituaries published by New York newspapers, accounts were given of [Stanwood's] experiments with ground wood and his unusual manufacture of wrapping paper from the wrappings of Egyptian mummies.' (Hunter gives the death date as 6 March 1914, the date of the obituaries themselves; the death date should be given as 4 March). The *Times* states only that Stanwood was 'said to have been the discoverer of the process of making paper from wood' and the brief obituary from the *Tribune* is similar (*New York Times*, 6 March 1914, 11; *New York Tribune*, 7). Only the extensive obituary in the *Herald* mentions mummy wrappings:

> He entered the paper manufacturing business with his father at an early age. That was when paper was made from rags and the industry had grown to such an extent that the manufacturers were forced to import their supplies. Large importations of mummy clothes were shipped here from Egypt and also rags from Italy. Because the health authorities were lax in those days the germs carried by the rags caused epidemics of cholera, it was said, among the rag sorters in the mills through the country ... It was to remedy this evil that Mr. Stanwood started to experiment with wood as a material for making paper. (*New York Herald*, 7)

The obituary does not attribute cholera to mummy clothes, but to rags (a much more probable explanation); nor does the detail of the Civil War have anything to do with the shortage. The sources for this information are not clear. The obituary states that Stanwood said 'to his friends' that his experiments were inspired by observing wasps – a motif of paper history generally associated with Réaumur. Stanwood had been living in Brooklyn for thirty or forty years, and his son's testimony, given after his own retirement, concerns a far-distant past.

22 P.M. Holt, 'Egypt and the Nile Valley,' in *The Cambridge History of Africa, vol. 5, From c. 1790 to c. 1870*, ed. John E. Flint (Cambridge, 1976), 34–5. The rail from Alexandria to Cairo and the Suez was begun in 1851 and completed in 1858.

23 Mark Twain, *Innocents Abroad*, ed. Guy Cardwell (New York, 1984), chap. 68, 504–5. I thank Prof. Jay Martin of the University of Southern California for this reference.

24 The documents are not at the Dard Hunter Paper Museum in Appleton, WI, although only Hunter's later correspondence is presently available. I thank Cindy Bowden of the museum for this information. I think this may be the same Isaiah Deck who authored a small geological pamphlet, 'Report on Certain Mineral Lands in the Island of Jamaica' (New York, 1854), but I have no other information about him. He is not listed in the standard biographical guides, nor in surveys of periodical literature. There are also no records for him in OCLC or RLIN, and only two in the National Union Catalogue. The *Nineteenth-Century STC* lists a number of short works by an Isaiah Deck written between 1837 and 1851 and published in England; most are geological.

25 See Hunter's 'Chronology,' *Papermaking*, 472–3, cross-referenced to 1855.

26 For mummies in literature, see, for example, Poe's 'Some Words with a Mummy,' and more generally John T. Irwin, *American Hieroglyphics: The Symbol of the Egyptian Hieroglyphics in the American Renaissance* (New Haven, 1980).

27 I thank Peter Hopkins of the Crane Paper Museum for taking the time to examine their files on 'Alternate Fibres.' Although he too knew of this legend (and claimed his source was not Hunter), there was nothing in these files to support it.

28 *First Annual Report of the State Board of Health* (Augusta 1886), 75. See the section on Bangor: 'The city was at that time [1849] in a very filthy state, and the sewage very imperfect' (106). In *Miscellaneous Documents of the Senate of the United States for the lst Session, 39th Congress* (Washington, D.C., 1866), several documents speak of an epidemic: one of 15 November 1865, from the Marquis de Montholon, speaks of the 'recent invasion of cholera in Egypt,' but the source of this disease again is not mummies. The Memorial of Doctor John Evans, Misc. Doc. 66, 23 December 1866, mentions an epidemic, possibly cholera, on the Mississippi, and associated with the 'obscure and filthy parts' of St Louis. A report by Charles A. Lee of Buffalo University Medical Dept. denies that the disease is contagious; rather it is spread by germs 'in privies and water-closets ... communicated by fresh dejections of those infected' (11).

29 The following essay was commissioned for an anthology of writings on irony in 1999, and appeared in French translation as 'L'histoire de l'ironie comme problème de bibliographie descriptive,' in *Poétique de l'ironie*, ed. Pierre Schoentjes, Collection Points (Paris, 2001). See also Joseph A. Dane, *The Critical Mythology of Irony* (Athens, GA, 1991).

Principal Works Cited

Allen, P.S., ed. *Opus Epistolarum Des. Erasmi Roterodami.* Oxford, 1906–.

Amelung, Peter. *Der Frühdruck im deutschen Südwesten, 1473–1500.* Bd. 1, *Ulm.* Stuttgart, 1979.

Anderson, Benedict. *Imagined Communities: Reflections on the Origin and Spread of Nationalism.* 1983; rev. ed. New York, 1991.

Baines, Paul. *The House of Forgery in Eighteenth-Century Britain.* Aldershot, 1999.

Baker, Donald C., ed. *The Manciple's Tale.* Variorum Chaucer 2/10. Norman, 1984.

Beal, Peter. *In Praise of Scribes: Manuscripts and Their Makers in Seventeenth-Century England.* Oxford, 1998.

Blades, William. *The Biography and Typography of William Caxton.* 2nd ed. New York, 1882.

– *The Life and Typography of William Caxton England's First Printer.* 2 vols. London, 1861–3.

Blake, N.F. 'Aftermath: Manuscript to Print.' In *Book Production and Publishing in Britain,* ed. Derek Pearsall and Jeremy Griffiths, 403–32. Cambridge, 1989.

– *Caxton and His World.* London, 1969.

– 'Geoffrey Chaucer: Textual Transmission and Editing.' In *Crux and Controversy in Middle English Textual Criticism,* ed. A.J. Minnis and Charlotte Brewer, 33–8. Cambridge, 1992.

– *William Caxton and English Literary Culture.* London, 1991.

Blake, Norman, and Peter Robinson, eds. *The Canterbury Tales Project: Occasional Papers,* vol. 1. Oxford, 1993.

Blayney, Peter W.M. *The Texts of King Lear and Their Origins.* Vol. 1, *Nicholas Okes and the First Quarto.* Cambridge, 1982.

Boghardt, Martin. 'Partial Duplicate Setting: Means of Rationalization or Complicating Factor in Textual Transmission.' *The Library,* ser. 6, 15 (1993): 306–31.

Bourdette, Robert E., Jr. 'A Sense of the Sacred: Richard Bentley's Reading of *Paradise Lost* as "Divine Narrative."' *Milton Studies* 24 (1988): 73–106.

Bowers, Fredson. *Principles of Bibliographical Description.* New York, 1962.

Bowers, Fredson, gen. ed. *The Dramatic Works in the Beaumont and Fletcher Canon.* 8 vols. Cambridge, 1966–92.

Bradshaw, Henry. *Collected Papers.* Cambridge, 1889.

Bühler, Curt F. *Early Books and Manuscripts: Forty Years of Research.* New York, 1973.

Burger, Konrad. *Buchhändleranzeigen des 15. Jahrhunderts.* Leipzig, 1907.

Campbell, M.F.A.G. *Annales de la typographie néerlandaise au xve siècle.* The Hague, 1874.

Catalogue of Books Printed in the Fifteenth Century Now in the British Museum. London, 1908–.

Dachs, Karl, and Wieland Schmidt. 'Wieviele Inkunabelausgaben gab es wirklich?' *Bibliotheksforum Bayern* 2 (1974): 83–95.

Dane, Joseph A. 'An Example of Netherlands Prototypography in the Huntington,' *Huntington Library Quarterly* 61 (1999): 401–9.

– 'Note on the Huntington Library and Pierpont Morgan Library Fragments of Donatus, *Ars minor (Rudimenta grammatices)* (GW 8995, GW 8996),' *Papers of the Bibliographical Society of America* 94 (2000): 275–82.

– 'Perfect Order and Perfected Order: The Evidence from Press Variants of Early Seventeenth-Century Quartos.' *Papers of the Bibliographical Society of America* 90 (1996): 272–320.

– *Who Is Buried in Chaucer's Tomb? Studies in the Reception of Chaucer's Book.* East Lansing, 1998.

Dane, Joseph A., and Thomas V. Lange, 'An Unrecorded South German Incunable at the Huntington with a Note on the Type (97mm/M44),' *Huntington Library Quarterly* 60 (1999): 470–4.

Darnton, Robert. 'What is the History of Books?' 1982. Repr. in *The Kiss of Lamourette: Reflections in Cultural History*, 107–35. New York, 1990.

Davies, Martin. 'Two Book-Lists of Sweynheym and Pannartz.' In *Libri tipografi bibliotheche: Ricerche storiche dedicate a Luigi Balsame*, 1: 25–53. Florence, 1997.

Davies, Martin, gen. ed. *The Illustrated ISTC on CD-ROM.* 2nd ed. London, 1998.

Dearing, Vinton A. 'The Poor Man's Mark IV, or Ersatz Hinman Collator,' *Papers of the Bibliographical Society of America* 60 (1966): 149–58.

De Grazia, Margreta. *Shakespeare Verbatim: The Reproduction of Authenticity and the 1790 Apparatus.* Oxford, 1991.

Dickinson, Donald C. *Henry E. Huntington's Library of Libraries.* San Marino, 1995.

Donaghey, Brian. 'Caxton's Printing of Chaucer's *Boece*.' In *Chaucer in Perspec-*

tive: *Middle English Essays in Honour of Norman Blake*, ed. Geoffrey Lester, 73–99. Sheffield, 1999.

Duggan, Hoyt N., et al., eds. *The Piers Plowman Electronic Archive*. Vol. 1, *Corpus Christi College, Oxford MS 201 (F)*. Ann Arbor, 2000.

Dunn, Thomas F. *The Manuscript Source of Caxton's Second Edition of the Canterbury Tales*. Chicago, 1940.

Eisenstein, Elizabeth. *The Printing Press as an Agent of Change: Communications and Cultural Transformations in Early Modern Europe*. 2 vols. Cambridge, 1979.

– *The Printing Revolution in Early Modern Europe*. Cambridge, 1983.

Empson, William. *Some Versions of Pastoral*. London, 1950.

Febvre, Lucien, and Henri-Jean Martin, *L'Apparition du Livre*. Paris, 1958. Trans. David Gerard and ed. Geoffrey Nowell-Smith and David Wootton. *The Coming of the Book: The Impact of Printing 1450–1800*. London, 1976.

Gaskell, Philip. *A New Introduction to Bibliography*. New York, 1972.

Gesamtkatalog der Wiegendrucke. Vols 1–7. Leipzig, 1926–38; vols 8 – Stuttgart, 1978–.

Goff, Frederick R. *Incunabula in American Libraries: A Third Census*. New York, 1964; repr. 1973.

Grafton, Anthony. *Commerce with the Classics: Ancient Books and Renaissance Readers*. Ann Arbor, 1999.

– 'Quattrocento Humanism and Classical Scholarship.' In *Renaissance Humanism: Foundations, Forms, and Legacy*, ed. Albert Rabil, Jr. Vol. 3, *Humanism and the Disciplines*, 23–66. Philadelphia, 1988.

Greetham, David. *Textual Scholarship: An Introduction*. New York, 1992.

Greetham, David, ed. *Scholarly Editing: A Guide to Research*. New York, 1995.

Greg, W.W. 'The Early Printed Editions of the *Canterbury Tales*.' *PMLA* 39 (1924): 737–61.

– 'The Rationale of Copy-Text.' *Studies in Bibliography* 3 (1950–1): 19–36.

– *The Variants in the First Quarto of 'King Lear': A Bibliographical and Critical Inquiry*. London, 1940.

Grendler, Paul F. *Schooling in Renaissance Italy: Literacy and Learning, 1300–1600*. Baltimore, 1989.

Haebler, Konrad. *Die deutschen Buchdrucker des XV. jahrhunderts im Auslande*. Munich, 1924.

– 'Der Gesamtkatalog der Wiegendrucke.' In *Fünfzehn Jahre Königliche und Staatsbibliothek. Dem scheidenden Generaldirektor Adolf von Harnack zum 31. März 1921 überreicht von den wissenschaftlichen Beamten der Preussischen Staatsbibliothek*, 278–84. Berlin, 1921.

– *Handbuch der Inkunabelkunde*. Leipzig, 1925.

– *Typenrepertorium der Wiegendrucke*. 5 vols. Halle, Leipzig, 1905–24.

Hain, Ludwig. *Repertorium bibligraphicum.* 4 vols. Stuttgart and Paris, 1826–38.

Hale, John K. 'Paradise Purified: Dr Bentley's Marginalia for his 1732 Edition of Paradise Lost.' *Transactions of the Cambridge Bibliographical Society* 10 (1991): 58–74.

Hammond, Eleanor Prescott. *Chaucer: A Bibliographical Manual.* New York, 1908.

Hanna, Ralph. 'The Application of Thought to Textual Criticism in all Modes – With Apologies to A.E. Housman.' *Studies in Bibliography* 53 (2000): 163–9.

– 'The Hengwrt Manuscript and the Canon of *The Canterbury Tales.*' In *English Manuscript Studies (1100–1700)* 1, (1989): 64–84.

– Reviews of *Facsimile of Oxford, Bodleian Library, MS Digby 86*, and *The Works of Geoffrey Chaucer and The Kingis Quair: A Facsimile of Bodleian Library, Oxford, MS Arch. Selden, B. 24. Huntington Library Quarterly* 61 (1998): 107–14.

Hellinga, Lotte. 'Further Fragments of Dutch Prototypography: A List of Findings Since 1938.' *Quaerendo* 2 (1972): 182–99.

Hellinga, Wytze, and Lotte Hellinga. *The Fifteenth-Century Printing Types of the Low Countries.* 2 vols. Amsterdam, 1966.

Hench, Atcheson L. 'Printer's Copy for Tyrwhitt's Chaucer.' *Studies in Bibliography* 3 (1950): 265–6.

Herring, Richard. *Paper and Paper Making, Ancient and Modern.* London, 1856.

Hessels, J.H. 'Prototypography.' In *Encyclopaedia Britannica.* 11th ed.

Hinman, Charlton. 'Mechanized Collation: A Preliminary Report.' *Papers of the Bibliographical Society of America* 41 (1947): 99–106.

– 'Mechanized Collation at the Houghton Library.' *Harvard Library Bulletin* 9 (1955): 132–4.

– *The Printing and Proof-Reading of the First Folio of Shakespeare.* 2 vols. Oxford, 1963.

Hirsch, Rudolf. *Printing, Selling and Reading (1450–1550).* Wiesbaden, 1967.

– 'The Size of Editions of Books Produced by Sweynheim and Pannartz between 1465 and 1471.' *Gutenberg-Jahrbuch* (1957): 46–7.

Holtrop, J.W. *Monuments typographiques des pays-bas au quinzième siècle.* The Hague, 1868.

Honemann, Volker, et al., eds. *Einblattdrucke des 15. und frühen 16. Jahrhunderts: Probleme, Perspektiven, Fallstudienn.* Tübingen, 2000.

Hunter, Dard. *Papermaking: The History and Technique of an Ancient Craft.* 2nd ed. New York, 1947.

– *Story of Early Printing: As Told in a Collection of Original Specimens.* Chillicothe, OH, 1950.

Isaac, Frank. *English and Scottish Printing Types, 1501–35, 1508–41.* London, 1930.

Jarvis, Simon. *Scholars and Gentlemen: Shakespearian Textual Criticism and Representations of Scholarly Labour, 1725–1765.* Oxford, 1995.

Johns, Adrian. *The Nature of the Book: Print and Knowledge in the Making*. Chicago, 1998.

Johnson, A.F. 'The Classification of Gothic Type.' In *Selected Essays on Books and Printing*, ed. Percy H. Muir, 1–17. Amsterdam, 1970.

– *Type Designs: Their History and Development*. London, 1934; 3rd. ed. London, 1966.

Kane, George. 'John M. Manly (1865–1940) and Edith Rickert (1871–1938).' In *Editing Chaucer: The Great Tradition*, ed. Paul G. Ruggiers, 207–29. Norman, 1984.

Karabacek, Joseph. *Das arabische Papier: Eine historisch-antiquarische Untersuchung*. Vienna, 1887.

Kenney, E.J. *The Classical Text: Aspects of Editing in the Age of the Printed Book*. Berkeley, 1974.

Kernan, Alvin. *Printing Technology, Letters and Samuel Johnson*. Princeton, 1987.

Koops, Matthias. *Historical Account of the Substances which have been used to describe events and to convey ideas, from the earliest date to the invention of paper*. London, 1800.

Lawton, Harold Walter. *Térence en France au XVIe siècle: Contribution à l'histoire de l'humanisme en France*. 2 vols. Paris, 1926.

Lenhart, John M. *Pre-Reformation Printed Books: A Study in Statistical and Applied Bibliography*. New York, 1935.

Levine, Joseph M. 'Bentley's Milton: Philology and Criticism in Eighteenth-Century England.' *Journal of the History of Ideas* 50 (1989): 549–68.

Lindstrand, Gordon. 'Mechanized Textual Collation and Recent Designs.' *Studies in Bibliography* 24 (1971): 204–14.

Loublinsky, B.C. 'The Book in Social History' *Vestnik Istorii Mirovoi Kultury* 4 (1959): 162–7.

Lounsbury, Thomas R. *The First Editors of Shakespeare (Pope and Theobald)*. London, 1906.

Love, Harold. *Scribal Publication in Seventeenth-Century England*. Oxford, 1993.

Malone, Edmond. *The Plays and Poems of William Shakespeare, in Ten Volumes; Collated verbatim with the most authentick copies*. London, 1790.

Manly, John M., and Edith Rickert. *The Text of the Canterbury Tales*. 8 vols. Chicago, 1940.

McGaw, Judith A. *Most Wonderful Machine: Mechanization and Social Change in Berkshire Paper Making, 1801–1885*. Princeton, 1987.

McKenzie, D.F. 'Printers of the Mind: Some Notes on Bibliographical Theories and Printing-House Practices.' *Studies in Bibliography* 22 (1969): 1–75.

McKerrow, Ronald B. *An Introduction to Bibliography for Literary Students*. Oxford, 1927.

McLuhan, Marshall. *The Gutenberg Galaxy: The Making of Typographical Man.* Toronto, 1982.

Molsdorf, Wilhelm. 'Die Photographie im Dienste der Bibliographie, mit besonderer Berücksichtigung Ierer Drucke.' *Beiträge zur Kenntnis des Schrift-, Buch- und Bibliothekswesens* 4 (1898): 83–9.

Munsell, Joel. *Chronology of the Origin and Progress of Paper and Paper-making.* 5th ed. Albany, 1876.

Myers, Robin. 'George Isaac Frederick Tupper, Facsimilist, Whose Ability in this description of work is beyond praise (1820?–1911).' *Transactions of the Cambridge Bibliographical Society* 7 (1978): 113–34.

– 'William Blades's Debt to Henry Bradshaw and G.I.F. Tupper.' *The Library,* ser. 5, 5 (1978): 265–83.

Neddermeyer, U. 'Möglichkeiten und Grenzen einer quantitativen Bestimmung der Buchproduktion im Spätmittelalter.' *Gazette du livre médiéval* 28 (1996): 23–32.

Needham, Paul. *The Bradshaw Method: Henry Bradshaw's Contribution to Bibliography.* Chapel Hill, 1988.

– 'Counting Incunables: The IISTC CD-ROM.' Review *The Illustrated ISTC on CD-ROM,* gen. ed. Martin Davies, 2nd ed., London, 1998. *Huntington Library Quarterly* 61 (1999): 457–529.

– 'Fragments in Books: Dutch Prototypography in the Van Ess Library.' In *'So Precious a Foundation': The Library of Leander van Ess at the Burke Library of Union Theological Seminary in the City of New York,* ed. Milton McC. Gatch, 85–110. New York, 1966.

– *The Printer and the Pardoner.* Washington, DC, 1986.

Oates, J.T.C. *A Catalogue of the Fifteenth-Century Printed Books in the University Library, Cambridge.* Cambridge, 1954.

Ohly, Kurt. 'Der gegenwärtige Stand der internationalen Inkunabelinventarisierung.' *Beiträge zur Inkunabelkunde,* N.F. 1 (1935): 8–30.

Ong, Walter. *Orality and Literacy: The Technologizing of the Word.* London, 1982.

Padley, G.A. *Grammatical Theory in Western Europe, 1500–1700: The Latin Tradition.* Cambridge, 1976.

Pearsall, Derek, ed. *The Nun's Priest's Tale.* Variorum Chaucer 2/9. Norman, 1984.

Pettigrew, Thomas Joseph. *A History of Egyptian Mummies.* London, 1834.

Pollard, Alfred W. *An Essay on Colophons with Specimens and Translations.* Chicago, 1905.

Pollard, Alfred W., and G.R. Redgrave. *A Short-Title Catalogue of Books Printed in England, Scotland, and Ireland, and of English Books Printed Abroad.* 2nd rev. ed. 3 vols. London, 1976–91.

Pollard, Graham, and Albert Ehrman. *The Distribution of Books by Catalogue from the Invention of Printing to A.D.1800, Based on Material in the Broxbourne Library*. Cambridge, 1965.

Preston, Douglas. 'Annals of Archaeology: All the King's Sons.' *The New Yorker*, 22 January 1996, 44–59.

Proctor, Robert. *Bibliographical Essays*. London, 1905.

– *An Index to the Early Printed Books in the British Museum: From the Invention of Printing to the Year 1500*. London, 1898.

Prothero, G.W. *A Memoir of Henry Bradshaw*. London, 1888.

Reichling, Theodor. *Alexandri de Villa-Dei Doctrinalis codices manu scripti et libri typis impressi*. Berlin, 1894.

Robinson, F.N., ed. *The Complete Works of Geoffrey Chaucer*. Boston, 1933; 2nd ed. 1957.

Robinson, Peter. 'Can We Trust the Hengwrt Manuscript?' In *Chaucer in Perspective: Middle English Essays in Honour of Norman Blake*, ed. Geoffrey Lester, 194–217. Sheffield, 1999.

– 'Is There a Text in These Variants?' In *The Literary Text in the Digital Age*, ed. Richard J. Finneran, 99–116. Ann Arbor, 1996.

Robinson, Peter, gen. ed. *Geoffrey Chaucer: The Wife of Bath's Prologue on CD-ROM*. Cambridge, 1996.

Ruggiers, Paul G., ed. *Editing Chaucer: The Great Tradition*. Norman, 1984.

Schwenke, Paul. *Die Donat- und Kalender-Type: Nachtrag und Übersicht*. Mainz, 1903.

Seary, Peter. *Lewis Theobald and the Editing of Shakespeare*. Oxford, 1990.

Senefelder, Alois. *A Complete Course of Lithography ... to which is prefixed a history of lithography, with preface by Frederic von Schlichtegroll*. Trans. A.S. London, 1819; repr. New York, 1977.

Sheppard, I.A. 'The Speculum Printer's Editions of Donatus.' *Gutenberg-Jahrbuch* (1954): 63–5.

Skeat, Walter W. *The Chaucer Canon, with a Discussion of the Works Associated with the Name of Geoffrey Chaucer*. Oxford, 1900.

Skeat, Walter W., ed. *The Complete Works of Geoffrey Chaucer*. 7 vols. Oxford, 1894–9.

– ed. *The Student's Chaucer*. New York, 1894.

– ed. *The Poetical Works of Thomas Chatterton with an Essay on the Rowley Poems*. 2 vols. London, 1871; repr. 1890.

Smith, Gerald A. 'Collating Machine, Poor Man's, Mark VII.' *Papers of the Bibliographical Society of America* 61 (1967): 110–13.

Smith, Steven Escar. 'The Eternal Verities Verified: Charlton Hinman and the Roots of Mechanical Collation.' *Studies in Bibliography* 53 (2000): 129–61.

Solopova, Elisabeth, ed. *Chaucer: The General Prologue on CD-ROM*. Cambridge, 2000.

Steele, Robert. 'What Are Fifteenth-Century Books About? IV.' *The Library*, ser. 2, 8 (1907): 225–38.

Sternberg, Paul R., and John M. Brayer. 'Composite Imaging: A New Technique in Bibliographic Research.' *Papers of the Bibliographical Society of America* 77 (1983): 431–45.

Tanselle, G. Thomas. 'Textual Criticism and Deconstruction.' *Studies in Bibliography* 43 (1990): 1–33.

Taylor, Donald S., ed. *The Complete Works of Thomas Chatterton*. 2 vols. Oxford, 1971.

Twyman, Michael. *Early Lithographed Books: A Study of the Design and Production of Improper Books in the Age of the Hand Press*. Williamsburg, VA, 1990.

Updike, Daniel Berkeley. *Printing Types: Their History, Forms, and Use: A Study in Survivals*. 2 vols. 2nd ed. Cambridge, MA, 1937.

Veröffentlichungen der Gesellschaft für Typenkunde des XV. Jahrhunderts. Berlin, 1907–39.

Voulliéme, Ernst. 'Nachträge zu den Buchhändleranzeigen des 15. Jahrhunderts in getreuen Nachbildungen herausg. von K. Burger.' In *Wiegendrucke und Handschriften, Festgabe Konrad Haebler*, ed. Isaak Collijn et al., 18–44. Leipzig, 1919.

Walsh, Marcus. 'Bentley our Contemporary: or, Editors, Ancient and Modern.' In *The Theory and Practice of Text-Editing: Essays in Honour of James A. Boulton*, ed. Ian Small and Marcus Walsh, 157–85. Cambridge, 1991.

– *Shakespeare, Milton, and Literary Editing: The Beginnings of Interpretive Scholarship*. Cambridge, 1997.

Warton, Thomas. *An Enquiry into the Authenticity of the Poems Attributed to Thomas Rowley*. London, 1782; repr. 1993.

Weeks, Lyman Horace. *A History of Paper-Manufacturing in the United States, 1690–1916*. New York, 1916.

Weiss, Adrian. 'Reproductions of Early Dramatic Texts as a Source of Bibliographical Evidence.' *TEXT* 4 (1988): 237–68.

Windeatt, B.A. 'The Scribes as Chaucer's Early Critics.' *Studies in the Age of Chaucer* 1 (1979): 119–41.

Zedler, Gottfried. *Von Coster zu Gutenberg: Der holländische Frühdruck und die Erfindung des Buchdrucks*. Leipzig, 1921.

– *Gutenbergs älteste Type und die mit ihr hergestellten Drucke*. Mainz, 1934.

Index

Abd al-Latif, 172, 177, 179, 180
Aldine British Poets, 164
Aldus Manutius, 57, 144–5; editions, 192
Alexander of Villa Dei, 59, 65, 69–74
Ames, Joseph, 12
Anderson, Benedict, 32
Annales, Groupe, 11, 28, 31–2
Antiquarius, Jacobus, letter to Politian, 62
Ashmole, Elias, 76, 119, 120
Ausgabe. See edition, definitions of

Bacon, Francis, 13
Baker, Donald C., 117, 118, 123
base text, defined, 115. *See also* editing
Beaumont, Francis, and Giles Fletcher, edition by Bowers, 90, 105, 107–8, 111
Beckett, Samuel, editions of *En attendant Godot*, 186–7
Bentley, Richard: edition of *Paradise Lost*, 5, 143, 148–54; edition of Terence, 154–8
best text editing, defined, 115. *See also* editing

bibliography: descriptive, 36, 39, 56, 99; enumerative, 56; analytical, 99–100
Bidwell, John, 170
bindings, 12, 60; binder's waste vs printer's waste, 61
Blades, William, 76, 82–7; Facsimile vs Imitation, 84–5
Blake, Norman, 115, 125, 126, 130
Blayney, Peter W.M., 98, 101–2, 106
book: defined, 4, 5, 8, 61; singularity, 9; relation to *le livre*, 30–1
book-copy: defined, 5; singularity 5; numbers of, 34, 36–40
book fragments, 38, 39; cataloguing of, 57–74
book history: methodology, 5; and categorization, 7
Book of Hawking, St Alban's, 75
Bourdette, Robert E., Jr, 149
Bowers, Fredson, 36, 99, 111. *See also* Beaumont, Francis, and Giles Fletcher
Bradshaw, Henry, 8, 61, 77, 79, 86, 130
Braudel, Fernand, 7, 14
breviaries, 75

Bridenbaugh, Carl, 11
British Library, 187; *Catalogue of Books Printed in the Fifteenth Century Now in the British Museum*, 12, 77–8, 79; type classifications, 27
Brusendorff, Aage, 140
Burger, Konrad, 33, 46, 76
Burkhardt, Jacob, 12, 74
Bussi, Giovanni Andrea, 46, 47

Camden, William, 119, 120
Campbell, M.F.A.G., 86
Canon Missae, 75
Canterbury Tales Project, CD-ROM edition, 124–42; aims, 126–7, 130
cataloguing, 9; of book fragments, 39, 57–75; meaning of catalogue entry, 186
Caxton, William, 26, 49–50, 51, 75; type 82–4, 86; Caxton sesquicentenary publications 12; two editions of *Canterbury Tales*, 124, 128, 134–9, 215nn31, 32
Chatterton, Thomas, 143, 163–9
Chaucer editions: of John Stow, 191; of John Urry, 76; of Thomas Wright, 115, 128; of William Thynne, 128; archetype for *Canterbury Tales*, 116, 125, 213n13; choice of copy-text and base manuscript 116; early editions, 123. See also *Canterbury Tales* Project; Chaucer Variorum; Manly, John M., and Edith Rickert; Robinson, F.N.; Robinson, Peter; Skeat, Walter W.
Chaucer manuscripts: Cambridge, Trinity College (Tc2), 136; Ellesmere, 115, 116, 117, 123, 125, 128, 129; Harley 7334, 128; Hengwrt, 114, 115, 116, 117, 123–4, 125, 128, 129, 132, 140; Pepys 2006, 140; Tanner 346, Bodley 638, Fairfax 16 [Oxford group], 140
Chaucer Society, transcriptions, 125, 126, 140, 141, 163
Chaucer Variorum, 114, 115, 116, 118, 125, 130, 132, 140
Chaucer's tomb, 76; epitaph, 118–22
cholera, 171, 181–2
Cicero, early editions, 47–9, 54–5, 75
'cladistics,' 125; vs stemmatics, 125
Clark Library, 90, 110
collation (editorial), 3; basis of collation, 96, 115–22, 132–3, 220n37; records of collation, 122–3
collators, optical, 88–97, 112; alternative methods, 91, 94, 95; and definition of variation 95–7; Hailey's Comet, 90, 92–4; Hinman, 90, 92–5, 96; Lindstrand comparator, 92, 94; McLeod, 90, 92–4; speeds, 91, 96; Sternberg and Brayer, 209n14; colometry, 143. *See also* Terence
copy-text, 111; defined 115; relation to printer's copy 136–7, 161; in Shakespeare editing, 161. *See also* editing
correction, at press, 100–1, 105–6; relation to 'correctness,' 102
Coster, Laurens, 14
Cowper, William, 98

Dachs, Karl, and Wieland Schmidt, 'Wieviele Inkunabelausgaben gab es wirklich?' 36, 37, 40–1
Darnton, Robert, 7
Dart, John, 119, 120, 121,
Da Spira, Vindelinus, 53; colophons of, 47, 48, 49
Deck, Isaiah, 171, 178–9

de Grazia, Margreta, 158
de Man, Paul, 18
de Réaumur, René Antoine Ferchault, 171
Derrida, Jacques, 20
de Worde, Wynkyn, 26
Dibdin, Thomas Frognall, 12
Donaldson, E.T., 127
Donatus: *Ars minor*, 39, 58, 59; difficulties of cataloguing 65–9; commentary on Terence, 148
Donne, John, 19
Dryden, John, 90, 130; 'State of Innocence,' 152–3
Dunn, Thomas F., 135–6

editing: base text, best text, and copy-text, 115, 117, 123, 126, 131–3, 140; basis for collation in, 117; diplomatic, 140; eclectic, 117, 123, 163, 169
edition (bibliographical): definitions of, 35, 55, 65, 67, 88, 187; lost, 43; sizes, 40, 42–51, 53, 58
Eisenstein, Elizabeth, 10–20
Elzevier Press, 192
Empson, William, 149
Erasmus, 5; and New Testament 145. *See also* Terence editions

facsimile, 6, 58; representations of early type 75–81; reproductions of Chaucer and Langland, 137, 139–41. *See also* Blades, William
Febvre, Lucien, and Henri-Jean Martin, *L'Apparition du livre*, 11, 60; estimate of numbers of incunables, 32–5, 42, 52, 53; on typefaces, 21–31
Folger Library, 90, 91–2, 96, 110

Foxe, John, 119

Gabler, Hans, 107–9, 111
Gardiner, Maine, cholera epidemic, 175–7, 180, 181–2, 185; physicians' reports, 182
Gaskell, Philip, 99–100
Geist, Bill, 'CBS Sunday Morning,' 183, 184
Gesamtkatalog der Wiegendrucke (*GW*), 35 36, 37, 40, 58; classification and measurement of type, 80–2; definitions of entries, 36, 56; estimates of number of editions 36–40, 42, 46; treatment of book fragments, 65–75, 80
Goff, Frederick., 86–7
Goldschmidt, E.P., 12, 61
grammar books, 38, 57–82
Greaves, John, 173–4
Greenhille, Thomas, 173
Greetham, D.C., 98–9
Greg, W.W., 98, 111, 151; on Caxton's *Canterbury Tales*, 135; definition of copy-text, 115, 161
Gutenberg, Johannes, 12
Gutenberg Bible, 32, 39, 57
Gutenberg Society, 12

Haebler, Konrad, 37, 42, 44–5, 46, 51
Hailey, Carter. *See* collators, optical
Hain, Ludwig, 36–7, 52, 53, 56, 73–4
Hale, John K., 148–9
Hale, Sarah, 120, 121, 122
Hammond, Eleanor, 140
Han, Ulrich, early editions, 54–5
Hanna, Ralph, 140–1
Hellinga, Lotte, and Witze Hellinga, *The Fifteenth-Century Printing Types of the Low Countries*, 77, 78, 79

Herodotus, 173
Herring, Richard, 172
Hinman, Charlton, 88; collator, 90, 92–5; *Printing and Proof-Reading of the First Folio of Shakespeare*, 91, 95
Hirsch, Rudolf, 47, 50, 51, 59
Hobson, G.D., 12
Holtrop, J.W., 77–9
Hunter, Dard, 170–5
Huntington Library, 62–3, 110; collection of incunables, 38, 55, 60, 75

ideal copy, 7, 36, 65, 81, 99, 187, 188
Incunabula Short-Title Catalog (*ISTC*), 6, 36, 41, 52–4, 56, 58
irony, as critical concept, 185–90
Isaac, Frank, 24–5
issue, 55, 65, 88, 187

Johns, Adrian, 11, 15–18, 20, 22, 82–3
Johnson, Samuel, 159
Juvenal, early editions, 52–5

Kane, George, 116, 117, 139
Karabacek, Joseph, 173
Ker, Neil, 12
Kernan, Alvin, 20
Koop, Mathias, 172

Lachmann, Karl, 150, 160
Lawton, Harold Walter, 148
Lenhart, J.M., 50–1, 59
Lerer, Seth, vii–viii
Lewis, Terry, 183–5
Library of Congress, incunable collection, 55, 60
Lincoln County Weekly, 183
Lindstrand, Gordon, 88. *See also* collators, optical

lithography: opposed to photography 81–2; in works of William Blades, 83–7. *See also* facsimile
London *Times*, 172, 178
Loublinsky, Vladimir, 34–5
Lounsbury, Thomas, 159
Love, Harold, 11, 19–21
Lucidarius, 59

Mainz, and early printing, 38. *See* prototypography
Malone, Edmond, 5, 158–63; collating and proofreading procedures in Shakespeare edition, 161–2
Manly, John M., and Edith Rickert, *Text of the Canterbury Tales*, 114–18, 122, 124–6, 132–3, 136, 137, 139; collating procedures, 117–18, 123
Mansion, Colard, 26, 27, 82–3
McKenzie, D.F., 105
McKerrow, Ronald B., 91, 98, 103, 111, 112
McLeod, Randall, 88. *See also* collators, optical
McLuhan, Marshall, 11, 13, 196n3
Melanchthon, Philip, 144
Michelet, Jules, 22
Milton, John, early editions, 148–57. *See also* Bentley, Richard
Moxon, Joseph, 17
mummies: as fuel, 171, 175–6; used in paper making, 173–85; the Wiscasset mummy, 181–5
Munsell, Joel, 171, 172, 174–5, 177
Myers, Robin, 83

Neddermeyer, U., 41–5
Needham, Paul, 36, 41, 52, 61
Netherlands and early printing. *See* prototypography

New Yorker, 171, 177
Nuremburg Chronicles, 14, 57

Ohly, Kurt, 35, 37, 39, 41
Oldham, J. Basil, 12
Ong, Walter, 10, 20

paper making, 171–85; material shortages, 171–2
Pearsall, Derek, 116, 118, 123
'perfecting process,' 103
Persius, early editions, 52–4
Peterson, Roger Tory, 87
Petrarch, Francis, 14
Pettigrew, Thomas, 173–4
Pierpont Morgan Library, incunable fragments, 63
Piers Plowman editions: Crowley, 92; SEENET, 137; Skeat, 163, 169
Pits, John, 119, 120, 121
Plato, myth of Thoth, 20
Plautus, early editions, 52–3
Pococke, Joseph, 174
Polifilo, *Hypnerotomachia*, 57
Politian, 62; collations of Terence, 144
Pollard, Alfred W., and G.R. Redgrave, *A Short-Title Catalogue of Books Printed in England ... (STC)*, 6
Pope, Alexander: *Dunciad*, 148, 154; edition of Shakespeare, 159, 163
press variation, 68, 97–109; relation to textual criticism, 110
print culture, 8, 10–21, 74; association with fixity, 3, 15–18, 21; assumption of coherence, 15; defined, 10, 13
Proctor, Robert, 12, 76, 77; system of type measurement, 78
prototypography, 62–82; and facsimile representation, 77–82

Rabelais, François, 189–90; typography of early editions, 29
railroads: mummies as fuel, 171, 177, 185
Reichling, Theodor, 71–2
Robinson, F.N., 114, 115, 130, 163
Robinson, Peter, 126, 128. See also *Canterbury Tales* Project
Rowe, Nicholas, 159–60, 163

Sammelband: defined, 55; examples, 62, 75
Schäffer, Jacob Christian, 171–2
Schaur, Johann, 29
Schoeffer, Peter, 45, 47
Schoenberg, Arnold, 40
Schwenke, Paul, 12, 66–7
scribal culture, 14, 19–21; defined, 13, 19
Seary, Peter, 159
Shakespeare, William, 112, 127, 142; *King Lear*, 98; version of *King Lear* by Nahum Tate, 152–4
Shakespeare editions: authority of quartos, 160, 163; First Folio, 91, 96, 160–2, 187; fourth folio, 159; by Malone, 143, 159–63; Q and F readings in *King Lear*, 162; by Theobald, Pope, and Rowe, 159–63
Skeat, Walter W.: eclecticism of editing, 163, 169; edition of Chatterton, 143, 163–9; edition of Chaucer 114, 125, 130, 163–4; *Student's Chaucer*, 115–18, 122, 123, 132; edi-tion of *Piers Plowman*, 163
Skinner, Stephen, 164
Speght, Thomas, 119, 120, 121
Spenser, Edmund, 19
Spurgeon, Caroline F.E., 128

Stanwood, I. Augustus, and Daniel
    Stanwood, 175–6, 225n21
state (bibliographical), 55, 65, 88,
    187; early and late states, 102–4,
    105–8
Stationers' Company archives, 18
Steele, Robert, 59
Sweynheim, Conrad, and Arnold
    Pannartz, inventory of early book-
    copies, 46, 47
Swift, Jonathan, 172, 179, 180
Syracuse *Daily Standard*, 174–5, 179,
    183

Tate, Nahum, 162–4
Terence: Bembo manuscript, 144;
    colometry, 144, 156–8; manu-
    scripts, 150
Terence editions: by Bentley, 154–8;
    early editions, 52–3, 142, 144–8; by
    Erasmus (Froben edition), 143–8;
    by Etienne, 145–8; by Faernus,
    154–5; by Hare, 157–8; by Melanch-
    thon, 144, 154; Oxford Classical
    Texts, 154–5
text: defined, 3, 6, 20–1; reproduci-
    bility, 3, 6, 8
textual criticism, 111–12, 128–9; basis
    of collation used in, 114–22;
    completeness of collation, 128, 131,
    150; relation to bibliography, 98,
    106; relation to press variation, 89,
    95, 96, 100, 102, 106–10. *See also*
    editing
Theobald, Lewis, 148; edition of
    Shakespeare, 159, 162, 163

Thynne, William, 128
Tonson, Jacob, 159; editions, 191, 192
Tupper, G.I.F., 83–7
Turner, Robert K., Jr, 105–6
Twain, Mark, 177, 185
Type Facsimile Society, 76
type measurement, 58, 78–82; and
    prototypography, 62–7
typography: categories of gothic,
    197nn20, 21; classification of type-
    faces, 22–9; fluidity of terminology,
    24–6, 28
Tyrwhitt, Thomas: and Shakespeare
    editing, 160, 161; essay on
    Chatterton, 163–7

Ulm, early printers, 29
Unwin, William, 98
Updike, Daniel, 24, 191
USA Today, 183, 184

*Veröffentlichungen der Gesellschaft für
    Typenkunde des XV. Jahrhunderts*, 76
Vollbehr, Otto, 55, 60
Voulliéme, Ernst, 46

Walsh, Marcus, 149, 154
Wiscasset, Maine, 183–5
witness, textual–critical, defined,
    127–8
'Woolley' photographs, 76
Wright, Thomas, 115, 128

Zainer, Johann, 29, 62
Zedler, Gottfried, 77–81

STUDIES IN BOOK AND PRINT CULTURE

General editor: Leslie Howsam

Bill Bell, et al., *Where Is Book History? Essays in the Emergence of a Discipline*

Hazel Bell, *Indexes and Indexing in Fact and Fiction*

Heather Murray, *Come, bright Improvement! The Literary Societies of Nineteenth-Century Ontario*

Joseph A. Dane, *The Myth of Print Culture: Essays on Evidence, Textuality, and Bibliographical Method*

William A. Johnson, *Bookrolls and Scribes in Oxyrhynchus*